Antonietta
"1990"

Sportsmanlike Driving

Eighth Edition

**American
Automobile
Association**

Falls Church, Virginia

**Webster Division,
McGraw-Hill Book Company**

New York   St. Louis   San Francisco   Auckland   Bogotá   Düsseldorf
Johannesburg   London   Madrid   Mexico   Montreal   New Delhi
Panama   Paris   São Paulo   Singapore   Sydney   Tokyo   Toronto

Editor: Carolyn E. Cranford
Managing Editor: Alma Graham
Coordinating Editor: Naomi Russell Onco
Design Supervisor: Margaret Amirassefi
Production Manager: Karen Romano
Photo Editing Supervisor: Rosemary O'Connell

Photo Editor: Alan Forman
Design: Function Thru Form, Inc.
Cover: Werner Müller/Peter Arnold Photo Archives

Library of Congress Cataloging in Publication Data

American Automobile Association.
  Sportsmanlike driving.

  Includes index.
  SUMMARY: Discusses the physical and mental qualities of a good driver,
traffic regulations, road safety and hazards, and automobile mechanics. Also
gives brief instructions for operating an automobile.
  1. Automobile driving. [1. Automobile driving]
I. Title.
TL152.5.A38   1980   629.28'3   79-11523
ISBN 0-07-001330-6

Contents

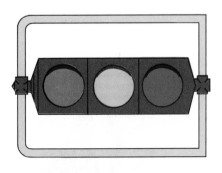

Preface

The eighth edition of *Sportsmanlike Driving* presents in a well-illustrated, easy-to-read format the information you need to become a safe, efficient driver. *Sportsmanlike Driving* brings together the most advanced information available on driving maneuvers and decisions, traffic laws, and vehicle control. This information will help you to make good driving decisions. The text focuses on factors relating to vehicles, drivers, and the highway—parts of the system with which you must learn to interact. One of the primary purposes of this book is to help you become more aware of the elements around you as you drive. These elements should influence your selection of speed and position in traffic. Another, broader purpose of this text is to help you develop the knowledge and skills to become a safe, effective user of the highway transportation system. You will need this knowledge and these skills not only as a driver of a motor vehicle but also as a pedestrian, a passenger, or a cyclist.

For you to get the greatest benefit from driver education, the course you are enrolled in should be scheduled so that your experiences in the car and in the classroom support each other. Lessons should be planned so that the knowledge you gain in class can be applied in the car the next day. Then, the experiences you have in the car can be discussed the next time you attend class.

In some cases, driver education courses and in-car experiences will not be scheduled in this way. Therefore, end-of-chapter projects are suggested that will let you apply driving concepts while you are riding as a passenger. In other cases, you can practice driving procedures, such as time-space gap evaluation, as a pedestrian. In addition to the projects suggested in the text, other parts of the *Sportsmanlike Driving* program are designed to bridge the gap between your class lessons, simulated driving, and in-car experiences. These aids include the *Tests*, the *Behind-the-Wheel Guide*, the *Project Workbook*, and the supplementary AAA Driver Improvement Program.

The importance of knowing where to find your car's controls and how to use them is obvious. Less obvious is the importance of proper seat- and mirror-adjustment and of safety-belt use. If your seat is improperly adjusted—too high or too low, too far forward or too far back—your ability to control your car is reduced. Failure to properly adjust both the inside and outside mirrors reduces the area you can see and often leads to dangerous actions. Failure to fasten your safety belt reduces your ability to control your car in an emergency situation.

One of the major marks of a good driver is the ability to spot in advance cues that show a problem may be developing. To control the risks involved in driving, you must know what to look for, where to look, and how to look. You must learn how and where to search for information. You must learn to evaluate the information available to you so that you can better predict the possible behavior of other highway users.

To make such evaluations, you will have to know and understand the purpose of traffic laws, signs, signals, and markings. You will have to be aware of the performance and handling characteristics of your car. You will also have to identify cues concerning other cars, trucks, buses, motorcycles, pedestrians, and bicyclists—cues that can alert you to possible problems.

first aid
station

In addition, you will have to evaluate the influence that roadway conditions, weather, and time of day may have on your ability to control your car. These factors can also influence your ability to identify and respond to traffic situations. So you must develop your perception, judgment, driving skills, and decision-making ability. Then you can learn to evaluate and predict driving situations and to make the best selection of speed and position.

Development of these abilities, however, does not guarantee that you will be a safe, efficient driver. Safe driving requires more than knowledge, the ability to control your car, and the ability to judge time and space needs. It also requires an awareness and consideration of factors that can have a negative effect upon your ability to drive.

telephone

For instance, traffic-accident investigations have shown that alcohol and other drugs are a contributing factor to more than half of all traffic fatalities. Yet, in spite of this evidence, many people continue to use drugs and then to drive. Many people do not understand the effects of alcohol or are misinformed. They are unaware, for example, that a can of beer, a glass of wine, or a shot of whiskey all contain the same amount of alcohol. Few people are aware that even low levels of alcohol in the bloodstream can have dangerous effects. Many drivers also do not realize the potential dangers associated with the use of nonprescription drugs, such as those drugs prescribed to relieve a cold.

The facts you learn and the skills you develop in driver education will add to the pleasure that comes with being a good driver. But only you can determine how you are going to drive. You will have to make that decision every time you get behind the steering wheel of a motor vehicle.

mechanical
help

Acknowledgments

The eighth edition of *Sportsmanlike Driving* was prepared under the direction of Dr. Francis C. Kenel. Dr. Kenel received a bachelor's degree in industrial engineering and safety, a master of arts degree in vocational education and traffic safety, and a doctoral degree in traffic safety and police traffic administration from Michigan State University. He has taught driver education, traffic safety, and accident prevention courses at both the high school and university levels. Dr. Kenel has been actively engaged in high school driver education and the preparation of driver education teachers for over twenty-five years. His special activities have included the development of learning modules in the area of perceptual development and information processing, as they relate to driving, and the design and operation of multiple-car driving ranges. He also served as a consultant to the Simulator Advisory Committees of the Allstate Insurance Company and the AETNA Casualty and Surety Company.

Before becoming director of the Traffic Engineering and Safety Department of the American Automobile Association, Dr. Kenel was professor and chairman for traffic safety and accident prevention, first at Illinois State University and more recently at the Safety Education Center at the University of Maryland. He also served on the Highway Traffic Safety Center staff at Michigan State University and taught driver education at Sexton High School in Lansing, Michigan.

Mr. Eugene Carney is an instructor at the Safety Education Center at the University of Maryland. Mr. Carney prepared the material for Unit IV, "Making Effective Driving Decisions," Unit VI, "Coping with Highway and Environmental Factors," Unit VIII, "Cooperating with Other Highway Users," and Unit X, "Performing Well at the Wheel."

Mr. Carney received a bachelor's degree in physical education and health education from the University of Maryland and a master of education degree from Frostburg State College. He completed additional graduate work in traffic safety and driver education at the University of Maryland.

Before joining the staff at the Safety Education Center at the University of Maryland, Mr. Carney taught driver education at Bethesda-Chevy Chase High School in Montgomery County, Maryland, for nineteen years. He served as consultant to the Maryland Department of Education during the development of the Maryland Driver Educa-

CROSS ONLY AT CROSS WALKS

tion Curriculum. He also served as consultant to the AETNA Casualty and Surety Company as a member of their Simulator Curriculum Advisory Committee. Mr. Carney has done extensive work in the development of concepts related to time-space management, risk assessment, and strategies necessary for the effective operation of a motor vehicle.

road
intersection

Mr. John D. DeLellis is an educational consultant for the Traffic Engineering and Safety Department of the American Automobile Association. He developed the end-of-chapter activities, questions, and projects for *Sportsmanlike Driving*. He also prepared the teacher annotations and was responsible for content editing of the *Behind-the-Wheel Guide* and *Project Workbook*.

unspecified danger

Mr. DeLellis received a bachelor of arts degree in English from Fordham University and a master of science degree in traffic safety education from Southern Connecticut State College. Before joining AAA, Mr. DeLellis taught driver education at North Rockland High School in Rockland County, New York. He has conducted workshops on "Driving-while-Intoxicated Countermeasures" throughout the United States.

A special thanks is extended to Mses. Vicki Tolson, Ellen Given, and Virginia Kulik for their efforts in manuscript preparation.

uneven
road

Supplementary materials for the eighth edition were developed under the direction of Dr. Harvey Clearwater, associate professor and director of the Safety Education Center at the University of Maryland, College Park. Dr. Clearwater received his bachelor's degree in social studies and English from the State University of New York at Albany. He received his master's degree in curriculum and traffic safety and his doctoral degree in curriculum traffic safety and police traffic administration from Michigan State University.

Before accepting the position at the University of Maryland, Dr. Clearwater taught driver education at Shaker High School, Latham, New York, and served on the staff of the Highway Safety Center at Michigan State University.

Dr. Clearwater was assisted by the following persons: Mr. Kenneth William Klecan, driver education teacher, Baltimore Polytechnic Institute, Baltimore City Public Schools; Mrs. Susan P. Klecan, driver education instructor, Northwestern High School, Baltimore City Public Schools; Mr. A. Powell Harrison, risk manager, Maryland National Park and Planning Commission; and the staff of the Safety Education Center at the University of Maryland.

Thanks are also due to all those who assisted in the development of the seven previous editions of *Sportsmanlike Driving*.

UNDERSTANDING THE NATION'S ROADWAYS

This unit gives students an understanding of our vast network of roadways. It discusses the need for cooperation among the users of the highway transportation system.

CHAPTER 1, "You and the Highway System," discusses
- how safe driving is like good sportsmanship.
- how the highway system is made of roadways, people, and motor vehicles.

CHAPTER **1**

YOU AND THE HIGHWAY SYSTEM

DRIVING AND SPORTS

The United States has a vast, complex network of streets, roads, and highways. This network can be used safely and efficiently only if all drivers, with their different goals and destinations, cooperate with each other and exercise a sense of courtesy and fair play.

Safe driving is sometimes called a team operation—like sports—because it requires team effort and sportsmanship. In fact, when you think about it, driving and sports are alike in several ways:

1. *Team cooperation in trying to reach a goal.* Highway users have to cooperate with each other, just as members of a winning team

must cooperate. In sports, the goal is to win—a game, a series, a match, a championship. "Winning" on a highway means the safe movement of people and goods from place to place.

2. *Regulated facilities*. Both driving and sports take place on regulated facilities. Both highway users and athletes must play by the rules. In sports, there are rules for the players and rules for the facilities (playing areas). In the highway transportation system, the traffic laws regulate the actions of the team members (drivers, cyclists, pedestrians). The facilities are the roadways, sidewalks, and parking areas regulated by signs, signals, and markings.

3. *Equipment*. In sports, equipment must meet certain design and construction standards. The same is true of cars, trucks, motorcycles, and other vehicles.

To be sure, there are some important differences between driving and sports: The immediate goal of an athletic team is to win a game. Highway users, on the other hand, have lots of immediate goals. These goals differ and often come into conflict. Each day, millions of drivers,

Roadway safety is based on (1) cooperation, (2) patience, and (3) courtesy among people who use the vast highway system.

cyclists, and pedestrians try to get to and from many different points. Often, their paths cross and their goals are in conflict. Unfortunately, some drivers think only of their own immediate goals. Once they reach a goal, they act as if to say, "I made it." They seldom seem to care about the goals or the safety of other highway users.

Another difference between driving and sports is that, unlike an athlete, you, the driver, are not preparing for only one game or series of games. Driving is an activity that you will probably take part in for the rest of your life. In organized sports, players' performances are constantly evaluated. Players who do not do well are dropped from the team. But a driver has to show only a minimum amount of skill and decision-making ability to get and keep a driver's license. Drivers are not carefully evaluated through all the years that they drive. They may lose their right to drive only if they are found guilty of major offenses time after time or if they are too seriously disabled to drive a motor vehicle safely.

The differences between sports and driving cause problems that make it most important for each operator of a motor vehicle to drive in a sportsmanlike manner. Emphasis must be put on cooperation, not on competition. This means that, as a driver, you must make every effort to drive safely. It means that you must know and obey the laws that regulate driving. You must learn to look for and adjust to the faults of other highway users. In short, sportsmanship in driving means that you help every other driver to become a winner.

The interstate highway system is made up of a network of modern roadways. These roadways link together most of the large cities in the United States.

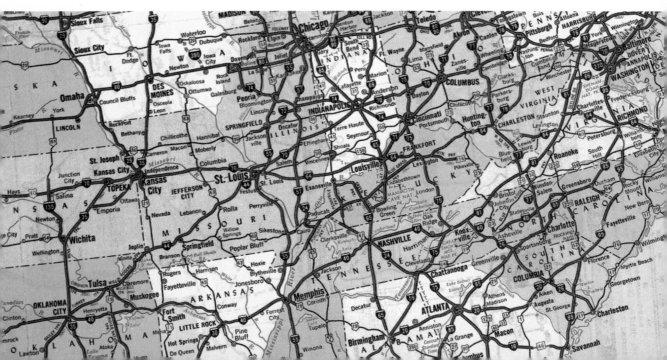

THE HIGHWAY TRANSPORTATION SYSTEM

To reduce the chance that you, as a driver, will make errors and cause collisions, you must know and understand (1) the major elements of the highway transportation system, (2) the part that each of these elements plays, and (3) how the failure of any of the elements can affect the operation of the system.

The highway transportation system is made up of vehicles, highways, and people. Each plays an important part in reaching the same goal: the safe and efficient movement of people and goods throughout this country. The system is large and complicated. As a result, problems can develop. Before you start to drive, you should be aware of the three parts that work together to make the system:

1. *Vehicles* (machines with wheels for carrying people or goods). Over 170 million cars, trucks, buses, and motorcycles move within the system. In addition, there are over 150 million bicycles, mopeds, and other special vehicles.
2. *Highways* (major public roads). There are more than 7 million kilometers (4.5 million miles) of highways. This includes both the roads and nearby off-road areas that are found in most parts of the country.
3. *Human beings* (both drivers and pedestrians). Nearly all of the more than 222 million people in this land can be counted as pedestrians. Many of them also ride the more than 105 million bicycles now in use. Also, over 150 million people are licensed to drive a motor vehicle.

When any part fails, the highway transportation system fails.

MOTOR VEHICLES IN THE SYSTEM

The highway transportation system is designed and operated to move people and goods by way of vehicles. These include bicycles; mopeds; large and small motorcycles; subcompact, compact, intermediate, and large automobiles. There are also small and large trucks and buses. When these vehicles are made, they are required to meet minimum safety standards.

However, they do not all "handle" the same way. In other words, each type of vehicle has its own performance capability. The vehicles accelerate, brake, and steer in different ways. For example, a large truck cannot pick up speed as fast as a small car. Vehicles differ also in how well they protect passengers in case of an accident. If there is a crash, a motorcycle does not protect as well as a large station wagon.

The *maintenance* (upkeep) of vehicles is the responsibility of each owner or operator. Some people take better care of their cars than others. Thus, the quality of upkeep runs from nearly perfect to dangerously bad. Before you drive or buy a car, you should be sure to check its condition. It is up to you, the driver, to keep the car you drive in the best possible shape.

Poor maintenance, of course, can cause trouble—not only for the driver but also for others using the highway transportation system. A vehicle that is not well maintained may break down in traffic and cause any number of problems, such as bottlenecks, or even collisions.

HIGHWAYS IN THE SYSTEM

A vast network of roads reaches into the smallest communities in this country. Without this network, the United States would be an entirely different place in which to live. Highways permit us to travel to and from school, work, shops, and vacations. They make it possible for supplies to be brought easily from one part of the country to another. In times of natural disasters, such as earthquakes and floods, highways can be used to carry out those who are threatened. It should be clear that highways are important to the health and welfare of our nation.

The improvement of the system of roads in the United States since 1947 has been dramatic. This has been especially true since the Federal Highway Act of 1956 was passed. This act provided funds for over 40,000 miles of the interstate system. Today, this system links nearly all

New highways must meet safety standards in design and construction.

cities that have 50,000 or more people. Highways in the interstate system must meet minimum design and construction standards. They must have, for example, 12-foot-wide lanes and a limited number of entrances and exits. In addition, they must have guard rails and wide, firm shoulder areas. But even these standards do not remove all the hazards from the interstate system.

The federal government also gives the states money to build and improve state and local highways. However, these roads, you will find, have far more hazards than do the interstate highways. For example, the lanes are not as wide, and there are many more entrances and exits. You will have to adjust your driving to meet these conditions.

A highway's design or condition may cause accidents or make a driver's errors worse.

To help drivers, there are signs, signals, and markings that give information about driving rules and potential hazards. They can tell the driver about environmental factors that could be hazardous. These markings can point out curves in the road, bumps or breaks in the pavement, or other conditions that will limit a car's traction or a driver's visibility.

PEOPLE IN THE SYSTEM

The people who use the highway transportation system are the single greatest cause of system breakdowns. Such breakdowns occur for many reasons. Sometimes people do not have enough knowledge on which to base good decisions. For example, a 2-year-old child who tries to cross a street is not able to judge the hazards. Furthermore, without guidance the child will not gain the information he or she needs to cross safely. Other highway users can cause the system to fail, too. A driver may panic and "freeze" on the brake pedal, not aware that steering control is lost when the brakes are locked.

Often drivers think that they will be all right as long as they do not break the law. As a result, they do not anticipate the actions of other users that may place them in danger. Such drivers fail to look for clues that can tell them that a problem is arising. Lacking information, they have not thought of ways to solve the problem. As a result, they do not know how to act in case of an emergency.

The purpose of this book is to help you prevent failures in the highway transportation system. Whether a breakdown in the system is caused by a vehicle, by highway conditions, or by driver error is not important. When there are such failures, drivers must do all they can to reduce the seriousness of the consequences.

A lot can be done to improve the highway transportation system. Drivers must learn to let others know what they plan to do on the road. All drivers must maintain their motor vehicle equipment. They must also see to it that their physical and emotional health is such that they are able to drive safely. Drivers must adjust their own needs and goals to benefit all the other users. How well they do these things will, in the end, determine the safety and efficiency of the system.

Drivers should keep in mind that vehicles of different sizes and shapes often use the same roads at the same time. These different types of vehicles accelerate, brake, and steer differently.

TO CONSIDER

1. What are some of the advantages of having a driver's license?

2. What responsibilities do you have as an operator of a motor vehicle? What are the duties of other highway-system users, such as pedestrians and cyclists?

3. Explain how driving is similar to organized sports. How is it different? The word "sportsmanship" can be applied to driving. Explain why this statement is true.

4. What is the purpose of the highway transportation system? How does it affect our daily lives?

5. Explain how a person's driving is affected by how well or how poorly a motor vehicle operates. How can vehicle maintenance affect the way you drive?

6. What are some of the reasons for failures in the highway transportation system?

7. Why must you cooperate with other highway users (drivers, cyclists, and pedestrians) when you drive? What can happen when drivers *do not* cooperate?

8. In your opinion, what part of the highway transportation system needs greatest improvement? Explain your answer.

PROJECTS

1. In a brief report, explain the purpose of the highway transportation system. List the main parts of the system and make a display that shows how the system has changed the way of life in this country. Use drawings, photos, and magazine clippings as a part of your report.

2. List three local, state, or national organizations that are trying to improve the highway transportation system. Make either a brief report on how each is trying to improve the system, or an in-depth report about the programs of *one* of the organizations.

3. Interview three people who drive and three who do not. Ask them what is more important for a driver: driving skill or attitude toward driving. Can you draw any conclusions from the answers they give?

PREPARING TO DRIVE

2 UNIT

This unit is about the various vehicle systems. It acquaints you with the checks and procedures you should follow each time you prepare to drive.

CHAPTER 2, "Driving Systems," tells you
- how to control the speed and direction of a car.
- how to keep track of the operation of some vehicle systems.
- how to increase driving comfort, safety, and security by adjusting your car's protective devices.
- how to improve your ability to see and signal other highway users.

We suggest that you review this chapter before your first in-car lesson.

CHAPTER 3, "Predriving Checks and Procedures," describes
- how to check for the visible signs that show the condition of your car.
- how to check for things in your path before you get into your car.
- how to adjust the driver's seat, mirrors, and safety restraints.
- how to get into and out of a parked car safely.

Practice each of these procedures before your first in-car lesson. When you know them well, you can use them to judge how other drivers are doing, too.

CHAPTER

2

DRIVING SYSTEMS

CD. Ditto
Driver — 2nd chap.

You are probably familiar with the various vehicle systems that you have seen drivers use. Some allow you to control the motion of the car, check on its condition, and communicate your path of travel to other highway users. Other systems provide for the safety and comfort of the passengers and some protection against theft of the vehicle.

You should learn where the instrument switches and control devices are and what they do. When you drive, you will have to steer and maintain speed without taking your eyes from the road. You will also have to find and adjust a number of controls and switches while you pay attention to the traffic around you.

PROTECTIVE SYSTEM

A car's protective devices help guard you from possible injury if there is a collision or sudden emergency maneuver. The driver and passengers do not have to do anything with some parts of the protective system, such as airbags, passive restraint belts, impact-resistant bumpers, side-bar door beams, and padding. But other devices, such as lap or seat belts, lap-and-shoulder belts, and adjustable head restraints, do require action on the part of the user.

SAFETY BELTS

Lap belts were the original restraining devices available on the car market. First, lap belts were *optional equipment* (something extra that a buyer decides to have installed in the car). Later, they became *standard* (required) front-seat equipment in new cars. The lap belts should be strapped snugly across the hips. They help keep you behind the steering wheel and in control of the car if you have to brake hard or swerve sharply. Shoulder safety belts are used with lap belts to provide added protection. These belts are strapped across the shoulder and the chest. They lessen the chance that you or your passenger will be thrown against the dashboard, through the windshield, or out a door which has sprung open as the result of a collision. A shoulder belt should not be adjusted tightly. You should be able to put your fist between the belt and your chest. These combination lap-and-shoulder safety belts became standard equipment in new cars in 1968.

Some cars have an ignition interlock system that prevents the engine from starting if the front-seat passengers are not buckled up. All

Head restraints prevent neck injury. Adjust your head restraint so that it reaches the back of your head, not the base of your skull. Safety belts prevent you from being thrown out of the car. Adjust your safety belt so that it fits comfortably.

cars manufactured since January 1, 1972, have a safety-belt warning light and buzzer that remind drivers to buckle up.

AIRBAGS AND PASSIVE SAFETY BELTS

Airbags and passive safety belts provide automatic protection in a collision. They have been shown to be very effective in reducing injuries in frontal collisions. The *passive safety belt* is a shoulder restraint which connects from the center of the seat to the door of the car. Unlike regular safety belts, neither passive safety belts nor airbags have to be fastened by the driver or passengers. However, the driver and passengers need a regular lap belt with a passive belt, or a combination lap-shoulder belt with an airbag, for the best protection in side collisions and rollovers.

DOOR LOCKS

Doors should be locked while you are driving your car. A locked door is less likely to open in the event of a collision. Also, it will not be accidentally opened by a car occupant while the car is in motion. In older cars, the front doors can be opened by lifting or pulling the door handle on the inside, even when the doors are locked.

HEAD RESTRAINTS

Head restraints help to prevent *whiplash* (neck injury). These front-seat safety devices are either fixed or adjustable. When you are riding in a car with an adjustable head restraint, make sure it is high enough to make contact with the back of your head, not with the base of your skull. Otherwise, serious injury could result in a collision.

COMFORT SYSTEM

Comfort-system devices make driving more comfortable and pleasant. They can help reduce tiredness and thus help you to drive more efficiently. If used in the right way, they may even help you when you need to respond to traffic hazards.

These systems are of two types. The first type includes devices that reduce muscle strain, such as the seat adjustments and cruise control. The second type can be considered climate-control devices, such as the heater, air conditioner, and the air vents.

SEAT ADJUSTMENTS

With proper seat adjustment, you should be able to reach all the car's controls and switches. You should adjust your seat so that you can look over the steering wheel and hood and see about 3½ meters (12 feet) of the road in front of your car. Also, your foot should rest comfortably on the *accelerator* (gas pedal). The brake pedal and clutch, if you are driving a manual shift car, should be within easy reach. Some cars have full-range power seats and adjustable steering wheels. Some equipment gives very tall and very short drivers a better opportunity to find a safe, comfortable position for driving. Even with a power seat or an adjustable steering wheel, you may still need pedal extensions or seat cushions to sit and drive properly. If you need cushions or pedal extensions in a driver-education car or a driving simulator, you are likely to need them in your own or your family's car.

CRUISE, OR SPEED, CONTROL

Cruise control lets you keep driving at a given speed without keeping your foot on the accelerator. You determine what speed you want to maintain, set the speed, and press a control button that is usually on the steering wheel or at the end of the turn-indicator arm. This causes the speed-control system to operate. In order to control the speed of the car manually again, you either touch the button or tap the brake pedal, but it takes practice to learn how to use it properly. There is a danger that a driver may become less alert when using speed control. Drivers sometimes fail to adjust the speed and drive into situations that need a quick response.

AIR CONDITIONER

The air conditioner lowers the temperature and humidity in the car. This helps to keep the driver alert. It reduces the drowsiness and discomfort brought on by hot, humid weather.

Nearly all air conditioners have a normal and a maximum setting for cooling the car. The normal air-conditioning setting cools air that is drawn in from the outside. The maximum air-conditioning setting provides faster cooling. It recirculates air that is in the car along with a small amount of fresh air that is drawn in from the outside. Some cars also have a bilevel setting. This setting provides conditioned air through the heater and the air-conditioner vents. In addition, it provides air through the defroster. This setting is very useful in rainy weather when fog appears on the windshield and side window glass.

HEATER AND DEFROSTER

These devices provide comfort and safety in chilly weather. The heater keeps car passengers warm. It should be adjusted to keep a moderate temperature. If the temperature inside the car is too warm, it can make the driver drowsy. The defroster defogs the windows, thereby giving you better visibility.

AIR VENTS

These vents are usually in the front-seat section of the car at the left and right sides. They let outside air flow into the vehicle to increase passenger comfort. You can select how much air you want to come in by adjusting the air-vent controls.

CONTROL SYSTEM

Control-system devices are used to start the car, to control its speed and direction, and to bring it to a stop.

STEERING WHEEL

You control the direction of your car with the steering wheel. When you drive, your hands should grasp the steering wheel at the 9-o'clock and 3-o'clock positions. If the seat is properly adjusted and your hands are on the wheel in this way, your upper arms should rest against your ribs. This reduces arm and shoulder strain and permits the best handling for steady, straight steering and for moderate turning. This position will also enable you to respond quickly in emergency situations when you have to make hard, fast reversals of the steering wheel.

ACCELERATOR OR GAS PEDAL

The speed of the car is controlled by the amount of gasoline that flows into the engine. You control the rate at which your car moves by the amount of pressure you apply to the *gas pedal* (the accelerator). Gradual acceleration is achieved by applying even, gentle pressure until your car is moving at the desired speed. Then you hold the pedal at the level necessary to maintain the speed. For most driving, this is the safest method. It also uses up less fuel than is needed for quick starts.

BRAKE PEDAL

When you step on the brake pedal, you can slow or stop the car. How fast the car stops depends on how hard you push down on the pedal. The amount of movement that takes place before the desired action begins to occur is called "play." There is normally some "play" in the foot pedal. If you press the pedal gently as the car moves, you will find that the pedal moves about 25 millimeters (an inch) or so before the car begins to slow down.

Power-assisted brakes make it easier to slow or stop the car. They increase the pressure beyond that exerted by your foot. Compared to regular hydraulic brakes, power-assisted brakes do not shorten the distance it takes to stop. As you use either regular or power brakes, you will adapt to the feel of them and learn how much foot pressure to apply. Remember, however, that when you change to a car with the other type of brakes, you will have to adjust the amount of pedal pressure you use.

Most drivers brake with the right foot, the same foot they use on the gas pedal. They prefer to brake this way because there will be no chance that they may press the gas pedal at the same time they brake. Other drivers find it quicker and more comfortable to brake with the left foot. To do this, they rest this foot on the floor near the brake, ready

The photo below shows a person properly applying the brakes. The left foot is on the floor and the right foot is on the brake.

for use.   In either case, it is important to learn to cover the brake as soon as a situation starts to develop that could become hazardous. If you choose to brake with the left foot, do not press both the brake and the gas pedal at the same time. This wears out the brake linings and interferes with the braking process. Also, do not drive with your left foot resting on the brake pedal. This keeps your brake lights on all the time, which confuses the drivers behind you.

PARKING BRAKE

This brake is also known as the *hand brake* or *emergency brake.* The parking brake holds the rear wheels; it is separate from the foot brake. This brake comes in one of three forms: (1) a small pedal located at the left of the foot brake, (2) a lever that is located below the dash and is worked by hand, (3) a lever mounted on the floor between the driver and the front-seat passenger. Most of the time, the parking brake is used to keep a parked car from rolling.

SELECTOR LEVER AND QUADRANT

Cars that have an automatic transmission come with a *selector lever* and *quadrant*. The selector lever lets you choose the gear in which you want to drive, and the quadrant tells you at a glance which gear the car is in. A pointer on the quadrant moves as you lower the lever. The symbols on a standard quadrant are:

P (park)	No gears are engaged. The rear wheels are locked when the car is in *park,* and the ignition key is removed. The engine should be started with the gear selector at *park.*
R (reverse)	*Reverse* gear is used for backing up. If the selector lever is on the steering column, you have to pull the lever toward you a bit and then move it down toward the floor to shift into reverse.
N (neutral)	In this position, the gears are not engaged, and the wheels are free to roll. As a result, the car may roll downhill if it is left in *neutral* and the parking brake is not set. You can try to start the engine with the selector in *neutral* if your car stalls while it is moving.

D (drive)	*Drive* is the basic forward gear. If the engine is set at a *fast idle*, the car may start to move as soon as you shift into *drive*. This will happen even if you do not press your foot on the gas pedal. To be safe, you should keep your foot on the brake pedal as you shift gears.
2 and 1 or L	These are lower drive gears. They allow the engine to deliver more power to the wheels at low speeds. You may choose these gears when you drive in mud or sand. They can also be used to climb steep grades, to hold a car back when driving down a long, steep hill, or to pull a trailer on a hill.

IGNITION SWITCH

In general, the ignition switch has five positions. They are *on*, *start*, *off*, *lock*, and *accessory (acc.)*. *On* turns on the electrical system, the ignition system, and the information gauges. You can read the gauges without starting the engine.   When you turn the ignition key to *start*, you engage a motor that starts the engine. In the *off* position, the engine stops, but you cannot remove the key from the switch. *Lock* locks the steering wheel, the ignition switch, and the automatic transmission. It also makes it possible to remove the key. *Accessory* lets you turn on the electrical equipment, such as the radio, without starting the engine.

VEHICLE-CHECK SYSTEM

In this system, lights and gauges on the dashboard allow the driver to check certain conditions of the car while it is running.

SPEEDOMETER AND ODOMETER

The *speedometer* shows, in kilometers or miles per hour, how fast the car is moving. As you drive, glance at the speedometer from time to time to check how fast you are going. The *odometer* shows the total number of kilometers or miles the car has been driven since the time it was purchased.

The lights and gauges on the dashboard help you to check the condition of your car while it is running.

AMMETER

This device is also called an *alternator gauge* or *light*. It tells whether the battery is being charged or discharged. If more electricity is drawn than is being generated, the gauge will show *D* (discharge) or the light will go on. If the battery is being charged, the gauge will show *C* (charge) or the light will stay off. The *ammeter* will show a discharge when the electrical system is in use and the engine is not running. It will also show a discharge if the engine runs too slowly for the alternator to charge the battery. A constant discharge light or gauge reading should warn you of possible trouble in the electrical system.

TEMPERATURE GAUGE OR WARNING LIGHT

This device, too, comes as a gauge or light. Either one shows whether the engine is running at the right temperature. A hot engine may be either the cause or the result of fluid leaking from the cooling system. Overheating can lead to serious engine damage.

OIL-PRESSURE GAUGE OR WARNING LIGHT

Either device shows the pressure at which the oil is being pumped to the moving parts of the engine. The gauge or light does not show

how much oil there is in the engine, but rather the operating pressure. When the light is on, the pressure is low. If the oil-pressure light comes on or the gauge drops, stop the car as quickly as you can.

FUEL GAUGE

This gauge shows the approximate amount of gasoline in the fuel tank. The markings usually read: *E* (empty), ¼, ½, ¾, and *F* (full).

PARKING-BRAKE LIGHT

This light flashes if the engine is turned on while the parking brake is set. This is to remind the driver to release the brake before trying to move the car. Not all cars have such a light. Late-model cars also have a light that shows when the fluid in the brake system is low.

HIGH-BEAM INDICATOR LIGHT

Usually, this light is located near the center of the speedometer. It goes on when you turn on the car's *high-beam* (bright) lights.

VISIBILITY SYSTEM

These are devices that help the driver see as much as possible, no matter what the weather or time of day. It is essential that you see the road ahead and the area bordering the path you wish to travel.

Highbeam headlights can temporarily blind other drivers. Do *not* use highbeams when (1) the car in front of you is close, (2) a car is passing you, (3) a car is approaching you from the opposite direction. Quickly switch to lowbeams.

HEADLIGHTS

Drivers must use headlights at night, during bad weather, and at any other time when visibility is poor. Headlights also help other drivers and pedestrians to see you. Usually, headlight beams can be changed from low to high or high to low by one of two methods: (1) by pressing your left foot on a button on the floor, (2) by pushing a switch on the turn-indicator lever. High-beam headlights should be used with care. They should not be used under these conditions: (1) when the car in front of you is close, (2) when a car is passing you, and (3) when a car is approaching you from the opposite direction.

When you turn on your headlights, the dashboard also lights up. This lets you see the selector quadrant, the speedometer, and the other dials and gauges. These lights can be made bright or dim by turning the knob on the headlight switch. The dashboard lights should be kept dim most of the time so that they do not make it difficult to see outside the car.

REAR-VIEW AND SIDE-VIEW MIRRORS

Up to a point, these mirrors allow you to see cars that are to the side and to the rear of your car. When they are set correctly, the two mirrors can do away with most, but not all, *blind spots* (areas which you cannot see). Many rear-view mirrors can also be adjusted to cut down on the glare from headlights of cars behind you when you drive at night.

WIPER-WASHER

Most cars have windshield spray nozzles and two-speed windshield wipers. Water from the spray nozzles (mixed with an antifreeze solution) helps the wipers clean the dirt from the windshield.

SUN VISORS

The sun visors can be moved to keep most of the sun's glare from your eyes. They should not be set, though, so that they block your view. For instance, they should not keep you from seeing overhead traffic lights. Also, they should not be used to store things, as these may fall and distract you.

DEFROSTER

The defroster clears the moisture or frost from the inside of the front and rear windows. When the defroster blows warm air, it keeps frost from collecting on the inside of the glass. It also melts ice or frost that may gather on the outside of the glass.

INTERIOR DOME LIGHT

In most cars, this light goes on when either of the front doors is opened. It can also be turned on and off by the headlight switch. This light should not be on when you drive at night. Any light in the car makes it difficult to see outside.

COMMUNICATIONS SYSTEM

These devices let other drivers know where you are and where you intend to go.

PARKING LIGHTS

These lights should be used only when your car is parked. They make your car more visible to other drivers. They are not designed to light the road in front of your car.

The lights on your car help you to give other drivers your position on the road. They also tell other drivers what you plan to do.

Front view

Rear view

Headlight \
Directional signal

Parking light

Directional signal
Taillight
Brake light

Rear license-plate light
and back-up light

HORN

A horn is a warning device. It should be used to tell others on the road that there may be danger. A gentle honk will usually be enough to get the attention of animals, pedestrians, or drivers. If you use it this way rather than sound a blast, the horn is less likely to startle people or animals into some dangerous move. Unnecessary use of the horn is against the law in many places.

DIRECTIONAL OR LANE-CHANGE SIGNALS

Directional (turn) signals tell other drivers that you plan to turn or move to the right or left. The signal control makes a light blink at both the front and rear of the car on the right or left side. To use these turn lights, move the turn signal lever in the same direction you will turn the steering wheel: up for right and down for left. The lights should go off automatically when the wheel straightens out after a turn. In most cars, you can hear the click of a turn signal. If the lights continue to flash after you have made your move, turn them off by hand. To do this, turn the lever back to the middle point.

To signal a lane change is almost the same. However, instead of switching the signal on, you lightly press and hold the switch in the desired direction. By not locking the signal in position, you eliminate the chance of leaving it on. The signal will go off after you release the switch.

In bright weather, the sun may shine on these lights and make them hard for others to see. If this happens, use hand signals. To signal

These are hand signals for a right turn, for a left turn, and for stopping or slowing down.

Right

Left

Stop

by hand, you must stick your left arm out the window. (1) Hold your arm straight out the window to signal a left turn. (2) Bend your arm up from the elbow to signal a right turn. (3) Bend your arm down from the elbow to signal slowing down or stopping. (You will have to use hand signals if your electric turn signals are not working. They are also used in a traffic situation, such as a close line of cars, in which a hand signal will be more visible to the other drivers.)

WARNING FLASHER

The warning (or hazard) flasher tells other drivers that a vehicle on or off the road ahead either has stopped or is moving very slowly. These flashers are usually worked by a switch on the steering column. This switch makes all four turn-signal lights flash at the same time. The turn-signal light on most cars will not work when the four-way warning flasher is turned on.

TAILLIGHT ASSEMBLY

This unit contains several lights: *red brake lights* that go on when you press the brake pedal, *red taillights* that go on when you turn on your parking lights or headlights, and *white back-up lights* that go on when you shift to reverse.

REAR LICENSE-PLATE LIGHT

This light goes on when you turn on your parking lights or headlights. This light aids in identifying vehicles, and under the law, all vehicles must have a rear license-plate light.

SIDE-MARKER LIGHTS

These lights also go on with the headlights. They help drivers to see your car when you are *intersecting* (crossing) streets.

ANTITHEFT SYSTEM

The devices in the antitheft system make it harder for anyone to break into or steal your car.

IGNITION BUZZER

The buzzer is designed to catch your attention and to remind you to take your keys when you leave the car. When the key is left in the ignition switch and the driver's door is opened, the buzzer sounds. This buzzer has two purposes: (1) to stop you from locking yourself out if you leave your keys in the car, (2) to remind you to take the keys from the ignition to reduce the chance of theft.

Always lock your doors and close the windows when you park your car. Use burglar alarms to frighten away thieves.

STEERING-COLUMN LOCK

When you turn the ignition key to the *lock* position, the steering wheel is locked in place. When this lock is on in a car with an automatic transmission, the steering wheel and the gear-selector lever will not move. In a car with a manual transmission, you usually can move the gear-shift lever, but you cannot turn the steering wheel.

DOOR LOCKS

Door locks keep people out. They also are a safety device because locked doors are less likely to open if there is a collision.

TO CONSIDER

1. Name the seven driving systems that will help you to drive a car properly, safely, and comfortably.

2. Give two reasons for wearing safety belts.

3. Locate and operate the warning flasher in the driver education car or the family car.

4. Describe the parts of the comfort system. How will using them properly help you to drive better?

5. What is the best way to reach and maintain a desired speed?

6. What information about the car is revealed by the dials and gauges in the vehicle-check system?

7. How can each part of the visibility system help you to see more of the roadway?

8. How can a driver use the communications system to warn other drivers of possible danger?

PROJECTS

1. Make a list of vehicle safety devices found in the visibility, communications, and protective systems of a new car that a 10-year-old car may not have.
   (Note: You can get this information from school and public libraries, car magazines, consumer magazines, car dealers, service stations, family members, insurance agents, and police officers.)

2. Visit a service station or a junkyard where collision-damaged vehicles can be found. Ask a mechanic or a service manager if it is possible to tell from the interior of such a car whether the people in it were wearing safety belts during the collision. If it is possible, ask what clues they look for. Report your findings to your class.

3. Contact a claims adjuster in the company that insures your family car. Ask if he or she can tell you how often safety belts are used in cases where a claim is made following an automobile accident. Report your findings.

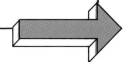

CHAPTER **3**

PREDRIVING CHECKS AND PROCEDURES

People who just get in a car and drive away show a lack of concern both for themselves and the car. They also show a lack of concern for the welfare of other people.

OUTSIDE CHECKS

When you go to your car, look for small children who may be playing near it—200 to 300 children under 6 years of age are killed each year while playing in the family driveway. Also look for such things as broken bottles or tree branches that may be under your car or in the path you plan to take.

Before you get into the car, check the headlights, windshield, tail-lights, and rear windows to see that they are clean and undamaged. Take notice of any damage to the car body , and look at the tires to be sure they have enough air in them. Note which way the front wheels are turned. If the front wheels do not point straight ahead, the car will move left or right as soon as you start to drive. If you are not ready for this kind of move to the side, it could cause an accident.

If you plan to drive far, take time to check under the hood before you start. Be sure to look at the water in the battery, the windshield-wiper fluid, the coolant in the radiator, and the engine oil level.

PREPARING TO ENTER

If your car is parked at the curb, check carefully for approaching vehicles. Be sure that other drivers see you before you walk into the street. Unlock the door, get in, close and lock the door quickly. A car door extends roughly a meter (3 to 4 feet) into the roadway when it is fully open. An open door can force other drivers to swerve to avoid hitting you. This could put you or them in danger. If you drive a car that has bench seats and a shift lever on the steering column, it may be easier to enter the car from the curb side.

Before you get into your car and drive off, look for children. They may be playing very near your car. Also, look up and down the street to locate children who might be playing in the street where you will be driving.

INSIDE CHECKS

Once you are in the car, you should follow a prestart routine. Make sure you know where the switches and controls are in your car. Their positions can vary among makes and models of cars. Your owner's manual may suggest that you do things in a way slightly different from what you will read here. The important thing is to set up a good routine and follow it. In general, a prestart routine should go like this:

1. Put the key in the ignition switch.
2. Check to see that all doors are locked.
3. Adjust the seat. For the best control, you should sit high enough to see over the steering wheel. You should be able to see the ground about 3½ meters (12 feet) in front of the car. Your foot should be able to rest easily on the accelerator and brake pedals (and the clutch pedal if you drive a manual shift car). You should be able to turn the steering wheel a full 180 degrees (a half circle) left or right. You should then be able to turn it 360 degrees (a full circle) in the opposite direction without changing your hand position on the steering wheel.
4. Adjust the head restraint. Pull up the head restraint so that it rests at the back of your head, not at the base of your skull. If you fail to adjust it this way, you may suffer a serious neck injury if there is a crash.

After you have adjusted your seat and head restraint, adjust the side- and rear-view mirrors.

5. Adjust the rear- and side-view mirrors for best vision. If your car has day-night mirrors, choose the day or night setting, as needed. You can adjust the outside mirrors by lining them up with the fenders. In the same way, the rear window can serve as a reference point when you adjust the inside rear-view mirror. A close check will show that even when the mirrors are set correctly, there are blind spots at both sides and to the rear of your car. These blind spots make it necessary for you to turn your head and check to the sides before you make any lane changes.

6. Check the insides of the windows to see if they need to be cleaned or defrosted.

7. Check to see that packages and other articles do not block your view and will not fly about in the event of a quick stop.

8. Check the ventilation and adjust the air vents, windows, or air conditioner as needed.

9. Fasten the safety belts. If the car has adjustable lap and shoulder belts, the following checks should be made:

   a. The lap belt should fit snugly across the hips.

   b. The shoulder belt should have just enough slack so that your fist fits between the belt and the middle of your chest.

   c. All passengers should have fastened their safety belts before you start the car.

PREPARING TO LEAVE

Before you leave a parked car, make sure that it is secured. The gear-selector lever should be in *park* in a car with automatic transmission or in *reverse* in a manual-shift car. Make sure that the parking brake is set. Turn off all accessories. Close all windows. Lock all doors after the passengers are out.

If you must get out on the street or traffic side, take care not to endanger yourself or other roadway users. A good habit to have is sometimes called *Look, Latch, and Leap. Look:* first check in your side-view mirror for any traffic coming on your side of the road. This check includes bicycles and motorcycles as well as cars, trucks, and buses. Look over your shoulder to double check. *Latch:* open the door only if it is safe to do so, and note any traffic near you. *Leap:* step out, close and

(a) **Look.** Check your rear-view mirror. Check your side-view mirror. Look over your shoulder for traffic. (b) **Latch.** Open the door when safe. Continue to look for traffic. (c) **Leap.** Step out. Quickly close and lock the door while still checking traffic.

lock the door as fast as possible to get clear of traffic. If you are getting out of the car on the curb side, you still must look. Pedestrians, bicyclists, or other obstructions may be too close for you to safely open the door. Far too often, drivers swing the door open, step out of the car, and then look to see if anything is coming.

You should follow these same steps when you get out of a car parked in a parking lot. Drivers who enter a space next to a parked car tend to direct their attention to getting into the space. Their main concern is that they do not hit the cars parked on either side of the space. They seldom pay attention to the people who are getting out of the cars alongside. As a result, they may fail to see a door opening or someone stepping out until it is too late to stop safely.

In this chapter, you have learned the steps to follow to adjust the various comfort and safety devices. Also, you have been given a checklist to follow each time you enter or leave a motor vehicle. You should practice making these checks and adjustments in your family's or a friend's car before you show up for your first driving lesson. Begin to watch and note how other drivers act. This will help you become more familiar with basic driving maneuvers.

TO CONSIDER

1. What predriving checks should you make before you enter your parked car?

2. What predriving checks should you make inside the car?

3. What are some of the reasons for making predriving checks?

4. What hazards can a driver cause by opening the street-side door of a car parked at the curb?

5. Explain why it is important to check behind a parked car before you back up.

6. To which position should the head restraint be adjusted?

7. Why must you check the sides as well as look in the mirrors when you make a lane change?

8. As a driver, are you responsible for seeing that your passengers wear their safety belts? Why or why not?

9. Why is it important to look behind your car before getting in and backing out of a driveway?

10. Describe a seating position that gives a driver the best control.

PROJECTS

1. Observe the way drivers enter and leave cars parked at the curb on the side of a street. How many drivers exit on the traffic side? How many of them check the traffic as they exit?

2. Spend a few minutes surveying drivers getting into their cars in the parking lot of a local business, such as a bank or food store. What percentage of the drivers you questioned use a seat belt for local trips? What reasons did the drivers give for using or not using safety belts?

3. Using your local library as a resource, review clippings or reports of auto collisions. When a cause is given, how often is it due to an error in predriving checks or procedures? An example is failure to fasten safety belts or to adjust inside and outside mirrors properly.

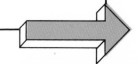

LEARNING BASIC MANEUVERS

UNIT

Unit III will help you master the skills you need in order to move, position, and control your car.

CHAPTER 4, "Basic Vehicle Control," tells you
- how to start your vehicle.
- how to speed up or stop smoothly and with control.
- how to maintain steering control while "tracking."

CHAPTER 5, "Space-Time Management," teaches you
- how to measure following distance and visual lead time.
- how much time you need to pass other vehicles.
- how much time you need to cross or turn at intersections.

CHAPTER 6, "Lateral Maneuvers," tells you
- how to merge onto and exit from an expressway.
- how to change lanes.
- how to change your position within a lane.

CHAPTER 7, "Turns," teaches you
- how to position your vehicle to prepare for a turn.
- where to start the turning movements
- how to steer so that you keep the most control.
- how to choose the best place for your car in the road ahead.

CHAPTER 8, "Driving a Car with a Stick Shift," teaches you
- how to drive a car with a manual transmission.

BASIC VEHICLE CONTROL

STARTING YOUR CAR

Make sure that you do all the predriving checks both inside and outside your car. After you have made any needed adjustments and have fastened your safety belts, you are ready to start the engine and prepare to move. It is again important that you get the habit of following a set way of doing things:

1. Make sure that the selector lever is in the right position—*park*—and that the parking brake is set.
2. Set the automatic *choke* (the valve that controls the air to the engine). To do this, press the gas pedal to the floor with your

right foot and then release it. This procedure feeds more fuel to the cylinders.

3. Place your left foot on the brake, press down hard, and hold it until you are ready to move.
4. Press the gas pedal down just a bit and hold it there.
5. Turn the ignition switch to *start*, let go of the key as soon as the engine is running, and let up on the gas pedal.
6. Let the engine *idle* (run in *neutral* gear) for a few seconds.
7. With your left hand, grasp the steering wheel. Decide which way you want to move and then, with your right hand, shift the gear selector lever to *drive* or *reverse*.
8. With your left foot still on the brake pedal, use your hand to release the parking brake.

You are now ready to make the car move. The next step is to learn to accelerate and brake smoothly. At the same time, you must learn the right way to position your car in a lane. You must be able to steer on straight streets, through curves and turns, both forward and in reverse.

Starting your car.

Make sure you are in park.

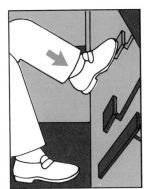

Make sure the parking brake is set.

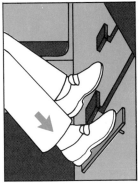

Press the gas pedal to the floor.

Place your left foot on the brake.

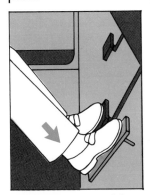

Hold the gas pedal down slightly.

Turn the ignition to start.

Shift to the gear you want.

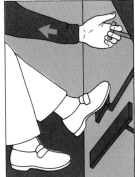

Release the parking brake.

ACCELERATING

For the best control of the gas pedal, the sole of your right foot should rest on the pedal, and the back of your heel should rest on the floor at the base of the pedal. To make the car pick up speed, press the pedal gently with the sole of your foot. Wearing high-heeled or platform shoes may make it difficult for you to control the gas pedal. If you wear these kinds of shoes, you should keep a pair of low-heeled or walking shoes in the car. Then when you drive, change your shoes. If you must, drive in your bare feet rather than with the wrong shoes. But first check your local traffic rules. While no state has a law that says you may not drive barefoot, some city authorities may not allow it.

BRAKING

For smooth braking, you need a sense of timing and the right pressure on the brake pedal. You may have problems if you

1. do not know when to press on the brake pedal.
2. cannot control the pressure you put on the brake pedal.

The amount of brake pressure you need to stop depends on many things. These include the size of the vehicle, its speed, the space it has in which to move, the type of brakes it has, and the road surface. With practice, you will learn to use just the right amount of pressure.

Watch the way experienced drivers brake to a stop. You can learn when to brake and how to stop more smoothly by watching what they do. For instance, at what point does the driver take his or her foot off the gas pedal and start to press on the brake? If you watch closely, you are likely to see that in a controlled stop, the driver applies pressure gradually. In that way, the pressure stays constant until the car slows down almost to a stop. At this point, the driver eases up slightly on the brake pedal and then uses pressure as needed to avoid a jerky stop.

The braking procedures used to stop on ice or under other emergency conditions are somewhat different. Even under such conditions, however, timing and application of controlled brake pressure remain the most critical factors.

TRACKING

Tracking means keeping the car moving on the path of travel you have chosen. This is done by making those steering changes needed to

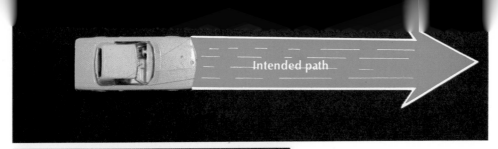

Intended path

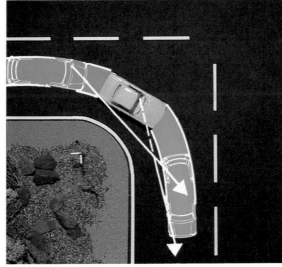

Look well ahead when you track in a straight line. Steer to a point in the center of your path.

Look through your intended turn to the point you want to reach. Always use the hand-over-hand steering for a smooth turn.

keep on the path. New drivers often fail to see slight or gradual changes in the position of the car. They do not correct their steering in time and, as a result, the car moves down the street in a series of jerks, left and right. To track smoothly, you will have to learn to steer to points well ahead on the road. You must choose these points on the basis of traffic conditions and where you want to go.

TRACKING IN A STRAIGHT LINE

The steering adjustments you will have to make on a straight road are small but critical. Because you may not be aware of gradual changes in the car's position, you may let it "wander" in its lane. When you try to correct this position, you may turn the steering wheel too much. This will cause the car to move too far in the opposite direction. To track smoothly, steer to a point in the center of your path. Look well ahead as you drive. Usually, only a slight turn of the steering wheel is needed to keep you on track.

To better understand how to steer smoothly, watch and question drivers when you are riding. See how much steering-wheel movement is needed to correct or maintain a car's position in a lane. You might ask the driver such questions as: Where in the path ahead are you looking? Why did you choose this lane? What made you decide to place the car in this lane?

TRACKING ON TURNS

Tracking smoothly through a turn requires much more steering-wheel movement than does lane positioning. Turning a corner smoothly requires the right timing and looking in the right places. Instead of keeping your eyes on the road immediately in front of the car, you should look beyond the turn to the point in the street that you want to reach. You must identify this point before you turn.

When you steer through a turn, you must consider several things. First, the rear wheels do not follow the same path as the front wheels.

Hand-over-hand steering: (a) Signal. Move your car into the correct position for turning. (b) With your left hand, push the steering wheel up, around, and down. Release your right hand when it reaches the bottom. (c) The left hand continues turning while the right hand crosses over it to the other side of the wheel. (d) The right hand then resumes turning as the left hand nears the bottom. Repeat as often as needed.

They have a smaller turning radius. As a result, you must allow extra space on the side of the car in the direction you are turning. You need this extra space so that your rear wheels do not hit the curb or other objects. Second, a different steering technique is required. To turn a corner, you should use *hand-over-hand steering*. This method of steering gives you the most steering control while you turn.

As you come to an intersection to make a right turn, for example, your hands should be on the upper half of the steering wheel at the 9 and 3 o'clock position. Grasp the steering wheel tightly with your left hand and push it up, around, and down toward the right. As your left hand nears the 3 o'clock position, reach across with your right hand and grip the steering wheel at the 9 o'clock position. With that hand, then pull the wheel up, across, and down. These movements are repeated as often and as fast as needed to bring the car where you want it to be. Correct your steering when necessary: If you have turned too sharply to the right, turn back a little to the left and then to the right again. Your steering judgment will improve with practice. To make a left turn, reverse the method described.

RECOVERING ON TURNS

When your car is about halfway through a turn, start to steer back to the straight-ahead position. Now, you should be looking at the point in the street you want to reach. You can return the steering wheel by one of two methods:

1. Reverse the procedure described in hand-over-hand steering.
2. Use the *controlled slipping* method. To do this, you let the steering wheel slip back through your hands. Then you tighten your hold on the wheel when the car is pointed in the direction you want it to go. Controlled slipping is sometimes difficult for new drivers to learn. This is especially true in cars that have power steering or in cars that are going at a very low speed. You may want to use the hand-over-hand steering method until you feel you have developed good vehicle control.

Poor recovery. The driver began recovery too late.

TRACKING TO THE REAR

Learning to track to the rear is also hard for many new drivers. At first, they may not know where to look, and they may fail to control steering and speed. To avoid making such errors, keep the following in mind whenever you back up.

LOOKING WHEN BACKING

You cannot see a great deal through the rear window. Head restraints and passengers block parts of your view. If you back up while you look into the rear-view mirror, the mirror restricts your view

When backing, turn your head so that you can see through the rear window. (a) Backing in a Straight Line: Brace yourself by placing your right arm and hand over the back of the seat. (b)(c) Backing to the Right and Left: Grasp the wheel in a 9- and 3-o'clock position.

even more. The best way to back up is to place yourself so that you can look in the direction you wish to go.

BACKING IN A STRAIGHT LINE

Turn your head and body to the right until you can see clearly through the rear window. Brace yourself by placing your right hand and arm over the back of the seat. If this is too awkward, hold onto the center console or passenger seat. Grasp the top of the steering wheel with your left hand and look through the rear window toward where you want to steer. Watch for pedestrians and obstacles.

BACKING AND TURNING

Turn your head and body until you can see through the rear side window in the direction you wish to go. Grasp the steering wheel with both hands in the 9 and 3 position, just as you would to turn while moving forward. Choose the point toward which you wish to steer. To change directions, turn the steering wheel hand-over-hand in the direction you want the back of the car to travel. Keep your speed low.

STEERING WHEN BACKING

You must move the steering wheel in the direction you want the car to go. Keep in mind that when you back up, the rear of the car becomes the front. It is the rear of the car that will move in the direction in which the steering wheel is turned. Again, the rear wheels of a car follow a path different from that followed by the front wheels. When you back and turn, the front of your car will swing in the direction opposite that to which you turn the steering wheel. As a result, there are two high-hazard points on the car when you back and turn it:

1. The rear side in the direction you are turning.
2. The front side opposite the direction you are turning.

KEEPING YOUR SPEED SLOW

It is important that you remember to back up slowly. Steering takes less effort and is more abrupt when you go backward. You must carefully control your speed of travel and steering-wheel movement. Speed and steering-wheel movement are even more critical if there is not much room in which to maneuver.

TO CONSIDER

1. What skills do you need for good tracking? What are some common tracking errors?

2. Explain why tracking on a turn is more difficult than tracking on a straight road.

3. What practices should you follow to avoid braking errors?

4. Why is it harder to steer when backing up?

5. What can you do to compensate for the difficulty of steering when you back up?

6. List and explain the steps you should always follow before starting your car.

7. Explain why care should be taken in selecting the shoes you wear if you plan to drive.

PROJECTS

1. Ride with an experienced driver and make notes about the way the driver makes steering corrections. Are the corrections smooth and gradual? Does the driver tend to "wander" across the road or within the traffic lane?

2. Make a chart of stopping distance required for different models and sizes of cars. Consult the magazines available in your school or local library.

3. Make your own checklist of things drivers should do in order to have the best control of their cars. Observe the driving of someone who you feel is a good driver. How closely does the person follow the guidelines for accelerating, braking, and backing? Has the person become careless? Report your findings.

CHAPTER 5

SPACE-TIME MANAGEMENT

To drive well in traffic, you need to position your car safely. First, choose a spot that lets you see the best—and be seen the most. Next, learn how to use your space by deciding upon the amount of time you will need to maneuver the car. And you must learn to judge the time and space other drivers and vehicles need to perform their maneuvers. Then you will be able to answer such questions as these:

- Am I looking far enough ahead?
- Is there enough space between my car and the one ahead?
- Can I stop in time if the vehicle ahead of me stops suddenly?
- Can I avoid a crash if the vehicle ahead of me has a collision?
- Do I have time to pass the vehicle ahead?
- How much time or distance does it take to stop my car?

- Do I have time to make a turn or to cross this intersection before an oncoming car gets here?

Once you have learned to judge time and distance, you will find driving in traffic much easier and safer.

SELECTING A POSITION IN TRAFFIC

To avoid accidents, you need to choose a spot in traffic where you can see and be seen. You also need to allow yourself enough *time* to react to danger. The road and traffic conditions that endanger you the most are the ones in front of you. If you follow another vehicle too closely *(tailgate)*, you may not have *time* and *space* enough to make a sudden stop or a fast change of lanes. So you need to keep a safe time-and-space gap between your car, the car ahead of you, and the car behind you.

The space gap between vehicles is called *following distance.* It is easy to convert following distance into seconds. Instead of car lengths, you use time to figure out whether you are far enough away from the car in front of or behind you. This system works whether you are driving fast or slow.

Choose a position in traffic that will allow you to keep a safe time-and-space gap between your car and the car ahead of you.

A 4-second following distance from the view of the driver.

A 4-second gap. When the rear of the first car passes the post, start to count from 1001 to 1004.

A 2-second following distance from the view of the driver.

A 2-second following gap. When the rear of the first car passes the post, start to count from 1001 to 1002.

2-SECOND FOLLOWING DISTANCE

In normal traffic and in good weather, a following distance of 2 seconds works well for cars. A gap of 2 seconds lets you see around the car ahead of you. It gives you time to change lanes fast if necessary. And it gives you time to brake to a stop if the car ahead of you brakes suddenly. But if you are behind a van or a large truck, 2 seconds is not enough time. You cannot see as well around a large vehicle. So when you follow large vehicles, stay at least 3 seconds behind them.

How can you judge a time gap of 2 seconds? It's easy. Watch the vehicle ahead of you in your lane. Wait until the rear of that vehicle passes a fixed point, such as a tree, a sign, a post, or an overpass. Then begin counting with "one-thousand-one." The front of your car should not reach the fixed point before you have said "one-thousand-two." If it does, you are following too closely. If the road is rough or if it is raining, you should increase your following distance to at least 3 seconds. If there is ice or packed snow on the road or if it is raining hard, a gap of 5 or 6 seconds may be needed. You can practice counting seconds when you ride in a car as a passenger.

4-SECOND PATH OF TRAVEL

The 2-second following rule works well if you must stop because the driver ahead of you brakes suddenly. If you are traveling at highway speeds and the road ahead is suddenly blocked by a crash or if a vehicle stops across your lane, a 2-second following distance would not give you enough time to stop. Then, the time needed to stop depends on your speed. At a speed of 50 km/h (30 mph), you can stop in about 2 seconds. If you are driving 90 km/h (55 mph), you will need nearly 4 seconds to stop. In addition, to stay out of a collision, you would have to have an *escape route*. A 4-second path of travel gives you the time to take an escape route. Always have an escape route in mind when you choose a position in traffic. Ask yourself two questions:

1. Based on road and traffic conditions, where do I want my car to be 4 seconds from now? This is called your *immediate path of travel*.
2. Where would I place my car 4 seconds from now if my path of travel were suddenly blocked? This is called your *alternate path of travel*.

You can set up a 4-second path of travel by counting. Pick a point ahead of you. Then, after the car in front passes the point, count from "one-thousand-one" to "one-thousand-four." Four seconds is the *approximate* time it will take to stop at speeds above 80 km/h (50 mph).

FOLLOWING DISTANCES AND GAPS

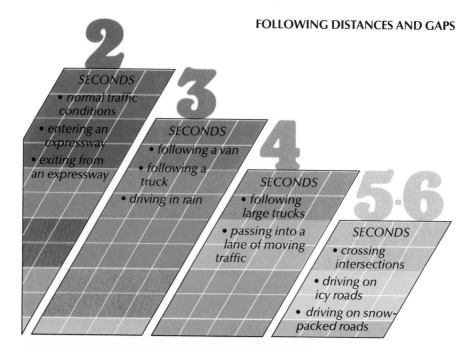

2 SECONDS
- normal traffic conditions
- entering an expressway
- exiting from an expressway

3 SECONDS
- following a van
- following a truck
- driving in rain

4 SECONDS
- following large trucks
- passing into a lane of moving traffic

5-6 SECONDS
- crossing intersections
- driving on icy roads
- driving on snow-packed roads

VISUAL LEAD TIME

You have learned that steering is easier if you look farther ahead. You should look at least 12 seconds ahead when you drive on city streets. At 50 km/h (30 mph), you are moving at 13 meters (44 feet) per second. At this speed, with a visual lead time of 12 seconds, you would be searching about *one block ahead*. This is far enough in the city.

If you are on an expressway driving at 90 km/h (55 mph), you may need to look 20 to 30 seconds ahead. Such a visual lead provides the time you need to safely choose an immediate path of travel. It gives you time to search the areas beside the road. It allows you the time to adjust your speed or to make lane changes well in advance of any problems. And it lets you find alternate paths if an emergency should arise.

You can find the 12-second visual lead time in the same way you find the 2-second following distance. Pick a point ahead of you. Start counting with ''one-thousand-one'' and count up to ''one-thousand-twelve.'' If you get to the point you chose before you reach ''one-thousand-twelve,'' you should look farther ahead. Remember, 12 seconds is a *minimum* visual lead for city driving.

VISUAL LEAD TIME

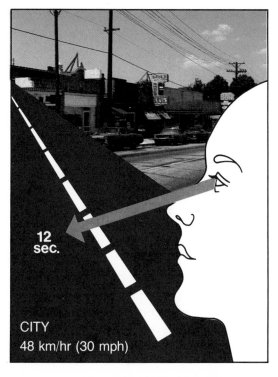

CITY
48 km/hr (30 mph)

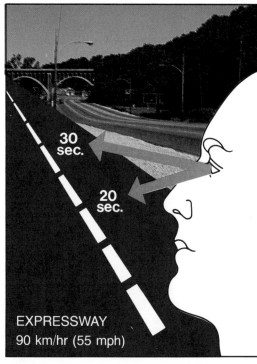

EXPRESSWAY
90 km/hr (55 mph)

ACTIONS TO AVOID

There are two actions that often affect a driver's visual search. They are staring at a fixed point and distractions.

STARING AT A FIXED POINT

Staring, no matter how far ahead, will not provide the information you need to plan a safe path of travel. Such action results in a narrow visual-search pattern. You must, therefore, learn to *scan* the road and roadsides ahead. You scan the road by moving your eyes back and forth between your car and your checkpoints ahead.   Look from one side of the roadway to the other. Search for clues that will assist you in selecting the safest and most efficient path of travel. You should also check to the rear. However, remember, the major source of problems is in front of you. But do have a plan for checking to the rear. A simple rule exists for making such checks: Anytime anything in front of you indicates that you may need to adjust speed or position, check to the rear for possible conflicts.

DISTRACTIONS

Many things may attract your attention. Unless you concentrate on driving, your visual lead may slip to as little as 3 or 4 seconds. A visual lead this short means that you are driving from crisis to crisis. The results of such visual habits can be observed as you see drivers making abrupt speed or lane changes or adjustments within their lane.

JUDGING THE TIME-SPACE GAP FOR PASSING

Passing another vehicle on a two-way roadway   can be dangerous. On a road that has only one lane going in each direction, you must check for cars coming toward you. You must also check behind, ahead, and to the side. Time and distance judgments become very critical for this type of maneuver.

When you start to pass another vehicle, an oncoming vehicle should be far enough away so that it seems to be standing still. If the road is flat and straight, vehicles will seem to be standing still when they are .8 kilometer (1/2 mile) or more from you.

There is another passing guide that involves counting seconds. It should take about 10 seconds to pass another car. Practice counting these seconds when you ride as a passenger with someone else. Start to count "one-thousand-one" when an oncoming car gets to the nearest point that you feel would still give you time to pass a car ahead. If you meet the oncoming car before you have reached at least "one-thousand-nine," the car was too close. If you counted higher than "one-thousand-fourteen," you allowed too much time.

How can waiting for too long a gap place you in danger? By failing to pass when you have enough time, you may anger the drivers behind you. As a result, other drivers may try to pass both you and the car you are following. This increases the risk of collision for all the drivers that are near you.

When passing on a two-way highway, make sure that the car coming toward you is far enough away so that the situation will not become hazardous. Signal that you plan to pass. Keep a 2-second following distance behind the car you are passing.

JUDGING THE TIME-AND-SPACE GAP AT INTERSECTIONS

Up to now, you have learned to judge the time-space gap between cars traveling in the same or in the opposite direction. Intersections require a similar set of space-time judgments. At intersections, you

51

must learn to judge gaps in traffic when vehicles are moving from the left and from the right of you. This is very important at intersections that have no signs or that have only yield or stop signs.

Most collisions at intersections occur when a car leaving a stop sign is struck from the right. This often happens because drivers approaching a stop sign look first to their left because that is the first lane of traffic they must cross. Drivers also tend to wait for a longer gap in traffic coming from the left than from the right. That habit places them in greater danger from vehicles coming from the right.

From a stopped position, it usually takes about 4 seconds to cross a street 7- to 9-meters (24- to 30-feet) wide. This means that you need at least a 5- to 6-second gap in traffic from both directions in order to cross. There is no simple rule for judging intersection time gaps for all speeds. For vehicles moving at 50 km/h (30 mph), a time gap of 6 seconds equals about half a block.

Try to determine a 6-second time gap. Stand at a corner and pick a car coming from the left. Start at "one-thousand-one" and count as the car passes through the intersection. How far does it travel by the time you count to "one-thousand-six"? Practice this counting a few times at the same place. What is the average distance that cars travel in 6 seconds? Cars coming toward the intersection from the right should be this far away before you would start to drive across the street.

When you have learned to spot a checkpoint for cars coming from the right, find a point in the same way for cars coming from the left. These two points can serve as a reference for streets where speeds and traffic conditions are similar. You will need to find different checkpoints for places with different traffic patterns and speeds.

TIME GAP   FOR A RIGHT-HAND TURN

To make a right turn at an intersection, you need a longer time gap than you would need to cross the intersection. From a dead stop, it takes about 6 seconds to turn right and to speed up to 50 km/h (30 mph). To be safe, you need a gap of 7 to 8 seconds between you and a vehicle coming from the left. This gap will allow the driver of that vehicle to keep a 2-second following distance once you are in the same lane and traveling at traffic speed.

On the open highway, speeds may be up to 90 km/h (55 mph). It takes more time, then, to reach the speed of traffic after you complete a turn. At highway speeds, you may have to increase the time gap for a right turn to 11 seconds or more. Use the method you have already learned. Pick a car that is passing through the intersection from the right. Find how far it goes in 11 seconds. The distance it goes is the gap you will need between your car and oncoming cars from the left.

TIME GAP FOR A LEFT-HAND TURN

A left turn is more dangerous than a right turn. When you make a left turn, you are faced with two hazards. Vehicles are moving toward you from the left and from the right. You must turn into the far lane while speeding up but while still moving at a low rate of speed. This takes time and increases the gap you need. At 50 km/h (30 mph), however, you need about 9 seconds. It will take 7 seconds to turn into the far lane and to come back up to speed. You will need 2 seconds more to make a following-distance gap between you and the vehicle closing in from the right.

To turn left onto a highway where traffic is moving as fast as 90 km/h (55 mph), you will need a gap of 13 or 14 seconds. This will allow you time to accelerate to highway speeds. It also includes a 2-second following distance for the vehicle behind you.

You need an 8-second gap between you and a vehicle coming from the left in order to make a right turn at an intersection. This gap will allow the vehicle behind you to keep a 2-second following distance when you are both in the same lane.

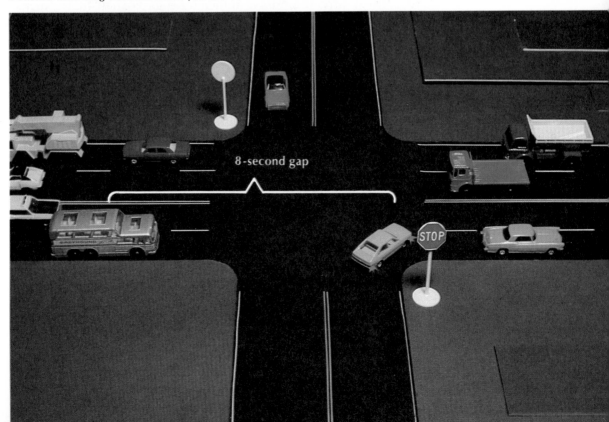

8-second gap

TO CONSIDER

1. What are three things which you must do to position your car safely in traffic?

2. Why is it important to keep an adequate time gap between your car and the vehicle ahead of you?

3. Describe the method explained in the text for keeping a 2-second following distance.

4. What is the purpose of the 4-second path-of-travel rule?

5. How can you measure your visual lead time?

6. How long should your visual lead time be on city streets? On an expressway? Explain your answer.

7. What are two time-space guides which you should use when passing other vehicles?

8. How can you make sure that you can safely pass another car on a two-way road?

9. Explain how you can judge the time gap needed when crossing an intersection.

10. Which turn requires a longer time gap: a left-hand turn or a right-hand turn? Give reasons for your answer.

PROJECTS

1. While riding as a passenger in a car, identify alternate paths of travel. Then ask the driver where he or she would go if the road ahead were blocked. Repeat the question in several driving situations. Do you and the driver always agree?

2. Stand near an intersection that is controlled by a stop or a yield sign. Do the drivers who are turning or driving through the intersection allow long-enough gaps in the cross traffic? Report on your findings.

3. Select a section of divided highway and conduct a survey. How many drivers use a 2-second following distance? Do the drivers who use less than a 2-second following distance tend to change lanes more often than those who use the 2-second distance?

CHAPTER **6**

LATERAL MANEUVERS

You are now ready to move onto the road. If you start from a roadside parking space, you have to move from there into a traffic lane. This sideways motion, either to the front or to the rear, is called a *lateral maneuver*. Lateral maneuvers can be within, into, out of, or across a traffic lane.

Lateral maneuvers are basic to driving. You may adjust your position by moving left or right within a lane. You may also move to another lane. These are the most common lateral maneuvers. Merging onto or exiting from an expressway are other kinds. Still others are pulling off a road onto a shoulder, parallel parking, and passing.

ELEMENTS OF A LATERAL MANEUVER

All lateral maneuvers require the same checks and procedures:

1. Check the path ahead and behind to see that it is clear. Is there enough space and time to perform the maneuver?
2. Check the mirrors. Is traffic closing in from the rear or from the next lane? Are any cars close enough to be a hazard?
3. Signal your intent to move left or right.
4. Make sure the lane you wish to enter is clear. Check over your shoulder in the direction in which you plan to move.
5. Adjust speed up or down as needed.
6. Move only when it is safe to do so.

Whenever you make a lateral maneuver, give special attention to

1. Speed adjustment, either through the use of the gas pedal or the brake.
2. The amount of steering that has to be done.
3. The time and space needed to enter or leave traffic.

When you make lateral maneuvers, check the path ahead and behind you to see that it is clear. Then (a) check your rear-view mirror, (b) check your side-view mirror, (c) signal, and (d) look over your shoulder to check blind spots. Adjust your speed and make your move.

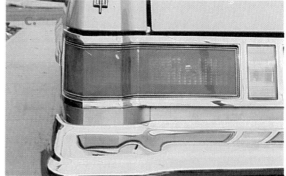

a.

b.

c.

When you enter a roadway from a parallel parking space, check the posted speed limit. Always check traffic to be sure you have enough room to make the maneuver.

ENTERING A ROADWAY FROM THE CURB

The simplest way to move from the curb is shown in A. The driver is about to enter a roadway where there is little or no traffic. The speed limit is 40 km/h (25 mph). Entering the roadway requires slight steering. Room to accelerate is available. There is barely any traffic.

In B, a truck is parked right behind the car. The driver must move forward in order to check traffic to the side and rear. Is there enough space to enter the roadway? The speed limit is 50 km/h (30 mph), but there is ample room to pick up speed. Little steering is needed because of the clear path ahead.

Situation C requires more accurate space-time judgments. The car parked in front and the car parked behind limit the space in which the driver can maneuver. The car's speed must be closely controlled. The speed limit is 70 km/h (45 mph). To allow the driver time to clear the car parked ahead, the gap in traffic must be much greater. Time is also needed to accelerate to the speed of the traffic in the lane.

You must take into consideration the time and space you need to position your vehicle. You must check in front of you, to the side, and to the rear. The time and speed needed for the maneuver depend on whether you are driving in traffic or pulling away from a roadside curb. You must also manage the space around your car when you are already in the stream of traffic.

CHANGING LANES ON THE HIGHWAY

On a multiple-lane highway, the same checks are required for positioning within a lane, lane changing, and passing. For this reason, the following discussion applies to all three maneuvers.

Assume that there is something close to the roadside 12 seconds ahead. Or assume that a slow-moving or wide vehicle is blocking your lane view. What should you do if you decide to change positions? First, you must make some checks. Will other vehicles, either behind or in front of you, be making the same move? Is there anything now in, or going into, the lane you wish to enter? Will other vehicles in the lane or lanes beside you try to enter your lane as you try to move out of it? Is anything approaching you fast from the rear?

While planning your move, make sure that you keep at least a 2-second following distance. Plan at least a 4-second path ahead. Check your mirrors and signal your intention to move. Just before you move, check over your shoulder in the direction in which you wish to move. Is there a 4-second gap in traffic in the lane you wish to enter? (Remember, a 4-second gap will give both you and the car behind you in the new lane a 2-second following distance.) If everything is all right, increase your speed a bit and steer into the new lane.

If the car on the left passes the car on the right, the passing driver will need a 4-second gap in traffic to safely enter the right lane. On an expressway, the driver can remain in the passing lane until such a gap occurs. On a two-lane road, a driver should not pass without enough space to reenter the right lane.

If you want to go back to your lane after you pass the other vehicle, repeat all the checks and signals. Before you move back into the lane, look into your inside rear-view mirror to make sure you can see the front of the vehicle which you just passed.

ENTERING AND LEAVING AN EXPRESSWAY

A lateral maneuver is harder to make when you are trying to enter or leave an expressway. Often, drivers are slowing to exit as other drivers are speeding up to enter. The two groups of vehicles must cross in what is known as a *weaving lane*.

Another problem may come up when you try to enter an expressway in which traffic is heavy or the entrance lane is short or curved. Here you may not be able to increase your speed to that of the traffic on the expressway. In either case, determining the safest speed and timing needed to merge will be very hard.

EXPRESSWAY ENTRY

As you get near the weaving lane, check for traffic ahead. Since vehicles ahead of you may slow or stop in busy traffic, keep a 2-second following distance. If a driver in front of you seems unsure, increase your following distance. Be ready to stop. Signal your intention to enter the expressway.

Check to the side and over your shoulder for possible conflicts. Look for vehicles signaling to exit. Check for a gap into which you can merge. Adjust your speed to that of the traffic flow. Keep checking the traffic ahead and the gap you plan to merge into. You must merge into the lane of traffic before you reach the end of the acceleration lane.

On some expressways, you will find a very short acceleration lane. In a few cases, there is no lane at all. Signs will tell you to stop or yield to through traffic. When you find this, you will need a much longer gap in traffic to enter. You must have more time to accelerate to the speed of the traffic on the expressway.

In a few cases, the acceleration lane merges into the far left lane of an expressway. This lane usually is used by high-speed traffic. Here you will have to make quick, accurate time and distance judgments. You will have to make early decisions. Then, you will have to accelerate quickly to bring the car smoothly into the lane of traffic.

EXPRESSWAY EXIT

First, know where you want to exit. Will you exit from the left or right side of the road? Place your car in the proper lane before you get to the exit. Can you make a simple lane change to a deceleration (slowing) lane and then reduce speed for the exit ramp? Will you have to pass through a weaving lane?

To help you to make these decisions, guide signs are placed about 2 kilometers (1 mile) ahead of the exits in urban areas. In rural areas, the signs are 2 and 3 kilometers (1 and 2 miles) ahead of the exits. Signs also show if the exit is on the left or the right side of the expressway. In general, the signs also show how many exit lanes there are. This should give you time to make changes in position and speed.

If you exit at a direct connection with a crossroad—such as at a diamond interchange—just make the lane changes. Be sure you change only one lane at a time, though. Signal your intention to exit. Steer into the deceleration lane. Slow down to the posted speed.

The drawing below shows the proper procedure for exiting from an expressway. The car leaving the expressway must pass through a weaving area. The car entering the expressway must also pass through the weaving area.

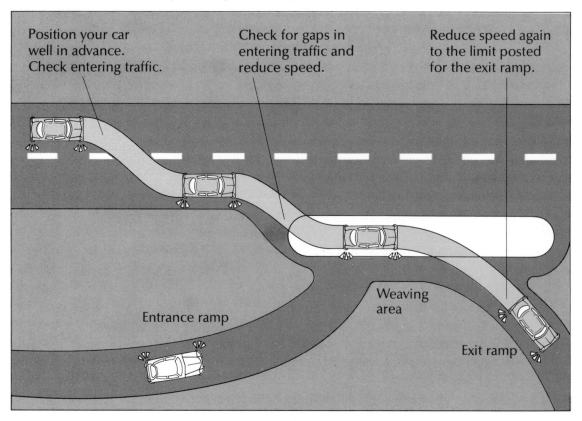

Position your car well in advance. Check entering traffic.

Check for gaps in entering traffic and reduce speed.

Reduce speed again to the limit posted for the exit ramp.

Entrance ramp

Weaving area

Exit ramp

An exit through a weaving area is a more difficult task. You are trying to move into the lane which leads from the roadway and slow down to exit. At the same time, drivers in the acceleration lane are entering the weaving lane (the same lane that you are using to exit) and trying to speed up to join the traffic lane. You should be driving in the lane next to the weaving lane. Turn your signal on well in advance to alert the drivers entering the roadway and the drivers behind you. Keeping a 2-second gap between you and the car ahead, check for a gap in the flow of vehicles on the entrance ramp. Adjust your speed so that you can steer your car into the gap in the weaving lane. Then complete your merge into the deceleration lane and move onto the exit ramp.

STEERING TO THE CURB

If you are going to park along a curb, let other drivers know what you intend to do. Move into the proper lane well in advance and signal that you are leaving the road. Use your turn signals, slow down, and flash your brake lights. You must use great care if you choose a parking space just past an intersection. When you slow down and signal as you approach the intersection, you could lead other drivers to think that you intend to turn. A car could pull out into your path as you go straight ahead. If other cars are near the intersection, just place your car in the lane and slow down. Do not use your turn signals until your car has entered the intersection.

PARALLEL PARKING

As you look for a parking space, keep an eye on the traffic around you. Concentrating on finding a parking space could cause you to fail to see sudden changes in traffic around you. It could also cause you to forget to check or signal while making a maneuver.

As early as you can, let other drivers know that you plan to go into a parking space. Put on your turn signal and flash your brake lights to warn other drivers that you intend to stop. Move over until your car is within 1 meter (4 feet) of the line of parked cars. Check to make sure that it is legal to park in the space. If it is, is the space large enough for your car? As a rule, the space must be at least 1.5 meters (5 feet) longer than your car. If the space is long enough, drive forward and steer left or right so that you have a space of ½ to 1 meter (2 to 3 feet) between your car and the parked car. If your car and the car you are parking behind are about the same size, stop when the center doorpost of your car is in line with the center doorpost of the car that you want to park behind. If there is a great difference in size, try to match up the positions of the back bumpers. (You would move ahead of the center doorpost of the other car if your car is longer. You would back up further if it is shorter.)

ENTERING A PARALLEL PARKING SPACE

From this point on, parallel parking is a lateral move to the rear. You must concentrate on and control both steering and speed.

Remember, keep your speed slow. When you want to stop to park, signal that you plan to do so. Check for traffic and pedestrians.

These are the steps for parallel parking.

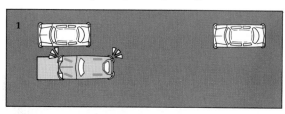

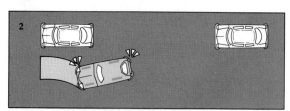

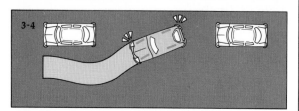

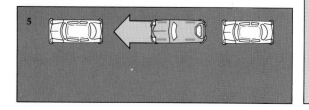

1. With your left foot on the brake pedal, shift to *reverse.* Check for traffic in the next lane. (Remember, when you back up, the front of your car will move in the opposite direction from that in which you turn the steering wheel.)
2. When you park on the right side of the street, turn the steering wheel at a smooth, steady rate all the way to the right as you move back slowly. (Keep your foot on the brake pedal.) Stop when the back of your front seat is in line with the rear bumper of the car you are parking behind. Start to move back slowly again and turn the steering wheel quickly and smoothly to the straight-line position. (If you fail to straighten your front wheels, the car will be at such a sharp angle that your rear right wheel will strike the curb. Do not turn the steering wheel too far to the left. If you do, your right front fender may hit the left rear fender of the parked car in front of you.)
3. Continue to go back with the wheels straight until your right front fender just clears the left rear fender of the car you are parking behind. At this point, your left rear fender should be in line with the inside edge of the left headlight of the car parked behind you.
4. Look over your left shoulder and move back slowly. As you move, turn the steering wheel quickly and smoothly all the way to the left. Continue to back up slowly. Stop just before you touch the car behind you.
5. Shift to *drive.* Move forward slowly. Turn the steering wheel all the way to the right. Go forward until your right front tire just touches the curb. At this point, your car should be centered in the space. It should also be parallel to and within .3 meter (1 foot) of the curb.

The illustration on page 62 shows parallel parking on the right. Parallel parking on the left is accomplished in much the same manner. The main difference between left-side and right-side parking is that at each of the checkpoints, you turn the steering wheel in the opposite direction. Since you can see each of the checkpoints more readily, you may find that parking on the left is easier than parking on the right.

The final step in parallel parking—turning the steering wheel to block the tire against the curb or toward the side of the road—is a safety measure. (It is required by law in some states.) This step may stop the car from rolling downhill or into the street. Always shift to *park* and set your parking brake whenever you park. This is especially important when you park on a hill. A parked car that is accidentally left in *neutral* without the parking brake set can be a hazard. The car could begin to roll out of control, endangering anyone or anything nearby.

Before you position your car to parallel park, make sure the space is big enough for your car. The space must be at least 1.5 meters (5 feet) longer than your car. When you back up, back slowly and check for pedestrians. Do not forget to check the traffic coming up behind you.

EXITING FROM A PARALLEL PARKING SPACE

To exit from a parallel parking space, move the car forward or back a little to bring the front tire away from the curb. Turn the steering wheel left or right until the front wheels point straight ahead. Move backward in the space until you almost touch the car behind you. At this point, reverse Steps 2 through 5 for entering a parallel parking space. Be sure to move your car slowly. Check for other cars before you pull out into the traffic lane next to the parking space.

LEAVING THE ROADWAY

You have dealt with steering to the curb and parallel parking. Like most other maneuvers, they are more complex when traffic is heavy. When there is little traffic, leaving the road may require no more than signaling, changing lanes, and braking to a stop. However, leaving the road to avoid a collision requires quick judgment and good control. In such a case, you may have to go off the road onto a shoulder. For the proper way to perform this maneuver, read Chapter 22.

TO CONSIDER

1. List the steps required in all lateral maneuvers.

2. What three factors must you pay special attention to when you make a lateral maneuver?

3. Describe the hazards of making a lateral maneuver to enter onto or exit from an expressway.

4. List the steps to take when parallel parking.

5. Describe a situation in which you would have to make a lateral maneuver *within* your lane.

6. Why is making a lateral maneuver harder when the time and space needed for the maneuver are limited?

7. Why is it a good idea to wait for a 4-second gap in traffic in the lane you wish to enter before changing lanes?

8. As a general rule, should you slow down, keep the same speed, or increase your speed a bit when changing lanes on an expressway?

9. Why is exiting through an expressway's weaving area a more difficult task than exiting where there is no weaving area?

PROJECTS

1. Observe traffic on an expressway entrance ramp for 15 minutes. Why are some vehicles unable to merge smoothly with traffic on the expressway? How could this problem have been avoided?

2. In an area with parallel parked cars, observe five to ten drivers entering the traffic from a parked position. How many of them fail to maintain an adequate gap to the rear? Make a record of your findings.

3. While riding with a friend or in the family car, count the number of lateral maneuvers the driver makes. Give a separate count for each different type, such as expressway merge, a lane change, or parallel parking. Choose the one maneuver that seemed the hardest. Describe what happened and give your reasons why it was the hardest.

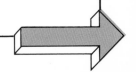

CHAPTER **7**

TURNS

Turns are another group of basic traffic movements. You have learned how to plan a safe path of travel and to move a car laterally. Now you must learn to judge the time and space you need to make turns under many different conditions. Although the basic steps are the same, turns vary in difficulty. They may be simple or complicated. Pulling into an angle parking space when no other cars are present is easy. However, backing out of that same spot could be a problem. The problem might be brought about when other cars are parked next to you and traffic is heavy. A turn from a one-way street onto another one-way street at an intersection controlled by a traffic signal is rather easy. But a turn into a multiple-lane, two-way highway without a traffic signal where traffic is moving at a high rate of speed requires difficult time and space decisions.

66

PREPARING FOR AN INTERSECTION MANEUVER

You must let other drivers know what you plan to do as you come to an intersection. You can tell them in a number of ways. First, place your car in the proper position in the correct lane well in advance. If you intend to turn, signal early. In the city in many states, you must signal at least 30 meters (100 feet) before you reach the place where you intend to make a turn. You must signal 60 meters (200 feet) ahead in rural areas in some states. It is best, though, if you warn other drivers even earlier. You should signal 45 to 60 meters (150 to 200 feet) ahead of your turn in town, and 90 to 150 meters away (300 to 500 feet) on the open highway.

As you approach an intersection, check for signs that control your movement. Is there a traffic signal light? A yield right-of-way sign? A stop sign? Are turns allowed? If turns are allowed, may they be made only at certain hours of the day or days of the week? May they be made only by certain types of vehicles? Are there special lanes for turning? Even before you have determined that a turn is allowed, slow down by pumping the brake pedal. The flashing brake light will warn the drivers in back of you that you plan to turn.

While all intersections are not the same, the following rules apply to most:

1. Unless you are told to do something else by a traffic sign, a signal, an officer, or road markings, make left turns from the farthest left lane of traffic. Make right turns from the farthest right lane of traffic.
2. Unless a traffic sign, a signal, an officer, or road markings indicate something else, turn into the nearest lane moving in the direction you wish to go.
3. Where turns are allowed from more than one lane, turn into the lane corresponding to the lane you left.

RIGHT TURNS

The steps for a right turn from a one-way or two-way street are the same whether the street you are turning into is one-way or two-way. Place your car in the proper lane. Signal that you plan to turn 30 to 60 meters (100 to 200 feet) before you reach the intersection. Stop behind the crosswalk or stop sign, about 1 to 1.5 meters (4 to 5 feet) from the

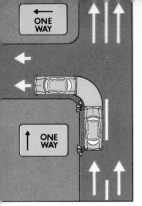

Left turn from a
one-way street into
a one-way street.

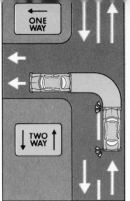

Left turn from a
two-way street into
a one-way street.

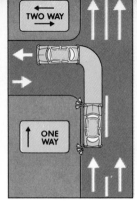

Left turn from a
one-way street into
a two-way street.

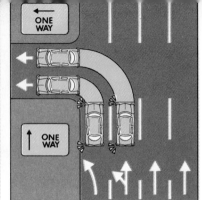

Left turn from a
multilane street into
a one-way street.

Turn from and into the correct lanes at an intersection.

side of the road. (Remember, the right rear wheel will have a smaller turning radius than the right front wheel. Unless you allow room, the rear wheel will strike the curb.)

Check for pedestrians or other obstacles in the path of travel you plan to take. Check for cars across the intersection that may be signaling to make a left turn. Move up until your front bumper is in line with the curb or edge of the road you wish to enter. Find a 7- to 8-second gap in the traffic to your left. Look through the turn to a point in the cross street to which you want to turn. You should then enter the first lane of traffic.

Accelerate to about 8 km/h (5 mph) as you turn the steering wheel hand over hand to the right. Choose a point 3 to 4 seconds in front of your car to which you want to steer. When the front of your car gets to a point about halfway through the turn, start to turn the wheel to the left (back to the straight-ahead position). Accelerate to the speed of traffic. Make sure the turn signal is off.

LEFT TURNS

LEFT TURN ON TWO-WAY STREETS

The steps for a left turn vary. They depend on what type street you are turning from and what type street you are turning onto. Left turns from a one-way street onto a two-way street require that you cross the lanes of traffic which are coming from your left. Left turns from a two-way street require that you also cross a lane of traffic coming toward you from across the intersection. Signal that you plan to turn 30 to 60

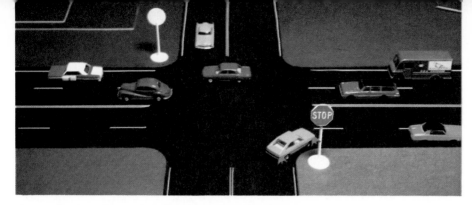

The car that is making a right-hand turn from the stop sign has the right to do so. There is no oncoming traffic in the lane in which the car is turning. The car at the opposite stop sign must wait. Traffic will not allow this car either to go forward or to turn.

When you are waiting at an intersection to make a left-hand turn, keep your wheels pointed straight ahead. If you are struck from behind, you will not be pushed into oncoming traffic.

meters (100 to 200 feet) before you reach an intersection. Stop your car next to the center line behind the crosswalk or stop sign.

Check for pedestrians or other objects in your path of travel. Check for cars across the intersection that may be coming straight through the intersection or are signaling a right turn. Check for traffic from the left. Find a 9-second gap to your right. Look through the turn to a point in the intersection to which you want to drive.

Move up until you are about one lane width away from the center of the intersection. Turn the steering wheel hand over hand to the left. Keep your speed at 8 to 15 km/h (5 to 10 mph).

Choose another point 3 to 4 seconds in front of your car to which you want to steer. When the front of your car enters the first lane beyond the center line, start to bring the steering wheel back to the straight-ahead position.

Accelerate to the speed of traffic and make sure the turn signal is off. Once you reach the speed of traffic, move into the proper lane.

LEFT TURN FROM A ONE-WAY STREET

If you are making a left turn from a one-way street into another one-way street, the procedure is similar to that followed for a right turn because you enter the first lane of traffic. If you are making a left turn from a one-way street onto a two-way street, the procedure is slightly different. You place your car in the far left-hand lane and turn into the first lane of traffic going in your direction.

ANGLE PARKING

In many parking lots and on some streets, angle parking is the only kind that is permitted. As a rule, when you park at an angle, you have little room and cannot see very much. You will have to be very careful getting in and out of an angle parking space.

When you look for a place to angle park, drive so that you can see as much as possible and have the most space in which to maneuver. Keep your car 1.5 to 2 meters (5 to 6 feet) from parked cars. Watch for any sign—such as brake lights or exhaust smoke—that tells you that a vehicle may be backing out of a parking space.

A. When you enter or leave an angle parking space, watch your left front bumper and your right rear fender or door. Move slowly. Check for traffic and pedestrians.

B. When you park at an angle, drive very slowly. Watch for brake lights and exhaust smoke from parked cars. This tells you that a car is about to back out. Use turn signals. Keep your car 1 to 2 meters (5 to 6 feet) from parked cars.

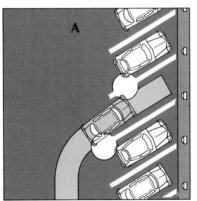
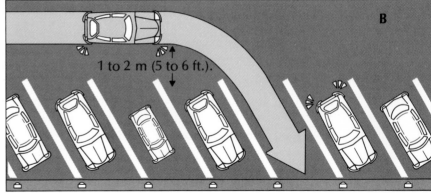

1 to 2 m (5 to 6 ft.).

ANGLE PARKING ON THE RIGHT

When you find an empty parking space, use your turn signal and slow to a speed of 5 to 8 km/h (3 to 5 mph). Keep at least 1.5 or 2 meters (5 or 6 feet) from parked cars. Drive forward until you can see along the left side of the car parked to the right of the space you want to enter. Quickly turn the steering wheel hand over hand all the way to the right. As the front of your car moves into the center of the parking space, turn the wheel to the straight-ahead position. Keep your speed slow. When the car is centered in the space, move up until your front wheels gently touch the curb. When you enter or leave an angle parking space, watch your left front bumper and your right rear fender or door. These are the points at which you can most easily hit the cars parked on either side of you.

EXITING FROM AN ANGLE PARKING SPACE

To leave an angle parking space, place your foot on the brake pedal and shift to *reverse*. Check for pedestrians, bicycles, and other vehicles. Move back slowly. Check your left front bumper so that you do not hit the car to your left. Check over your right shoulder for traffic. When your rear window is in line with the rear bumper of the car parked to your right, check traffic again. If the lane is clear, turn the wheel all the way to the right as you go back slowly. As your car centers in the traffic lane, straighten the front wheels. Shift to *drive* and drive forward.

ANGLE PARKING ON THE LEFT

Angle parking on the left requires almost the same checks and steps as angle parking on the right. The differences are

1. you turn the steering wheel the opposite way.
2. the danger points are now your right front bumper and your left rear fender.

PERPENDICULAR PARKING

Sometimes, parking spaces are marked at a 90-degree angle. Parking lots marked this way provide more spaces. This is the most dangerous kind of parking. The problem again is that it is hard to see at an angle, and there is little room in which to maneuver. When you look for such a parking space, stay alert for parked cars that are starting to pull out. Watch for brake lights or exhaust smoke.

ENTERING A PERPENDICULAR PARKING SPACE ON THE RIGHT

When you find a parking space, signal and slow to a speed of 5 to 8 km/h (3 to 5 mph). If the space is on the right, move to a spot 2 to 2½ meters (7 to 8 feet) away from cars parked on your right. Drive forward until your front bumper is in line with the left side of the car parked to the right of the space that you want to turn into. Quickly turn the steering wheel hand over hand to the right. Check carefully to be sure your left front bumper will clear the parked car, then move forward slowly. As your car centers in the space, turn the wheel back to the

Use your turn signal and slow down to indicate that you want to park. Drive forward until your front bumper aligns with the side of the car you are parking along side of. Check your rear fender. Turn into the space. Stop just short of the curb.

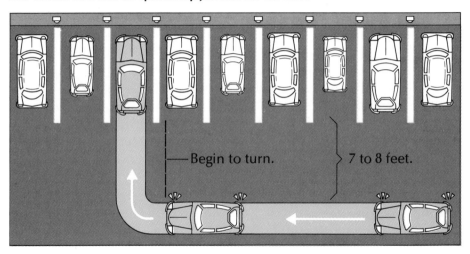

When you exit from a perpendicular parking space, drive slowly. Check sides and rear for pedestrians and traffic. Check your front bumper and the rear of cars opposite the direction you are turning. Make sure your front bumper does not hit the rear bumper of the car beside you.

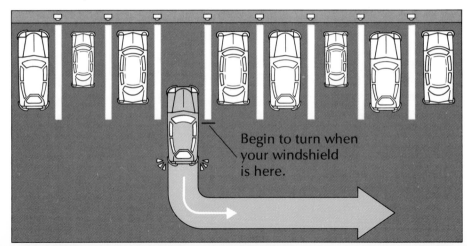

straight-ahead position. Check your right rear fender to see that it does not scrape the rear bumper of the car on your right. Drive forward slowly and position your car in the center of the space. Stop just short of the curb or of the car parked in the space in front of you. Shift to *park* and lock your car.

ENTERING A PERPENDICULAR PARKING SPACE ON THE LEFT

Entering a perpendicular parking space on the left requires almost the same checks and steps used when entering one on the right. The differences are

1. you turn the steering wheel in the opposite way.
2. the danger points are your right front bumper and your left rear fender.

EXITING FROM A PERPENDICULAR PARKING SPACE

When you back out of a perpendicular space, you will not be able to see much to the sides and the rear of your car. To be safe, you must go at a very low speed. After you shift to *reverse* and are moving backward, keep your foot lightly over the brake pedal. Keep checking to the sides and rear for vehicles, pedestrians, and other obstacles. Move straight back until your windshield is in line with the rear bumpers of the cars parked to either side. Start to turn your steering wheel slightly left or right, depending on which way you want to back up. Check to make sure that your front bumper does not strike the rear of the car opposite the direction in which you are turning. Back up until your front bumper clears the rear bumper of the car beside you. Check to the rear and turn the wheel quickly in the direction you wish to turn. As the car centers in the lane, turn the wheel quickly the opposite way to straighten the front wheels. Stop and shift to *drive*.

TURNABOUTS

Turnabouts are moves that allow you to reverse direction. When they are done on a city street, they create potential hazards. The degree of hazard depends on several factors:

1. The field of vision.
2. Width of the street.
3. Number of vehicles.
4. Speed of traffic.

73

Do not make turnabouts on curves, on hills, at crosswalks, at busy driveways, or at intersections. Such turnabouts are very dangerous and illegal. Where turnabouts are legal, make the one that is easiest and least hazardous.

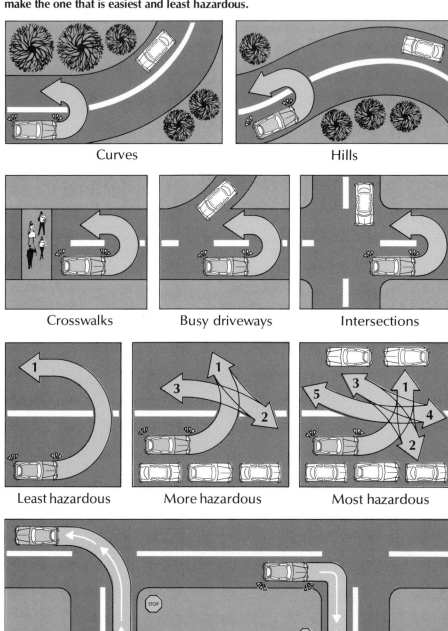

Curves

Hills

Crosswalks

Busy driveways

Intersections

Least hazardous

More hazardous

Most hazardous

Go around the block when turnabouts are illegal.

In some places, turnabouts may be illegal. Often, signs will let you know. All turnabouts involve risks. In some cases, going around the block will be faster and safer. However, there are times when you will have to make a turnabout—for example, when you find yourself on a dead-end street or in other areas where you cannot circle the block.

TWO-POINT TURN

The least hazardous way to reverse direction is to back into a driveway. This is called a *two-point turn*. First, signal to show that you plan to stop. Then follow these steps:

1. Stop ½ to 1 meter (2 to 3 feet) from the curb. The rear bumper of your car should be just past the driveway or alley that you wish to back into.
2. With your foot on the brake, shift to *reverse*. Check to the rear of your car for traffic, pedestrians, and other objects that may be in your path.
3. If the way is clear, look over your right shoulder into the driveway or alley. Then, as you go back slowly, turn the steering wheel fast all the way to the right.
4. As the rear of the car enters the driveway or alley, start to turn the steering wheel back to the left. Stop when the front of the car is clear of the traffic lane. The front wheels should now point straight ahead.
5. Shift to *drive*. Check traffic. Signal a left turn, and, when it is safe to do so, leave the driveway.

Two-point turn by backing into a driveway or an alley. This method is the least hazardous for making a two-point turn.

Two-point turn by heading into a driveway or an alley. This is a more hazardous method of making a two-point turn. Here, you have to back into the street and come to a stop in the through-traffic lane.

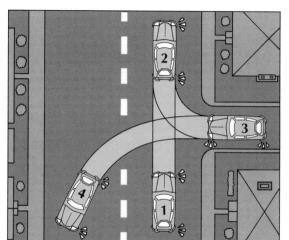

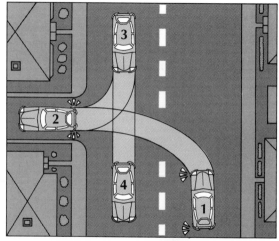

There is another, more hazardous way to make a two-point turn. To do it, you head into an alley or driveway. You then back into the street and come to a stop in the through-traffic lane. The steps in this maneuver are as follows:

1. Make sure you can see well in all directions as you choose a driveway or alley on the left.
2. Turn on your left-turn signal and check for traffic. When traffic is clear, turn into the driveway or alley. Stay as close as you can to the right side of the driveway.
3. Stop when the rear bumper clears the edge of the road. The front wheels of your car should be straight.
4. Shift to *reverse*.
5. Check for traffic and look over your right shoulder into your path of travel to the rear.
6. As you move slowly to the rear, turn the steering wheel quickly all the way to the right. Be sure to keep the car in the first lane of traffic.
7. When you are halfway through the turn, start to straighten the steering wheel.
8. Stop with the front wheels turned straight ahead.
9. Shift to *drive* and accelerate to traffic speed.

Reverse instructions in Steps 2, 5, and 6 if you choose a driveway or alley on the right. When making this type of turnabout, you must look for traffic in both directions. You must back across traffic in the first lane. Then, you must come to a full stop in the lane of traffic moving in the opposite direction. This type of turnabout must be done as quickly as possible. You must constantly look for cars in all directions while completing the maneuver.

U-TURN

A U-turn is the easiest turnabout to make. But you need a wide street in which to do it. (Also, it is illegal in some places.) If you must make a U-turn, pick a place where you can see well and other drivers can see you. To make a U-turn, do the following:

1. Stop your car as far to the right of the road as you can.
2. Check for traffic from both ways, and then signal a left turn.
3. Make sure there is a large time-space gap in both directions. Check traffic as you move forward. At the same time, turn the

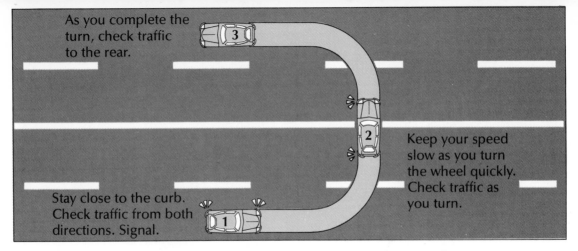

As you complete the turn, check traffic to the rear.

Keep your speed slow as you turn the wheel quickly. Check traffic as you turn.

Stay close to the curb. Check traffic from both directions. Signal.

The U-turn is the easiest turnabout to make. This maneuver requires a wide street. When you make a U-turn, pick a place where you can be seen by other drivers.

steering wheel hand over hand all the way to the left.

4. As you finish the turn in the far right lane headed in the new direction, straighten your wheels. Check for traffic to the rear.
5. Accelerate to the speed of traffic.

THREE-POINT TURN

The hardest and most hazardous turnabout is a *three-point turn*. This turn should be used only when

1. the street is too narrow for a U-turn.
2. there are no driveways or alleys to turn into.
3. traffic is very light.
4. visibility is very good.

The three-point turn is hazardous because when you make it, you must stop your car twice. Each time you stop, you block a traffic lane. If you must make a three-point turn, make these checks first:

1. Be sure that you are not near an intersection, a curve, or a hillcrest. If a fast-moving car appeared suddenly, you would be helpless, since you would be stopped in or across a lane of traffic.
2. Check the height of any curbs at the side of the road. The front and rear of your car may go well over the curbs during this maneuver. High curbs could damage your car.

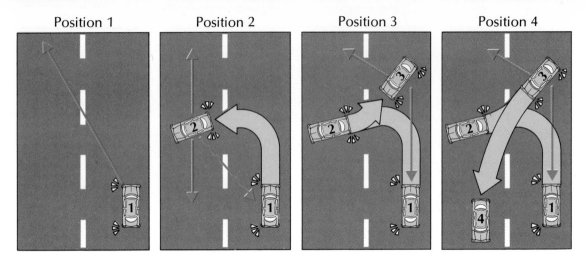

| Position 1 | Position 2 | Position 3 | Position 4 |

The three-point turn is the most difficult and most dangerous type of turnabout.

3. Pick a spot without trees, telephone poles, fire hydrants, or other objects near the curb. Such objects are hard to keep in sight while you back up and turn. You must also check for traffic from both ways.
4. Move the car slowly and the steering wheel quickly.

Once you have made these checks, do as follows:

1. Stop close to the right-hand edge of the pavement or curb.
2. Again, check both ways for traffic. Wait for a gap that is long enough to complete the maneuver.
3. Put on the left-turn signal and check over your left shoulder before you start the turn.
4. Move the car forward slowly. Turn the steering wheel very quickly to the left to bring the car into the opposite lane.
5. When the front tires are about 1 meter (4 feet) from the edge of the pavement or the curb, turn the steering wheel hard to the right. Stop the car just short of the road edge or curb.
6. Shift to *reverse* and back up slowly, holding the wheel, which is turned to the right. During the last meter (4 feet) or so before stopping, turn the steering wheel quickly to the left. Keep looking back until you have stopped the car.
7. Shift to *drive* and move the car slowly forward, completing the turn to the left. Check traffic and proceed.
8. If needed, repeat Steps 6 and 7 to complete the turn.

Both turns and turnabouts require close control of speed and steering. For each maneuver, you must make accurate judgments of the time and space you need. You can start to develop these judgments by watching other drivers as you ride with them.

78

TO CONSIDER

1. Describe some hazards you should be alert for when making a left turn at a busy, four-way intersection.

2. What are the hazards of perpendicular parking?

3. List and describe three kinds of turnabouts.

4. What factors would you consider in choosing a place to make a U-turn?

5. Identify hazards you should check for before making a three-point turn.

6. What are the steps you should take to let other drivers know that you plan to turn at an intersection?

7. What information should you check for as you approach an intersection where you plan to turn?

8. Name three general rules that would apply to most intersection turns.

9. Why do you need more time for a left-hand turn than for a right-hand turn?

10. What are two points to watch for when entering or leaving an angle parking space?

11. What factors determine the amount of risk there is in a turnabout?

PROJECTS

1. Prepare a poster showing step-by-step maneuvers in making a three-point turn.

2. Observe traffic turning left at a four-way, four-lane intersection. How many drivers turn into the wrong lane? What hazards, if any, do they cause? Make a presentation to your class.

3. Observe a number of turnabouts on a well-traveled roadway. Did the drivers seem to give themselves enough time and space for the turnabouts? Did any of them have any problems? If so, prepare a diagram showing the troublesome maneuver. Prepare a diagram showing a similar maneuver that was completed with no difficulty.

DRIVING A CAR WITH A STICK SHIFT

Learning to drive a car with a stick shift (hand-operated gear shift) is not difficult after you have learned to drive a car with an automatic transmission. What will be new is learning to use the clutch pedal with the gear-shift lever and the gas pedal at the same time. When you start to drive a car with a stick shift, you will need longer gaps in traffic. This space will give you time to use the clutch smoothly, both when starting from a dead stop and when shifting gears while the car is in motion. To shift smoothly, you must listen to the sound of the engine, feel the car vibrate, and check the speedometer. In short, you have more things to do when you drive a car with a stick shift.

Shifting gears *manually* (by hand) takes extra time and effort. When you drive a stick-shift car and you see a hazard ahead, you must act early. You must give yourself extra time to shift gears up or down and change speed or lane position. Once you have shifted gears, you will be able to give your full attention to driving. After the gears have been shifted, driving a stick shift is the same as driving a car with an automatic transmission.

The transmission is made of a set of gears. The direction in which the motor vehicle moves and its speed are determined by the choice of gears. There are several gears for forward movement and one gear for reverse movement.

When you drive a car with an automatic transmission, you move a gear selector lever to the position you want. The transmission then changes gears automatically. When you drive a car with a stick shift, you must change gears by hand. You have to start in low gear and shift to higher gears as you pick up speed. You will then have to shift from high to low as you slow or stop.

The gear-shift lever can be found either on the steering column or on the floor over the transmission. When and how often you shift gears depends on the size of the engine and the type of manual transmission there is in your car. Some cars have a three-speed transmission. This means that there are three forward gears plus a reverse gear. A car with a four-speed transmission has four forward gears and a reverse. Some cars and many trucks have more forward gears.

To shift gears when the engine is running, you must push the *clutch pedal* to the floor and hold it there. This disconnects the engine from the transmission. The transmission is in turn connected to the drive shaft. The drive shaft provides the power to make the wheels turn. When the clutch pedal is up and the transmission is in gear, the engine is, in a sense, locked to the transmission and drive shaft. When the clutch is pressed to the floor, the connection is broken and you can shift from one gear to another.

The clutch pedal and the gear-shift lever must be used together. There are times, though, when you may use the clutch pedal alone, such as when you stop from a very low speed. *Never try to move the shift lever without pushing down the clutch pedal.*

The secret of smooth clutch operation is to sense the *friction point*. This is the point where, as you let the clutch pedal up, the clutch and the other parts of the power train begin to work together. At this point, you must be very careful as you continue to let the clutch pedal up. You must now match the upward movement of the clutch with an increase in pressure on the gas pedal.

If you have learned to control a car that has an automatic transmission, it should not be difficult for you to learn clutch control. The easiest way to get a "feel" for the friction point is to start by using the reverse gear. Since *reverse* is the lowest gear, a lesser sense of feel is needed to control the friction point. Once you have developed this feel, shifting from one gear to another is quite simple.

You change gears by moving the stick-shift lever (gear-shift lever). The gear shift is found either on the steering column or on the floor of the vehicle.

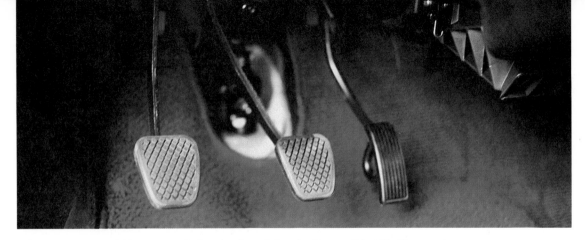
When you want to shift gears, push the clutch pedal to the floor and hold it. You must use the clutch pedal along with the gear-shift lever.

GETTING READY TO DRIVE

When you are settled in the driver's seat, look down for the foot pedals. You must learn where they are so that you do not have to look to find them as you drive. There are three pedals. The clutch pedal is on the far left. The brake pedal is in the middle. The gas pedal is the long, thin one on the right. Remember, the clutch pedal must be pressed and held to the floor each time you start the car, shift gears, or stop. You must be able to reach it and the other pedals easily. To do so, you may have to change your seat position or use pedal extenders.

STARTING THE ENGINE

Before you start the engine, *make sure the parking brake is set.* Then do as follows:

1. With your left foot, push the clutch pedal to the floor and hold it there. (If the engine has not been on for awhile, push the gas pedal to the floor and let it up. This sets the automatic choke, which feeds more fuel to the engine.)
2. Make sure the shift lever is in *neutral*. If it is not, the car will move suddenly when you start the engine.
3. Press lightly on the gas pedal and turn the ignition key clockwise as far as it will go. You will hear the *starter* begin to turn the engine. Be sure to let go of the key as soon as the engine starts to run. When you let go of the key, it will spring back to the *on* position. (Never use the starter when the engine is

Clutch-pedal and accelerator-pedal movements must be coordinated.

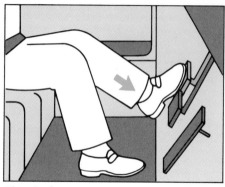
Clutch down.

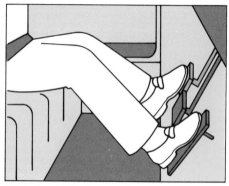
Clutch at friction point.

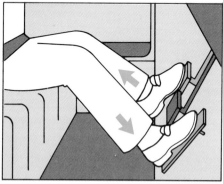
Passing friction point–additional pressure applied to accelerator.

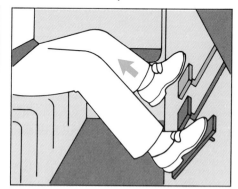
Foot is removed from clutch pedal.

running. If you are not sure the engine is running, press gently on the gas pedal.) When the engine is running, you can remove your foot from the clutch pedal. Move your right foot from the accelerator to the brake pedal.

To stop the engine, turn the key to the left to the *off* position.

Starting a car with a stick shift.

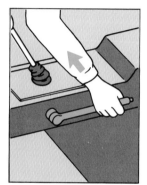
Be sure the parking brake is set.

Press and hold down the clutch pedal.

Make sure the shifting lever is in neutral.

Turn the key and start the engine.

PUTTING THE CAR IN MOTION

After the engine is going, follow these nine steps to put the car in motion:

1. With your right foot, press on the brake pedal. With your left foot, press the clutch pedal to the floor.
2. Shift to *low* (first) gear.
3. Release the parking brake.
4. Check the mirrors for traffic.
5. Before you move the car, look over your shoulder to check the blind spot. (Do this each time you start your car so that it becomes a habit.)
6. Signal your intention to move. Look ahead through the path of travel. *Do not look at your feet.*
7. Let the clutch pedal up slowly until it gets to the friction point. Hold the clutch pedal at the friction point for a moment.
8. Move your right foot from the brake to the gas pedal and press down gently.
9. At the same time, slowly let the clutch pedal up all the way.

If the car jerks forward, you have made one of two errors: (1) you have not let up the clutch pedal the right way; (2) your right foot is bouncing on the gas pedal. In either case, press the clutch pedal to the floor. Again, bring the clutch pedal up as far as the friction point and press on the gas pedal. Practice letting the clutch pedal up to the friction point until you can make the car move smoothly. If you feed too little gas to the engine, the car will stall and you will have to start again. If you feed too much gas to the engine, it will "race." This can damage the clutch and engine.

STOPPING FROM LOW GEAR

To stop from *low* or *second* gear at speeds of less than 15 km/h (10 mph), follow these steps:

1. Check the mirrors for traffic.
2. Signal for a stop with the brake lights or by a hand signal.
3. Press the clutch pedal to the floor. This will keep the car from jerking.
4. Take your foot from the gas pedal.

Putting a stick-shift car in motion.

1. Press clutch pedal to floor. Keep firm pressure on brake pedal.

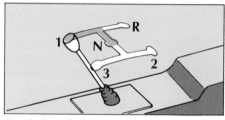

2. Shift to low (first) gear.

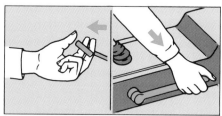

3. Release parking brake.

4. Check mirrors.

5. Check over shoulder.

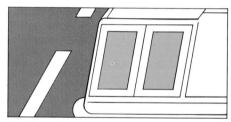

6. Signal.

7. Let clutch pedal up slowly.

8. Move right foot to gas pedal. Press down gently.

9. Slowly release the clutch pedal all the way.

5. Move your right foot to the brake pedal. Push down slowly until the car comes to a stop.
6. Keep your foot on the brake pedal and shift to *neutral*.
7. Set the parking brake. Take your foot off the brake.

SELECTING GEARS

The gear positions let the driver choose the power and speed needed for various kinds of driving.

Low, or *first*, gear gives the power needed to get the car in motion. With careful use, this gear can also move your car through mud, sand, water, or deep snow.

Second gear lets you go as fast as 25 to 40 km/h (15 to 25 mph). Just how fast depends on the size (horsepower) of the engine. It also depends on whether the car has a three-, four-, or five-speed transmission. *Second* gear can also be used to start on ice or to drive in heavy snow. This gear works to brake the car as it goes down hills, as long as the road is not slippery.

Third gear, in cars with a three-speed transmission, is used for all speeds over approximately 40 km/h (25 mph). If a vehicle has a four- or five-speed transmission and a small engine, *third* gear is used at speeds up to 50 to 60 km/h (30 or 40 mph).

Fourth gear is used for driving at speeds above 55 km/h (35 mph) on flat roads. When driving up hills, you may have to wait until you reach 65 km/h (40 mph) before you shift to *fourth* or *fifth* gear.

SHIFTING FROM LOW TO SECOND GEAR

Once your car is moving smoothly in low gear, you must shift to *second* gear. Continue to watch the road and traffic ahead. Without taking your eyes from the road,

1. pick up speed until your car is moving at 25–30 km/h (15–20 mph). (This speed will keep the car moving while the clutch pedal is pressed down.)
2. press the clutch pedal to the floor. (This should be done an instant before you let up the gas pedal.)
3. let up the gas pedal.
4. move the gear-shift lever through the *neutral* position into *second* gear.

1. Accelerate to about 30 km/h (20 mph).

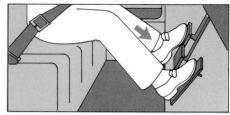

2. Depress clutch pedal and an instant later. . .

3. Release gas pedal.

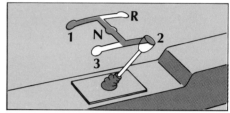

4. Shift from low to second gear.

5. Release clutch pedal. Wait an instant while you press gas pedal.

6. Release clutch pedal completely.

Shifting from low to second gear in a stick-shift car.

5. let the clutch pedal up to the friction point and hold it for an instant while you press down slightly on the gas pedal.
6. let the clutch pedal up all the way.

SHIFTING FROM SECOND TO THIRD GEAR

To shift into *third* gear, your car should be running smoothly in *second* gear. As you scan the road ahead,

1. speed up to about 40 or 50 km/h (25 or 30 mph).
2. press the clutch pedal to the floor.
3. let up the gas pedal.
4. shift from *second* gear through *neutral* to *third* gear.
5. let up the clutch pedal smoothly. At the same time, press the gas pedal down slowly.
6. move your foot from the clutch pedal to the floor.

1. Accelerate to 40 to 50 km/h (25 to 30 mph).

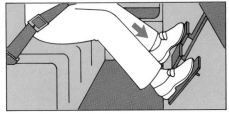

2. Press clutch pedal and an instant later . . .

3. Release gas pedal.

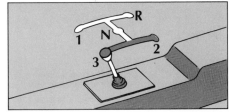

4. Shift from second to third gear.

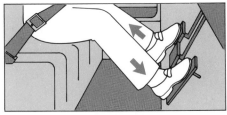

5. Release clutch pedal. Wait an instant while you press gas pedal.

6. Release clutch pedal completely.

Shifting from second to third gear in a stick-shift car.

Speeding up to 40 or 50 km/h (25 or 30 mph), as in Step 1, keeps the car moving while the clutch pedal is pressed down. (It also keeps the engine from "laboring" when you shift to *third* gear.)

STOPPING FROM THIRD GEAR

To stop from *third* gear, follow these steps:

1. Check the mirrors for traffic.
2. Signal for a stop.
3. Let up on the gas pedal.
4. Press the brake pedal. Slow your speed to about 15 to 25 km/h (10 to 15 mph).
5. Press the clutch pedal to the floor.
6. Continue to brake. Ease up on the brake pedal slightly just before the car comes to a full stop. Then press down on the brake pedal again. To keep the car from moving, hold the pressure on the brake pedal.

1. Check rear-view mirrors.

2. Signal for stop.

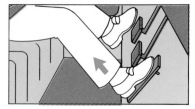
3. Release foot pressure on gas pedal.

4. Press brake pedal, slowing car to 15 to 25 km/h (10 to 15 mph).

5. Depress clutch pedal to floor.

6. Continue to brake.

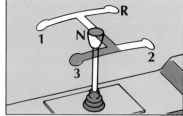
7. Shift to neutral.

8. Apply parking brake. Remove feet from clutch and brake pedals.

Stopping from third gear in a stick-shift car.

7. Move the gear-shift lever to *neutral*.
8. Set the parking brake and take your feet from the clutch and brake pedals.

Note the order of Steps 4 and 5. It is the reverse of the order for stopping from *low* or *second* gear. To stop in *third* gear, you press down on the brake pedal before you press down on the clutch pedal. When you take your foot off the gas pedal in order to brake, the engine speed slows. This helps to slow the car. If you press down on the clutch pedal too soon, you lose the braking power of the engine.

SHIFTING FROM THIRD TO SECOND GEAR

Sometimes, you will want to *downshift* (to go from a higher gear to a lower gear). Shifting from *third* to *second* gear increases the engine's power and slows the car's speed. Always shift to *second* if you feel the engine is struggling because the car is moving too slowly. You may have to downshift when you go up a steep hill or when you are driving in slow-moving, heavy traffic. Always downshift when you turn corners. Downshift on long, steep downhill roads. Downshifting makes use of the braking power of *second* gear. After you shift to *second* gear, you can pick up or slow your speed more easily and quickly than you could in *third* gear. Downshift before you reach a speed that is too slow for *third* gear. For instance, if you are going to make a turn, complete the downshift before you reach the corner. If you downshift early, you will be able to have both hands on the steering wheel when you start to turn. Do the following to downshift from *third* to *second* gear:

1. If you are moving faster than 40 to 50 km/h (25 to 30 mph), take your foot from the gas pedal and press down on the brake.
2. When your speed is down to about 50 km/h (30 mph), press the clutch pedal all the way to the floor.
3. Shift from *third* to *second* gear. (If you are going uphill, shift quickly, or else you will lose speed.)
4. Let up the clutch pedal to the friction point. At the same time, adjust the pressure on the gas pedal as needed.

Shifting from third to second gear in a stick-shift car.

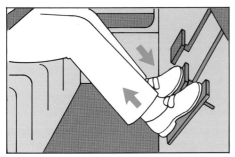

1. Release gas pedal and press brake pedal.

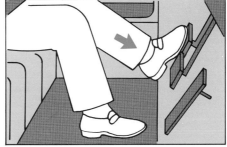

2. Press clutch pedal to the floor.

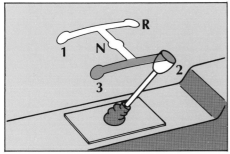

3. Shift from third to second gear.

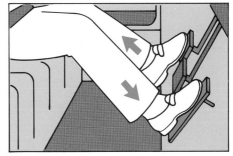

4. Release clutch pedal to the friction point. Press down gas pedal as necessary.

Going uphill

Going downhill

On turns

Downshifting increases the engine's power and decreases the car's speed.

The emergency downshift.

Practice downshifting in your car until you develop a feel for the proper engine speed.

Cars that have four- or five-speed transmissions shift from *third* gear to *fourth* or from *fourth* to *fifth* the same way they shift to *third*. The shift into *fourth* gear should be done at about 55 or 60 km/h (35 or 40 mph). Downshifting from a higher to a lower gear is done the same way as shifting from *third* to *second* gear.

THE EMERGENCY DOWNSHIFT

Downshifting from *second* to *low* gear is difficult unless you are moving very slowly. You can shift down into *second* or *third* gear, though, at almost any time or speed. When you shift from *third* to *second* gear to slow your speed on a long or steep hill, you still will have to use your brakes. The braking power of your engine will not be enough. Follow these steps:

1. Press down on the brake pedal to slow your speed.
2. Press the clutch pedal to the floor.
3. Shift quickly to *second* gear.

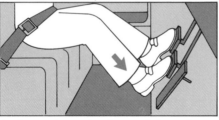

1. Press down brake pedal to slow your speed.

2. Press clutch pedal to floor.

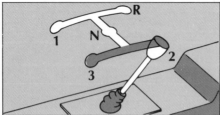

3. Shift quickly to second gear.

4. Let clutch pedal up, moving slowly through friction point.

5. Brake as needed.

4. Let the clutch pedal up. Now, move smoothly through the friction point.
5. Use the brake pedal as needed.

It is best to practice shifting gears, up or down, away from traffic. It is important that you learn to shift smoothly before you try to drive a stick-shift car in heavy traffic.

STARTING ON A HILL

Your car may roll back when you stop uphill. In a vehicle with an automatic transmission, you just step on the brake as needed with your left foot. When you are ready to move, step on the gas until the engine starts to pull the car forward. Then you take your foot from the brake pedal and move ahead. In a car with a stick shift, rolling back is more of a problem:

1. After you stop the car, set the parking brake.
2. When you are ready to move, press the clutch pedal to the floor and shift to *first* gear.

1. Once the car is stopped, set parking brake.

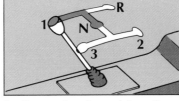

2. Press clutch pedal to floor and shift to first gear.

3. Grasp parking brake, but do not release it.

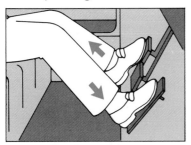

4. Let clutch pedal up to friction point. Gently press gas pedal.

5. Release parking brake slowly when you feel car pushing forward.

6. Increase pressure on gas pedal. Release parking brake. Let up clutch pedal.

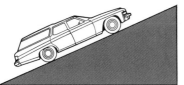

Starting on a hill.

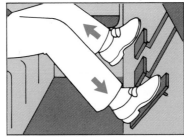

7. Accelerate in first gear.

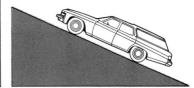

3. While you keep one hand on the steering wheel, grasp the parking brake release.
4. Let the clutch pedal up to the friction point and press gently on the gas pedal.
5. Release the parking brake when you begin to feel the car pulling forward.
6. Press on the gas pedal and let up on the clutch pedal.
7. Accelerate in *first* gear until you have gained enough speed to shift gears.

Important: You must accelerate just enough to move the car forward the instant that the clutch pedal is at the friction point and the parking brake is let go. If you let the parking brake go too soon, the car will roll back. If you do not feed the engine enough gas, the car will stall. If the car stalls or starts to roll back, push the brake pedal down and set the parking brake. Then shift to *neutral* and begin again.

STOPPING ON A HILL

Parking a car on a hill adds one more step to your parking procedure. Before you turn off the engine, shift into *reverse* gear and set the parking brake. Let the clutch pedal up after you turn off the ignition. The clutch and transmission, working together in a stick shift car, do the same thing that the *park* gear does in a car with an automatic transmission. The power train is "locked." Even if the parking brake should fail, the car will not move.

Stopping on a hill.

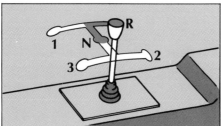

1. Shift to reverse gear.

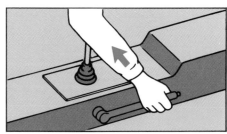

2. Set parking brake.

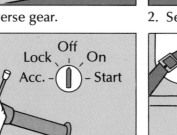

3. Turn off ignition.

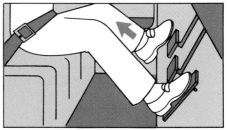

4. Release clutch.

TO CONSIDER

1. What factors make driving a car with a stick shift more complex than driving a car with an automatic transmission?

2. Explain why you would need longer time gaps in traffic for a stick-shift car than for one with an automatic transmission.

3. Define the "friction point."

4. Describe the procedures for shifting gears up and down.

5. What steps do you take to make an emergency downshift?

6. In what gear would you leave a stick-shift car if you parked on a hill? Explain your answer.

7. What is the easiest way to get a "feel" for the friction point?

8. Describe two errors that can make the car jerk forward.

9. What is the fourth gear normally used for?

10. What can happen if your foot slips off the clutch while you're stopping at an intersection with your car in gear?

11. What should you normally do when you feel the engine about to stall?

12. If you need to stop while on an uphill part of the road, what should you do to get your car moving without rolling back?

PROJECTS

1. Question three drivers of cars with stick shifts and three drivers of cars with automatic transmissions. Ask them about the advantages and disadvantages of driving each type of car. If they could make the choice again, which type of car would they select?

2. Ask an auto sales person what the advantages and disadvantages are of buying a car with a stick shift. What are the advantages and disadvantages of buying a car with an automatic transmission? Ask an auto mechanic the same questions. What points do they agree on? Where do they disagree?

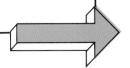

MAKING EFFECTIVE DRIVING DECISIONS

UNIT

Unit IV deals with the information you, the driver, must accurately gather to make good driving decisions. It discusses how good decision making helps prevent those situations that could cause collisions.

CHAPTER 9, "Perception," tells you
• how to gather traffic information.
• how to organize a search.
• how to prevent closing movements from developing into collisions.

CHAPTER 10, "Decision Making," discusses
• how to minimize risk.
• how to minimize collision potential through vehicle control.
• how to simplify traffic situations.

PERCEPTION

Many driving errors occur because drivers fail to notice what is happening on or near the roadway. Other errors occur because drivers interpret information incorrectly. To avoid errors and make the best driving decisions, you must learn how to gather and interpret information that relates to driving.

SEEING WHAT WE WANT TO SEE

People often fail to notice a lot of what goes on around them. Most of us tend to see only the things we expect to see. This can cause problems when we drive. We may not notice warning signs in the driving environment. In this way, we may fail to see something that is important to safe driving. We may also fail to see some actions that other drivers take because they are unexpected. Remember that other roadway users do not always act the way we think they should.

ORGANIZING A SEARCH

Good driving decisions depend on how well you gather and interpret information.

First, search the area in and near your intended path of travel 4 seconds ahead. Problems in this area develop quickly. Next, search at least 12 seconds ahead. If there are possible conflicts, you will have time to decide how to respond. This should reduce the chance that you will make bad decisions.

MAKING A SELECTIVE SEARCH

Our minds do not interpret everything we see. Therefore, we must learn to look at things selectively. When you drive, search for things with collision potential. Your first concern should be those things in or near your path with which you could collide—vehicles, pedestrians, animals, or fixed objects. Things that move are more dangerous than those that do not. Those things near your path are more dangerous than those farther away.

Be aware of places where your vision is limited. Crests of hills, curves, large vehicles, shrubbery, and buildings can prevent you from seeing important objects. Limited visibility should alert you to the possibility of trouble as you drive.

In making a selective search, be extremely cautious of places where your vision is limited. Also, beware of objects that move. Search the roadway and its shoulders for signs giving information about the condition of the road.

SEARCHING BY CATEGORY

You can improve your ability to gather information by grouping like objects into these four basic categories:

1. *Signs, signals, and roadway markings.* These items provide information about the road and the driving environment. They guide you in making driving decisions by warning you of such hazards as curves or steep hills. This information is usually accurate and easy to understand.
2. *The highway.* Search the road and the road shoulder for information about their design, construction, maintenance, and surface conditions. Check for visual obstructions. Look for objects on the road and the area bordering it that could possibly cause a collision. Identify other paths of travel that you could take if you had to leave the road.
3. *Motorized vehicles.* Information about motor vehicles is more difficult to gather and evaluate. Cars, motorcycles, trucks, and buses all handle differently. They are also cared for differently. A driver near you on the road may not know his or her vehicle's capabilities very well. The driver may not be able to drive well enough to deal with some situations. Look out for such drivers. Adjust your speed or position to protect yourself against their possible actions. Keep in mind, too, that drivers of certain kinds of vehicles are less predictable than others.
4. *Nonmotorized highway users.* Pedestrians, bicyclists, and animals are the least protected of all highway users. They should be watched carefully whenever they come near the roadway.

Always search the path you intend to drive. Check your side- and rear-view mirrors for other roadway users. Correct your speed and position for the possibility of bicyclists or pedestrians entering onto the road into your path.

ESTABLISHING A PATTERN FOR SEARCHING

Develop an effective search pattern and then use it. Search at least 12 seconds ahead of your car. Look for objects or situations on, near, or approaching the roadway. What you find in your search should influence your selection of speed and position. Check to see whether your immediate path, 4 seconds ahead, is clear. Has there been any change in the position of hazards that you identified earlier? Make sure that you have at least 2 seconds between you and vehicles ahead of you. Also, check the space between your car and any vehicles in the lanes next to you.

Visual checks in any direction other than your path ahead should be brief. After a quick check of the mirror or a fast look over your shoulder to check the rear, return your attention to the path immediately ahead. If a brief glance behind you does not provide enough information, do not stare. If there is no immediate problem in the path ahead, check the mirrors or look over your shoulder again as needed.

Vehicles closing from the rear or traveling beside you can create hazards, especially if you have to slow down or change lanes. Be sure to check your rear-view and side mirrors before you reduce your speed or move to the side. Also, take a quick look over your left shoulder. Make sure that no one is in your blind spot. Checking traffic to the sides and rear should become a habit. Learn also to check the instrument panel while you drive. Note what your speed is, understand what the gauges tell you, and then quickly return your attention to your path of travel.

ANALYZING INFORMATION

Usually, highway users act as expected. Some highway users, though, may not. Their errors often lead to collisions.

To avoid accidents, learn to expect the unusual. Be able to answer the following questions: (1) What actions by other highway users could lead to a collision? (Identify possible *closing movements*. These are actions by other highway users that may lead them across your path.) (2) How would a closing movement affect your safety? How likely is it that this event will occur? (3) If a collision should occur, what are the possible consequences? When you know of possible dangers in advance, you are better able to prepare for them.

Highway construction and maintenance signs are orange with black symbols or lettering. They warn drivers of hazards created by roadway workers. Always reduce your speed until you clear the construction area.

CLOSING MOVEMENTS

Closing movements are actions that can lead to a collision. Here are some that can end up as accidents:

1. *Possible rear-end collision.* You are rapidly *closing in* (gaining) on the car ahead of you. You would be unable to steer around the vehicle if it stopped. In addition, another car is *tailgating* you. (The vehicle behind you is following dangerously close.) This reduces your possible paths of escape in an emergency.
2. *Vehicles entering your path.* A vehicle parked at the curb or in a driveway may pull into your path. A vehicle at an intersection or approaching a merging lane may head for you.
3. *Possible head-on collision.* An oncoming vehicle may pull into your path. The other driver may have made a turn, passed another vehicle, or simply drifted into your lane.
4. *Possible sideswipe.* A passing vehicle cuts back into your lane before completely passing you.
5. *Hitting a pedestrian or animal.* A pedestrian or animal near the road steps or runs into your path.
6. *Possible collision with an off-road object.* Traffic conditions force you to leave the road just at the point where a light pole, tree, or traffic sign is standing.

Closing movements are more likely to happen when your field of view is limited. Curves, hills, bushes, or other large objects or signs may hide hazards. So can fog, darkness, heavy rain, or snow. Be especially prepared when these elements are present.

PROBABILITY AND CONSEQUENCES

When you are in a traffic situation that has closing potential, adjust your speed or position in response to (1) the *chances* (probability) and *consequences* (results) of a collision.

Suppose you are driving at 90 km/h (55 mph) on a two-lane highway through gently rolling farm country. You notice a fenced field ahead to your right. Several cows in the field are running toward the fence. The consequences of a collision with a cow are usually severe. But the probability of the cows breaking through the fence is quite low. So the cows require little attention as a collision threat. Suppose now that wild deer are heading toward the road. This situation has a different level of risk. The consequences of a collision with a deer can also be severe. There is a high probability, too, that a wild deer will leap the fence. In this situation, you must adjust your speed to meet the threat. The difference in the level of risk, then, is the difference in the probability that the collision will occur.

You will often be faced with several possible hazards at once. The difficulty this causes is shown in the following example. You are driving at 50 km/h (30 mph) on a two-way street. Coming toward you is a steady line of cars. A young child is riding a bike alongside the road. The child is having trouble pedaling and is weaving.

It is clear that you should slow down. You should also move as close to the center line as you can. There is a chance that one of the cars may cross the center line, but the probability is quite low. Of greater concern is the bike rider who is having trouble steering in a straight line. This increases the probability that the bike rider may enter your path of travel. After slowing down, all you can do is give the bike rider as much room as possible and be ready to stop quickly.

The most difficult decisions occur when there is no chance of avoiding a collision. If you do not panic, however, you can often reduce the consequences of a collision. For example, you are driving at 90 km/h (55 mph) on a road that has two 3.5-meter (12-foot) lanes in each direction.

A vehicle that is passing could sideswipe you if it cuts back into your lane too quickly. Learn to recognize closing movements so that you can react in time to prevent a collision.

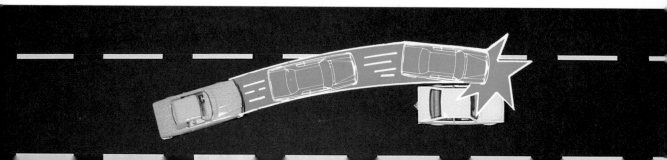

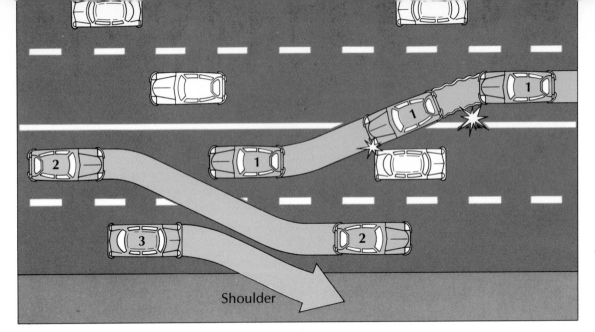

If you cannot avoid a collision, you may still be able to reduce its consequences. In this case, car #2 can avoid a head-on collision with car #1 by not braking. Instead, car #2 can move into the right lane. Car #2 may sideswipe the car already in the right lane (car #3). But the consequences will be less serious than a head-on collision would be.

Traffic is heavy in all four lanes. You are driving in the inside lane 2 seconds behind the car ahead. Suddenly, the left front tire of an oncoming vehicle blows out. The driver slams on the brakes. The oncoming car skids across the center line and hits the left rear fender of the car ahead of you. It continues to skid straight down your lane toward you. If all you do is brake, you will not prevent a head-on collision—the worst kind. To reduce the consequences of the collision, move as far as possible to the right. Ideally, the driver in the right lane sees the situation and moves to the right as well. With 7 meters (24 feet) of roadway, there would be room for three cars to be side by side. With proper steering control and 1 to 2 seconds to respond, you could move right 2.5 to 3 meters (8 to 10 feet). This would allow you either to avoid the skidding car or to be struck at an angle. If that car on your right does not move over, you may sideswipe it as you make your maneuver. But the consequences of a sideswipe are less serious than those of a head-on collision that might involve many vehicles.

In judging the probability of a collision and deciding what to do, consider all likely consequences. The number of factors may seem almost unlimited. But two should help you decide what to do. The most important is the extent of personal injury that may result. (How many people are involved? How seriously would they be injured?) The second is the amount of property damage that may occur.

TO CONSIDER

1. Why do drivers sometimes fail to notice a hazard? Why is it risky at times to assume that other drivers will act in a certain way?

2. What is the advantage of organizing your visual search (the way you look about) in traffic?

3. How can a driver conduct a "selective search"? Why should you be more alert in areas where visibility is limited?

4. What is the purpose of searching by category? Describe the four major categories. Why do drivers of certain kinds of vehicles tend to be less predictable than others? What hazards should you be alert to when slowing down or changing lanes?

5. Define *closing movements*. What closing movements can result in a collision?

6. How can you judge the amount of risk that a closing movement will create? Where would closing movements most likely occur?

7. Describe two situations in which you are faced with several potential hazards at the same time. How would you handle them? When there is no chance of avoiding a collision, what factors should you consider in trying to reduce the consequences of the collision?

PROJECTS

1. Ride with someone over a frequently traveled road. Record everything you notice that has to do with driving, including traffic signs, pedestrians, and vehicles. Ask the driver which potential hazards she or he noticed. If the driver did not notice some, explain why you think this happened.

2. While riding in a car, try to predict what others on the highway will do. Take notes on what you see. Compare your predictions with what happens. How often were you correct?

3. While riding as a passenger in an urban area, make a list, during a 5-minute period, of potential hazards near your intended path. Give reasons why each item is a hazard and tell what action—if any—the driver took to cope with the hazard.

DECISION MAKING

DECISIONS AND DRIVER RESPONSE

Good drivers make safe driving decisions. To make good driving decisions, you must learn to

1. *minimize* (reduce) the risk related to any hazard by
    a. developing good search habits so you will be aware of problems as they arise.
    b. selecting a speed and position that will increase your chances of responding properly to dangerous events.
2. *simplify* situations. Separate one hazard from another. The number of risks you have to respond to at one time will be more manageable.

3. minimize one risk without increasing another. When you are faced with a number of conflicts, *compromise*. That is, weigh the risks, and react to your best advantage.

MINIMIZING RISK

REDUCING THE CHANCE THAT A HAZARD WILL MOVE INTO YOUR PATH

Any dangerous event can lead to a collision. Such events may be started by other drivers. Some may arise from your own actions. It is to your advantage to try to reduce the number of such events. One way to do this is to improve your ability to judge time-space gaps.

Time-space gap problems can develop whenever you enter a stream of traffic. They can arise when you pull from a curb, change lanes, merge, or turn right or left at an intersection. You can reduce time-space problems by influencing the behavior of other highway users.

1. Let other highway users know what you plan to do by using your horn and directional signals. The information you provide will help others avoid conflicts with you. This will reduce the chances of a collision.
2. The placement of your vehicle can inform others of your intentions. By obeying traffic laws that regulate lane positioning, you can let other drivers know where you plan to go.

If you signal your intention to pass in advance, the car you wish to pass will be able to move to the right to give you more room to make the maneuver. This action minimizes risk.

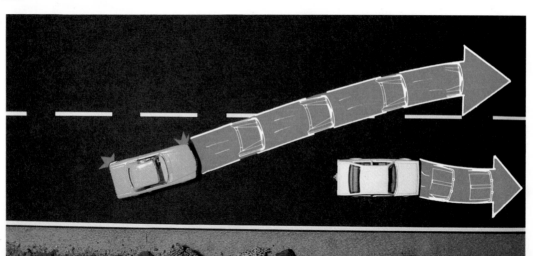

3. Make others especially aware of your presence in hazardous or emergency situations. You can signal danger by driving with your headlights on during daylight hours or by using hand signals or your car's emergency flashers. However, make sure that these signals do not confuse other motorists.

These actions can reduce the chance of trouble arising from the unexpected actions of others. They also offer protection against your own errors in judgment. But they cannot substitute for proper control of speed and position.

SELECTING SPEED AND LOCATION

Any event that has collision potential is dangerous. Those events that develop well ahead of your car may require only a simple, routine response. Those that develop in your immediate path may be more difficult to handle. First consider your present speed and road position. Then determine how you can best respond to the situation.

Whenever you approach parked cars, increase the space between your car and the parked cars. This will give you extra time to adjust your speed and position should any of the parked cars suddenly pull out, or should someone open a door to get out of one of the parked cars.

MANAGING RESPONSE TIME

Too often, drivers fail to anticipate dangerous events. As a result, their speed and road position make it very difficult to respond.

An effective visual search is important in managing response time. The sooner you are aware that you may be on a collision course, the sooner you can respond.

The time you have to respond can also be increased by keeping as much distance as possible between your car and all hazards. These include other vehicles, pedestrians, animals, and fixed objects.

Usually, a slight adjustment of both speed and position is better than a major adjustment of one or the other. For example, if you are approaching parked vehicles, move a little farther away from them and slow down slightly. These actions will give you extra time to respond if a person or vehicle should move away from the curb.

To avoid a collision, make speed and position adjustments as early and as gradually as possible.

SPACE MARGIN

Keeping your distance from potential hazards is called maintaining a *space margin*. Keep a space margin between your car and other vehicles, pedestrians, and fixed objects (parked cars, road signs, walls, buildings, and fences). Also keep a space margin between your car and potentially hazardous places, such as a hidden driveway (one that is blocked by trees or shrubbery). At first, you may see nothing in the driveway as you approach. Then suddenly a driver pulls out just far enough to check traffic, partly blocking your path of travel. To avoid such a problem, anticipate hazards that may be hidden from view and provide a space margin for them. In the case of a hidden driveway, move into the left lane if there is one. If there is no left lane, move close to the center line.

MINIMIZING COLLISION POTENTIAL THROUGH VEHICLE CONTROL

Steering, braking, and accelerating are affected by the kind of road surface on which you are driving. Adjustments in speed and road position have to be made when you drive from one surface to another or when you are driving in rain or snow.

Traction is the friction between your car's tires and the road surface. As traction is reduced, your vehicle becomes more difficult to control. There are a number of things that reduce traction, including underinflated tires, tires with little or no tread, dirt, sand, gravel, wet leaves,

Tailgating blocks your visual lead and can result in a rear-end collision, as below. Do not tailgate. The car you are tailgating might brake suddenly, and you will have no room to make an emergency maneuver.

Water reduces traction. During or after heavy rains, water may collect (1) at underpasses, (2) near cliffs, (3) in potholes, and (4) at the foot of hills. If you drive through deep puddles, pump the brakes and drive slowly.

oil, water, snow, ice, bumps, and holes in the road. High speed reduces traction, too.

In some instances, conditions that reduce traction (and thereby vehicle control) will be found only on sections of a road. There may be a patch of ice or a pile of wet leaves on your pathway. If possible, avoid driving over or through that spot.

A loss of traction increases the risk of losing control of your vehicle. If conditions are extreme, you may have difficulty maintaining speed and direction. Slowing down reduces the risk of losing control of your vehicle. Changes in speed or direction should be made gradually. Abrupt changes increase the chance that you may lose control of your car.

INERTIA

A natural force that affects vehicle control is *inertia*. Inertia is the tendency of a car in motion to resist any change in direction. You can feel this resistance when you make a turn. When you turn right, your body feels as if it were being pushed to the left. Your body is being pushed in the same direction in which the car was moving before you made the right turn. To make a turn from a straight path of travel, forces must be used that will let you change your direction and reduce your speed. The steering wheel, brakes, and accelerator—together with the friction between the tires and the road—create this force.

Good friction is of the utmost importance when you make a turn. Without it, your car could go into a skid.

111

SELECTING YOUR SPEED

Speed is a major factor in maintaining vehicle control. Selecting a speed would be easy if all you had to think about was the speed limit. Unfortunately, in most situations there are hazards to consider, too. Until you are an experienced driver, decisions about speed will be hard to make and errors will occur.

A speed that is acceptable in one situation may be unacceptable in another. For instance, if an adult pedestrian is far off the road, you may be able to drive past him or her safely at 80 km/h (50 mph). A small child close to the road would be much more of a hazard, and you would have to reduce your speed considerably.

SIMPLIFYING SITUATIONS

Often, drivers have to deal with several hazards at once (*multiple-hazard conditions*). These conditions increase the chance of collision. But not all multiple-hazard conditions are difficult. For example, suppose you are driving on a residential street. There are a few potholes, one or two parked cars in each block, and a few pedestrians. Any of these elements could become a problem, so you must keep track of each. But there is no real danger here. There are more difficult multiple-hazard situations. If possible, avoid having to deal with too many hazards at one time because

1. the more hazards present, the greater the chance that difficulties will develop.
2. the more hazards that occur at one time, the less likely it is that there will be enough maneuvering space.
3. the more hazards that are present at once, the greater the chance of making bad decisions.

You cannot prevent hazards from arising. But you can simplify situations. Then, you will not have to deal with too many hazardous situations at one time.

You often have enough control over a situation to keep two or more high-risk situations from developing at once. You do this by anticipating multiple hazards. For example, you may be driving on a narrow two-way road. You see a pedestrian walking on your side of the road. There is a truck coming toward you. By adjusting your speed, you can avoid passing the pedestrian and the truck at the same time. If either does something unexpectedly, it will now be easier for you to move

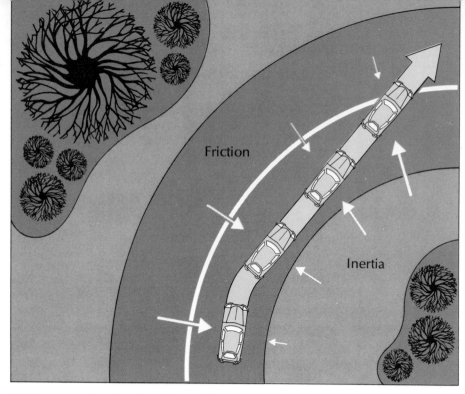

Friction acts against inertia. As long as there is more friction than inertia, you can make a turn.

away. You have simplified the situation by separating the hazards.

There are other ways you can avoid dealing with more than one hazard at a time. For example, do not pass a bicycle as you enter a blind curve on a narrow, two-way road. Doing so could bring you into conflict with an oncoming vehicle.

COMPROMISE

In complex traffic situations, a decision about one hazard may conflict with a decision on another. For example, a conflict may arise when you try to simplify your path of travel. Suppose you are about to meet an oncoming car. At the point where you expect to meet the car, there are cars parked on the right. If you increase your speed, you will meet the oncoming car where a pedestrian is standing. If you decrease your speed, you will meet the oncoming car on a narrow bridge.

Such situations point up the need for compromise. Your decision may not reduce risk as much as you like. But it should reduce risk as much as possible.

A conflict can arise when you are trying to maintain a sufficient time gap both in front and to the rear of your car. Suppose you are followed

Following too closely will not get you to your destination any faster. Try not to bunch up or drive with a pack in traffic. If the traffic flow is heavy and is traveling at a moderate speed, reduce your speed, as the car in the far left lane is doing. This will put a space cushion around your car and leave you a way out of a possible hazard.

by a tailgater on a two-way highway. If you speed up, you may dangerously reduce the time-space gap ahead. The best thing to do is slow down gradually. Keep these points in mind: (1) traffic flow rarely exceeds safe speeds by more than 8 km/h (5 mph). If you drive slightly slower, you will increase the gap in front of you without having much effect on the traffic behind. (2) Rear-end collisions usually occur when vehicles reduce speed sharply, not when speed is reduced gradually or slightly. (3) Under the law, you are more *liable* (legally responsible) for collisions that involve the front of your car than for those that involve the rear of your car.

Sometimes, a vehicle will follow you so closely that it becomes an extreme hazard. In this case, move well to the right and slow down gradually. This will encourage the tailgating driver to pass. If this does not work, you may have to pull off the road to allow the driver to pass you.

You should position your vehicle between hazards on either side of your vehicle according to how dangerous each side is. If they are about the same, leave equal space on both sides. If the hazards are not the same, give greater space to the one that presents the greater risk. When you adjust your position, take care not to surprise other drivers. Signal your movements early and change your position gradually. If possible, make the adjustments within your own lane. Whenever you leave your lane, you increase the risk of having a collision. There may be a vehicle in your blind spot.

TO CONSIDER

1. Why is decision making such an important part of good driving?

2. Define the terms "minimizing risks" and "simplifying situations." Give an example of each.

3. Discuss three techniques you can use to minimize risks.

4. Explain why it is best to avoid having to deal with many hazards at one time.

5. Give examples of ways in which drivers should compromise by adjusting vehicle speed and position.

6. How can you influence the behavior of other highway users?

7. Define the term "inertia."

8. What factors should you consider when selecting a speed?

9. Which factor has more influence on your response time in a crisis—your vehicle's *speed* or its *position?* Explain your answer.

10. Why is your judgment (about the speed and position of your car) less accurate under conditions of reduced traction?

PROJECTS

1. Construct a mock-up of a busy intersection, or use a traffic board if one is available. Set up a situation that requires a driver to compromise. Ask five of your classmates, one at a time, how they would handle the situation. Then prepare a diagram of the response each person makes, listing his or her reasons for the specific actions taken. Present your findings to the class.

2. Observe traffic in three different areas where trees, buildings, or curves block drivers' views. Of the drivers you observe, how many adjust their speed or position to compensate for the limited visibility?

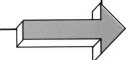

UNDERSTANDING MOTOR VEHICLES AND TRAFFIC LAWS

UNIT

Unit V discusses some of the legal responsibilities you must accept in order to drive. It also discusses those traffic regulations that reduce the risk of collisions.

CHAPTER 11, "Administrative Laws," tells you
- how to get a driver's license.
- how to fulfill your legal responsibilities as a driver.
- how to prove vehicle ownership.
- how to provide for minimum standards of car maintenance.
- what to do at the scene of an accident.

CHAPTER 12, "Traffic Laws," explains
- the rules of the road that govern a driver's behavior.

CHAPTER 13, "Signs, Signals, and Roadway Markings," discusses
- how to recognize the function and purpose of traffic control signs and signals.
- how to interpret roadway markings.

CHAPTER

POINT SYSTEM

11

ADMINISTRATIVE LAWS

Each state has laws that regulate the licensing of drivers and the registering of motor vehicles. There are also laws that set standards of financial responsibility for drivers and owners. Other laws regulate the minimum equipment and care a vehicle must have. These are called *administrative laws*. They are designed to keep track of who owns a vehicle, who has a license, and the violations of traffic laws that drivers commit.

In their laws, the states try to follow the standards for rules of the road and motor vehicle equipment that are suggested in the Uniform Vehicle Code. Thus, the laws in all parts of the United States are as alike as possible.

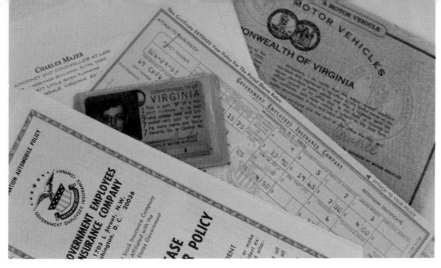

Administrative laws are carried out at the state level.

DRIVER'S LICENSE

Before you can get a license, you must take some tests. These tests find out if you meet minimum standards of vision, hearing, and physical condition. You will also be tested to see if you know the basic rules of the road. Then you will take a driving test that measures how well you can perform basic driving maneuvers. If you pass each of these tests, you will qualify for a driver's license.

THE POINT SYSTEM

To keep your license after you get it, you must meet certain standards. Otherwise, your license may be revoked or suspended. To *revoke a license* means to take it away permanently. To *suspend a license* means to take it away temporarily. Each state has rules and procedures for revoking or suspending a driver's license.

Most states use a point system. Where such a system is used, each violation of a traffic regulation has a number of points assigned to it, depending on how serious it is. When a driver is found guilty of violating a law, a report is sent to the state Department of Motor Vehicles, which assigns that number of points to the driver's record.

A driver who gets more than four or five points within a period of time (usually 2 years) may be sent a warning letter. One who gets six or seven points may have to go for an interview at the Department of Motor Vehicles. A driver with eight to eleven points may be called in for a hearing. This could lead to a suspension of the driver's license.

After the suspension is over, if the driver is convicted of further violations and gets more points, the driver's license generally will be revoked. Some regulations are so important that if you are found guilty of violating them you will lose your license automatically. Examples are driving under the influence of alcohol or drugs, leaving the scene of an accident in which there has been an injury, and using a motor vehicle in a crime.

These rules vary from state to state. The system is designed to make people drive more carefully. The right to drive can be taken away from those who do not obey the law.

NATIONAL DRIVER REGISTER SERVICE

In 1960, the United States Congress established the National Driver Register Service. The register stores the names of drivers whose licenses have been suspended or revoked. The motor vehicles department of a state may ask the service about the driving record of a person

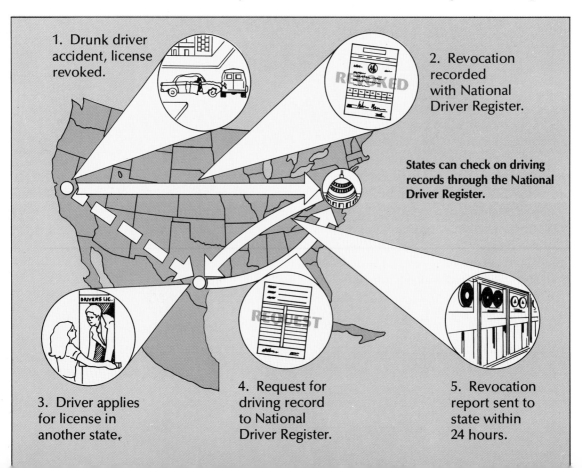

1. Drunk driver accident, license revoked.

2. Revocation recorded with National Driver Register.

States can check on driving records through the National Driver Register.

3. Driver applies for license in another state.

4. Request for driving record to National Driver Register.

5. Revocation report sent to state within 24 hours.

who applies for a license. States can find out, for instance, if an applicant has had a license revoked or if the applicant could not get a license for health reasons.

CERTIFICATE OF TITLE

Almost every state issues a certificate of title when you buy a car. It identifies the make, style, serial and engine numbers, and owner. Before a vehicle can be sold, the seller must prove ownership. You may buy a car without having a license to drive it.

VEHICLE REGISTRATION AND LICENSE PLATES

The states also register motor vehicles and issue license plates. You must own a vehicle before you can register it. When it is registered, the Department of Motor Vehicles gives the owner a certificate of registration and license plates or tags. The certificate identifies both the car and the owner. It must be in the vehicle any time the vehicle is in use. The license plates allow the police and others to identify a car. Some police departments now have computer systems that they can use to check on stolen or abandoned vehicles instantly.

RESPONSIBILITIES WHEN INVOLVED IN AN ACCIDENT

If you are involved in an accident or you are the first at the scene of an accident, be very careful when you help someone who has been hurt. Unskilled handling, particularly when there are broken bones, may make the injury worse and may even cause death. For example, if a person with an injured spine is moved, she or he could become paralyzed or die. It may be best not to move an injured person unless you have been trained to do so or unless you must (away from fires, for instance). However, you should stop any bleeding as well as you can. Then try to make the victim comfortable.

LEGAL RESULTS

If you break a traffic law at the time of the accident, you may be penalized in several ways. You may be fined and have to pay court

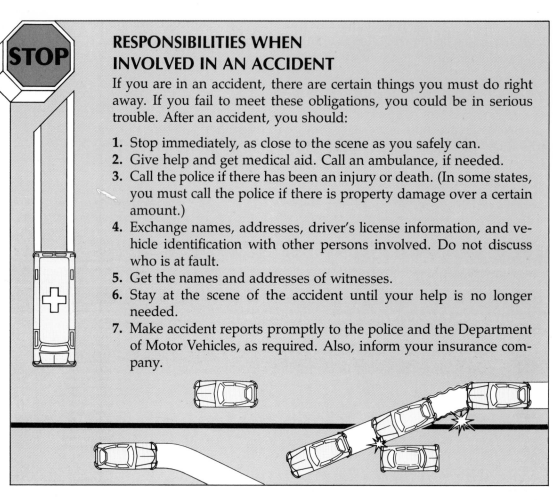

RESPONSIBILITIES WHEN INVOLVED IN AN ACCIDENT

If you are in an accident, there are certain things you must do right away. If you fail to meet these obligations, you could be in serious trouble. After an accident, you should:

1. Stop immediately, as close to the scene as you safely can.
2. Give help and get medical aid. Call an ambulance, if needed.
3. Call the police if there has been an injury or death. (In some states, you must call the police if there is property damage over a certain amount.)
4. Exchange names, addresses, driver's license information, and vehicle identification with other persons involved. Do not discuss who is at fault.
5. Get the names and addresses of witnesses.
6. Stay at the scene of the accident until your help is no longer needed.
7. Make accident reports promptly to the police and the Department of Motor Vehicles, as required. Also, inform your insurance company.

costs. Your license could be suspended or revoked. You could even be sent to jail.

You may also be sued for damages if there are injuries or property damages. Damages awarded by courts in injury or death cases may come to hundreds of thousands of dollars. If the sums are more than your insurance covers, you have to pay the rest yourself. People have lost their cars, homes, and other possessions as the result of such cases. Others have had part of their wages taken for years.

ARRIVING AT THE SCENE OF AN ACCIDENT

If you come upon an accident on the highway, use good judgment. If the police have taken charge, do not stop unless you are asked to do so. You do not want to get in the way of the police, ambulance, and other emergency vehicles. If you are trained to help and you are needed, park the car well out of the way of traffic. Then walk back to the accident.

ACCIDENT INVESTIGATION

When the police investigate an accident, they must gather all the evidence they can find. They note the final position and direction of

If you are the first to arrive at an accident, park your car ahead of the collision. Do not pull up behind it. Your car may block the collision from the view of emergency vehicles.

travel of the vehicles involved. They check the condition of the drivers, road, and vehicles. They will usually measure the skid marks, and they will ask witnesses what they saw. Often, some *violation* has been committed (law has been broken) when an accident takes place. If so, one or more of the drivers may get a *citation* (ticket) for a violation.

MOTOR VEHICLE INSPECTION

Vehicle failure can cause accidents. Because of this, all states have laws that say you must keep your car in good working condition. A number of states have inspection laws to make sure that vehicles meet minimum standards. Some states require inspections at set times of the year. In other states, inspections are done by police spot-checks.

Since failures in vehicle systems can cause accidents, some states require yearly inspection of all motor vehicles. The exhaust system, when improperly functioning, affects the operation of the car. It also causes air pollution.

Where laws require inspection, states may choose to check vehicles at state inspection centers or at private garages approved by the state. These inspections usually include tests of the brakes, lights, horn, exhaust systems, steering and suspension, directional signals, tires, and *emission-control* (antipollution) devices. If any part is not working properly, it must be repaired in a given period of time. The owner must show proof of the repairs before the car can be certified as having passed the inspection.

TO CONSIDER

1. Why does the United States have national standards for motor vehicle and traffic laws?

2. What are the reasons for vehicle registration and insurance?

3. Explain how a person gets a driver's license. What are some reasons why a person's license might be suspended or revoked?

4. How does the point system work in your state?

5. What do police look for when they investigate an accident? Why would a driver get a ticket as a result of an accident?

6. What would you do if you came to a bad accident?

7. Why should injured people at the scene of an accident *not* be moved unless you have no choice (if, for example, there is a fire)—and then, only with the greatest care?

8. Describe the purpose of the National Driver Register Service.

9. What is the purpose of motor vehicle inspections?

PROJECTS

1. Find out from your state's motor vehicles bureau what tests you must pass to get a driver's license. Do you think the tests are good measures of driving performance and knowledge? Would you change the tests if you could? If so, how?

2. Ask judges, police officers, drivers, and nondrivers their opinions about suspension and revocation laws. Do you agree or disagree with their opinions? Should the laws be changed?

3. Visit your nearest vehicle inspection station. Find out what items are inspected, and why. Ask an inspector what major defects he or she finds when checking cars. How does the inspector think motorists could take better care of their cars? Report your findings to the class or make a display that shows which items are inspected.

TRAFFIC LAWS

Traffic laws are rules for drivers. They help you to predict what other drivers will do. For example, you expect all drivers to signal a lane change, and you expect that drivers on cross streets will not drive through red lights into your path.

Unfortunately, you cannot depend on highway users' obeying the law all the time. Drivers or pedestrians may ignore or not know some traffic laws. Also, people make mistakes. So you must stay alert.

To make highways as free from accidents as possible, you must do more than just strive to obey the laws. Whenever you can, make up for the faults of other users as well.

RULES OF THE ROAD

Directions from a police officer, a sign, a signal, or a marking on the road take priority over rules of the road. There is one more rule to

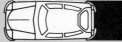

RULES OF THE ROAD

Some rules of the road apply in all parts of the United States. They lead to a safer and more orderly flow of traffic. Rules are:

1. Drive to the right of the center of the road except to pass vehicles moving in your direction.
2. Pass to the right of vehicles coming toward you.
3. Pass vehicles going in the same direction as you are only when it is safe to do so.
4. Allow vehicles that are gaining on you to pass.
5. If you drive slowly, keep to the right-hand lane when there is more than one lane.
6. Signal when you intend to reduce speed, stop, turn, change lanes, or pass.
7. Always drive at a speed that fits the existing conditions.

remember: It is always against the law to drive under the influence of alcohol or other drugs.

RIGHT-OF-WAY

Where the paths of motor vehicles, pedestrians, and cyclists cross, there is the chance of a conflict. Who has the right-of-way?

Right-of-way rules require one person to yield—that is, to let another go first. It is very important that drivers know and obey the right-of-way laws in the states where they drive. Not knowing or disobeying these laws can lead to accidents. In some towns and cities, pedestrians at crosswalks legally have the right-of-way, and drivers must yield to them. Another common right-of-way rule states that highway users must yield to emergency vehicles. When you see flashing lights or hear a siren, move as far to the right as you can. Drivers of emergency vehicles must also drive in a reasonable manner. (Serious accidents have been caused by emergency vehicles speeding or passing through red lights.)

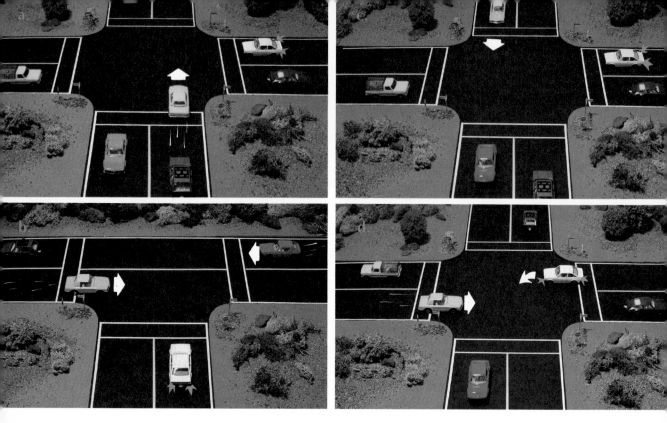

You must yield the right-of-way (a) to vehicles already in the intersection, (b) to traffic on the main thoroughfare, (c) to vehicles on the right, (d) before turning.

The Uniform Vehicle Code suggests several basic right-of-way rules that all drivers must obey:

1. If two vehicles, at the same time, come to or enter an intersection not controlled by a traffic sign or signal light, the driver on the left shall yield to the driver on his or her right.
2. Drivers shall yield to pedestrians crossing legally at intersections or at marked crosswalks between intersections.
3. A driver who intends to turn left shall yield the right-of-way to vehicles coming the other way if they are so close that they are an immediate hazard.
4. A vehicle coming out of a driveway or alley shall yield the right-of-way to vehicles on the street and to pedestrians.
5. When moving to the left or right into a lane being used by other drivers, a driver must yield to any vehicle that is passing or is so close that it presents a hazard.

SPEED LIMITS

Some states have fixed (or absolute) speed limits to guide drivers. Other states have flexible limits. Since speed-limit signs cannot be changed easily when there are changes in the road, the traffic, or the weather, think of posted speed limits as the maximum speed in the best of conditions.

FIXED SPEED LIMITS

Fixed limits set the maximum or "absolute" speed. Drivers may not exceed the posted speed limit for any reason. A driver who does so can be arrested and made to pay a penalty. You could also be penalized for driving so far below the posted speed limit that you cause traffic congestion or back-up. Under bad road conditions, though, you may drive below the fixed speed limit for the sake of safety.

States that use fixed speed limits usually do so for two reasons:

1. The limits can be set by experts to best fit road and traffic conditions in that area.
2. It is easier to enforce fixed limits.

You must yield the right-of-way to emergency vehicles. When you see flashing red lights or hear sirens, move as close to the side of the road as you can.

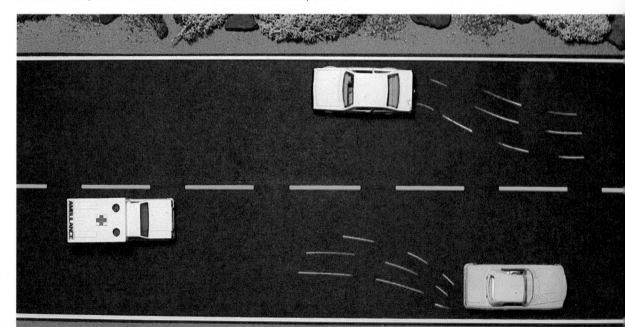

FLEXIBLE SPEED LIMITS

Flexible (or *prima facie*) speed limits are based on the idea that no one speed is best under all conditions. The posted speed is the speed that is recommended under ideal conditions. A reasonable maximum speed depends on the type and condition of the road and on such things as the traffic, weather, and light. Drivers who are charged with driving over the posted limit can use the defense that their speed was not too fast for existing conditions. The court must then decide if the driver is right. Of course, no driver may legally exceed 90 km/h (55 mph), which the federal government has established as the highest allowable speed limit.

A driver can be arrested for speeding even if she or he is driving slower than the posted limit. The officer who makes the arrest must show the court that the car was being driven too fast for the existing conditions. For example, a road may have been icy or the traffic may have been heavy.

With a flexible speed limit, one can also be arrested for driving too slowly. In this case, the officer must show that the speed was so slow as to cause danger to other drivers.

THE BASIC SPEED RULE

Nearly all states have put some version of the basic speed rule in their traffic laws. This rule states: "Always drive at a speed that is

Maximum/minimum speed limit signs are used on high-speed roads. They keep the flow of traffic moving smoothly.

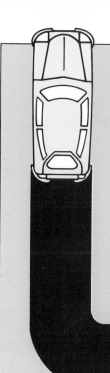

FACTS ABOUT SPEED

Lots of people think that too much speed is the greatest cause of accidents. While others may disagree, there are some facts about speed that cannot be argued.

1. The higher the speed, the less time the driver has to spot hazards and take action.
2. The higher the speed, the greater the time and distance it takes to stop.
3. The higher the speed, the greater the chance the car will skid or roll over on a turn.
4. The higher the speed, the greater the danger if there is a blowout.
5. The higher the speed, the greater the force of impact in a collision.
6. The higher the speed, the greater the personal injuries and property damage in a collision.

reasonable and proper for existing conditions." So no matter what the posted speed limit, you must select a speed that is safe. The right speed at any time is determined more by the situation than by the posted limit—fixed or flexible.

DAY AND NIGHT SPEED LIMITS

Because it is hard to see in the dark, some states post different speed limits for the day and for the night. Lower speeds at night give drivers more time to search for visual clues and to spot hazards.

MINIMUM SPEED

Minimum speed limits are posted on all interstate highways and on some heavily traveled state and local roads. The minimum speed limit is designed to keep traffic moving and to reduce the chance of collisions between vehicles going at different speeds. But, when driving conditions are poor, you may drive slower than the minimum limit.

The faster a car is moving when it collides with another car or a fixed object, the greater the bodily injuries to the driver and passengers.

SPEED ZONING

One speed limit cannot meet the conditions found on all sections of a road. So speed zoning is used. Surveys are made by traffic engineers, who decide what speed is best for the road under normal conditions.

Regardless of the posted limit, you must drive at a speed that is safe. If weather or visibility conditions are bad, reduce speed.

Signs are then posted to tell drivers of the speed limit in each zone. Whole sections of a highway may be zoned at one speed. Lower speed limits may be set for curves, intersections, school zones, business and residential districts, or other special areas.

DRIVING WHILE INTOXICATED

Alcohol and other drugs seriously reduce one's ability to drive. Therefore, it is illegal to drive anywhere while under their influence. Even if you have a doctor's prescription, driving under the influence of drugs is against the law. Such laws are not limited to driving on a highway.

A court of law must determine whether a driver is guilty of *driving while intoxicated* (DWI). An officer who suspects a driver is *intoxicated* (drunk) must first make an arrest. To convict the driver in court, the officer has to show evidence that the driver was intoxicated. This evidence includes the officer's notes about the way the person was driving, the time, the date, and the place. Usually, the results of a chemical test that show the amount of alcohol or drugs in the driver's blood must be presented to the court. (Some states permit the use of a test for alcohol before an arrest has been made. But, in most states, tests for *blood-alcohol concentration* [BAC]—the amount of alcohol found in the blood—can be given only after an arrest.)

CHEMICAL TESTS FOR INTOXICATION

Chemical tests for the presence of alcohol or other drugs can consist of an examination of breath, blood, or urine samples. The breath test is the one most often used to find the BAC. It is usually done with a device called a *breathalyser* and must be given by trained persons.

BLOOD-ALCOHOL CONCENTRATION

In nearly all states, a driver who is arrested and has a BAC of 0.10 percent can be charged with driving while under the influence of alcohol. (A BAC of 0.10 percent simply means that there is 1 part of alcohol for every 1000 parts of blood.) When the BAC gets as high as 4 or 5

Drinking and driving can result in accidents such as the one shown above. Drivers should give their full attention to their vehicles and paths of travel. If you must drink, ask someone who has not been drinking to drive.

parts per 1000 (a BAC of 0.40 or 0.50 percent), a person may go into a deep coma or die.

Most states have a lesser offense called *driving while impaired*. A driver may be charged with this offense when the BAC at the time of arrest falls between 0.05 percent and 0.10 percent. A BAC of 0.05 percent may seem low, but it takes only a small amount of alcohol to impair your ability to drive. A person with a BAC of 0.05 percent is twice as likely to be involved in a traffic accident as a driver with a BAC of 0 percent. With a BAC of 0.10 percent, a driver is six times as likely to be involved in a collision. This figure rises to twenty-five times as likely when the BAC reaches 0.15 percent.

IMPLIED CONSENT

Under the *implied consent law*, any driver arrested for being drunk must agree to take a chemical test for the presence of alcohol. If a driver will not take the test, the state Department of Motor Vehicles usually has the right to take away the driver's license. In most states, a suspension under the implied consent law is for 3 to 6 months.

Police officers often carry portable units to test the blood-alcohol level of motorists. A driver who has a blood-alcohol level of 0.10 percent can be charged with driving under the influence of alcohol.

TO CONSIDER

1. List five of the seven rules of the road. Why is it important that these basic rules be the same throughout the United States?

2. Describe three situations in which there would be right-of-way conflicts. How should each of the conflicts be resolved?

3. Why do we have minimum and maximum speed limits? List six facts about speed that should be considered when choosing a speed at which to travel.

4. Why is speed a cause of many traffic accidents?

5. When could a driver be stopped for speeding even though he or she is driving at or below the posted speed limit? What kind of hazards can such a driver cause for other highway users?

6. Explain the laws relating to driving while intoxicated.

7. What is the purpose of traffic laws? How do they help you predict what other drivers will do?

8. What can happen to a driver who is arrested and then refuses to take a chemical test for BAC?

9. What does a reasonable maximum speed depend on? Why do some states use "fixed" and "flexible" speed limits?

10. Explain the difference between "driving while intoxicated" and "driving while impaired."

PROJECTS

1. Interview a police officer. Ask what methods he or she uses to enforce speed laws. Is enforcement stricter in some places than in others? If so, why? What are the main problems the officer must face in enforcing speed limits? Report your findings to the class, adding your own conclusions.

2. Get in touch with your local police department. Arrange to be part of a "Ride-Along" session to watch how police officers enforce traffic laws. (Note: There may not be such a program in all places. If your town has one, you may have to get clearances from your parents and the police to be in it.)

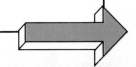

CHAPTER

13

SIGNS, SIGNALS, AND ROADWAY MARKINGS

Signs, signals, and markings tell drivers about rules or laws and warn them of hazards. Drivers need good information to make the right decisions. Traffic signs have standard shapes and colors that have special meanings. If drivers know these meanings, they can recognize and understand signs from far away. This gives a driver more time to react to hazards ahead. Study the signs, signals, and markings on the following pages. Learn to know them at a glance.

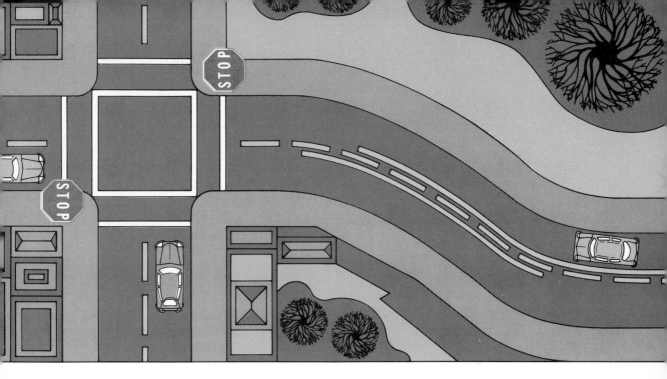

REGULATORY SIGNS

Regulatory signs tell drivers what they can and cannot do. These signs are usually rectangular shaped. Exceptions are stop signs, yield signs, and railroad crossbucks.

STOP SIGN

This sign is always a red *octagon* (eight-sided figure) with white lettering. It is found at intersections. The *stop* sign tells drivers to come to a *full* (complete) stop. It tells a driver who has the right-of-way.

Stop at a stop sign before any part of your car is in the intersection or crosswalk. After your car has come to a full stop, you may go when it is safe to do so. Usually, stop signs are placed so that drivers can see them well in advance. When drivers slow down before they arrive at a stop sign, they alert cross traffic and vehicles behind them that they intend to stop. This gives the drivers in the vehicles behind a chance to note speed changes and to respond gradually. It also tells traffic on the cross street that the driver is stopping. This allows drivers on the cross street to pay more attention to other conflicts they may have to face.

At an intersection in which all the streets are controlled by stop signs, the first vehicle to get there should be given the right-of-way. Other drivers should then take their turns.

YIELD SIGN

The yield sign is a triangle with red letters on a white background. A *yield* sign requires that a driver be ready to give the right-of-way (stopping if necessary). Yield signs can be found at points where streets cross or merge.

The yield sign does not always require a complete stop. Slowing down may give a driver enough time to complete a move safely. Whatever move is made, it should not break the flow of traffic in the lanes being crossed or entered. If traffic is heavy, the driver must come to a full stop and wait until the move can be made without breaking through cross traffic.

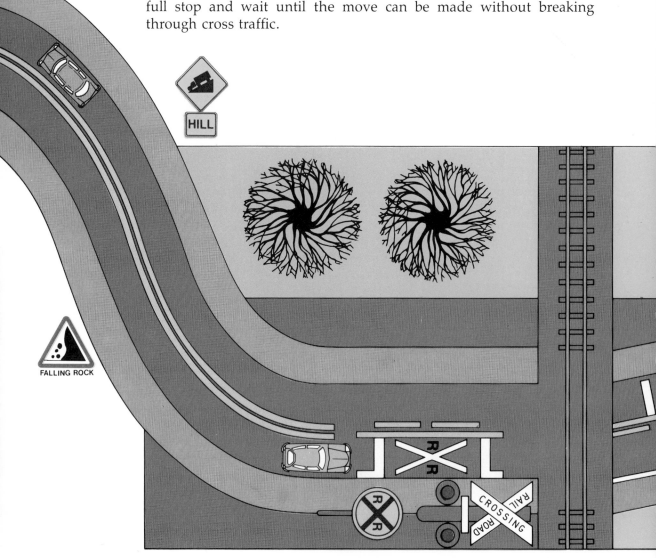

RAILROAD CROSSINGS

Railroad crossings have a number of signs. One sign is a round, yellow *warning* sign with a black RR and black X on it. It is found several hundred feet before the railroad crossing. Another sign is a large, white X called a *crossbuck*. This sign is placed a few feet from the railroad tracks. A small rectangular sign just below the crossbuck shows how many tracks there are at the crossing.

Railroad crossings that get heavy train traffic may have a gate or barrier that is lowered across the road to stop cars when a train nears the crossing. A pair of red lights with the crossbuck mounted on a post flashes when the train is approaching.

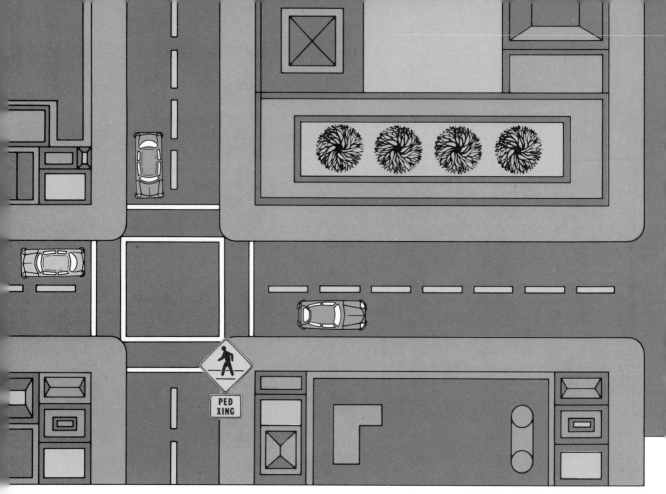

Accidents at railroad crossings can be very serious because of the size and speed of trains. Approach railroad crossings with great caution even if the lights are not flashing and the gates are not down. (The lights and gates could be broken.) If there are no lights or gates at a railroad crossing, approach it with still more caution.

OTHER REGULATORY SIGNS

There are many other kinds of regulatory signs. These include speed-limit signs, parking signs, *wrong-way* signs, *one-way* signs, and *do-not-enter* signs. There are also warnings against littering, unnecessary noise, and making unlawful driving maneuvers. The size and color of some signs will vary from one city or state to another. When you drive in unfamiliar places, you must watch carefully for signs. If you do not recognize regulatory signs or if you fail to notice them, you are not excused from having to obey them.

INTERNATIONAL TRAFFIC SIGNS

International traffic signs are being seen more frequently. These signs have pictures and symbols instead of words. They can be easily understood in any country.

WARNING SIGNS

A warning sign is yellow and is either diamond-shaped or round. It has black letters or symbols. *Warning signs* alert drivers to possible dangers. Drivers should prepare to change their speed or position.

Among the dangers that these signs warn of are hills, curves, school or railroad crossings, intersections, merging traffic, and bad road surfaces.

Construction and *maintenance signs* are also warning signs. They are diamond-shaped, too, but they are orange instead of yellow. They warn drivers that road crews are working on or near the road.

INFORMATION SIGNS

Information signs serve as guides and direct drivers to service areas. These signs all have symbols that can be easily recognized. *Guide signs* include route markers and destination signs showing directions and mileage. They may also show points of interest or recreation. *Service signs* tell drivers about such things as food, gas, and rest areas.

SLIPPERY WHEN WET

MERGE

US 38   5 mi.   8 km.
Greenville   40 mi.   64 km.
St. Louis   125 mi.   200 km.

EXIT
25
M.P.H.

DO NOT
ENTER

RAMP
30
M.P.H.

SPEED
LIMIT
55

TRAFFIC-CONTROL SIGNALS

RED, YELLOW, AND GREEN TRAFFIC LIGHTS

The most common traffic signal is the three-lens red, yellow, and green light. These lights may be on posts at the corners of intersections or hung over the roadway. When the _red lens_ (usually the top light) is lit, you must _stop_ your car. There may be a line that shows where to stop. If not, you should stop before the intersection. Do not go beyond the crosswalk.

When the _yellow lens_ (the middle light) is lit, you should proceed with caution or stop if necessary. When you come to a traffic signal, you must think about the time and distance you need to stop. Also, keep in mind the traffic in front and in back of you. Will you be able to brake to a stop before you reach the intersection? If you stop, will the driver behind you crash into you? Will you be able to speed up to get through the intersection if necessary to avoid being hit? In other words, are you at the _go_ (continue) or the _no-go_ (stop) position? Some drivers wait until after the yellow light comes on before they make a _go_ or _no-go_ decision. They often find themselves entering the intersection on a red light, still trying to make up their minds.

When the _green lens_ (most often at the bottom) is lit, you may go through the intersection if it is clear. If the light has just turned green, you should yield to any cross traffic or pedestrians already in the intersection. As you near a green light, note how long it has been green. If the green light has been on for some time, it is called a _stale_ green light. There is a good chance the light will soon turn yellow.

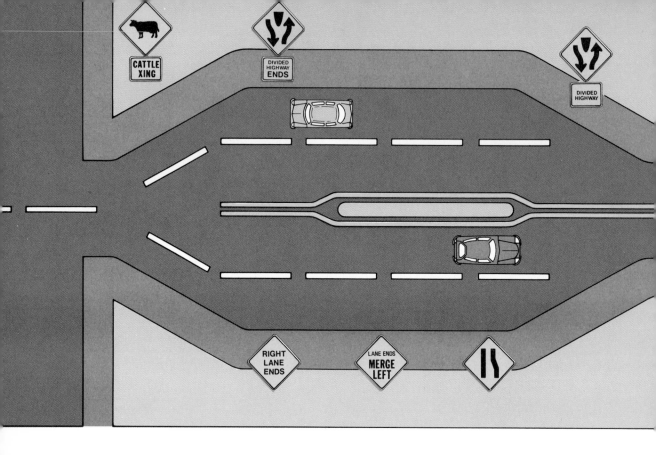

RIGHT AND LEFT TURN ON RED

In all but a few areas, right turns are permitted when the traffic light is red. A small number of areas permit a right turn on red only if a sign is posted.

Many areas also permit left turns on red lights. A left turn on red generally may be made only if the driver is turning from a one-way street onto another one-way street. (Check your state driver's guide for the rules in your state.)

When turning either left or right on a red light, drivers must first make a full stop. They must make sure that the way is clear of both pedestrians and cars.

WALK/DON'T WALK SIGNS

Walk/Don't Walk signs are traffic lights for pedestrians. Pedestrians may not walk against a steady DON'T WALK signal. They may start

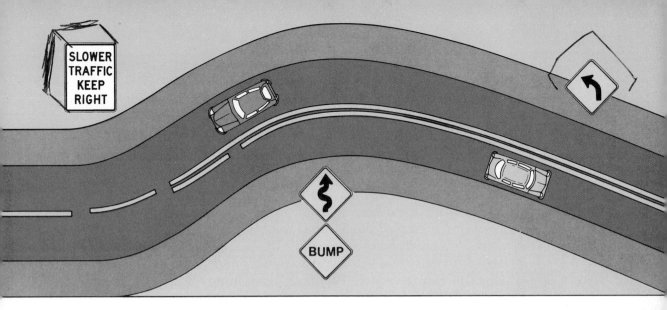

across the street only on a WALK signal. A flashing DON'T WALK light means that there is not enough time to cross the street safely. It can also alert drivers that the green traffic-signal light is stale.

RED, GREEN, AND YELLOW ARROWS

Besides red, yellow, and green lights, a traffic signal may have red, yellow, and/or green arrows. Whereas the *round green lens* tells the driver to go in any direction, a *green arrow* permits movement only in the direction shown by the arrow. A *yellow arrow* means that movement in that direction is about to end. A *red arrow* means that it *prohibits* (forbids by law) movement *only* in the direction of the arrow. (Traffic in a turning lane, for example, may not turn.)

FLASHING RED LIGHTS

A *flashing red light* means come to a full stop before proceeding. It is found at hazardous intersections where there is not enough cross-street traffic to warrant a red-yellow-green traffic light.

FLASHING YELLOW LIGHTS

A *flashing yellow light* signals a possible hazard. It means slow down, check traffic, and proceed with caution (prepare to stop). The flashing yellow light may be used in many places, such as intersections, fire houses, and school zones. Determine the purpose of the light as you approach it.

SPECIAL LANE-CONTROL LIGHTS

Sometimes, there are changes in the direction of traffic flow. For instance, some lanes may be used by traffic going one way in the morning and the other way in the evening. To help avoid the hazard of head-on collisions, signal lights may be hung over the lanes. If the signal is a *green arrow* or a *green X*, the lane is open to traffic facing the signal. If the signal is a *yellow X*, traffic flowing in the direction of the signal is about to end. If the *yellow X* is flashing, then that lane is for use of left-turning vehicles only. The lane is closed to those vehicles facing a *red X* signal.

PAVEMENT MARKINGS

Markings on the pavement are used alone or with signs and signals in places where a driver might not see signs or signals.

LANE AND CENTER-LINE MARKINGS

The most common roadway markings are lane lines and center lines. These lines may be yellow or white. A *solid* or *broken yellow line* divides traffic traveling in *opposite* directions. A *solid* or *broken white line* separates traffic going in the *same* direction.

A *solid white* line is used where extra caution must be taken. If a *solid yellow* line is used, you cannot legally cross it. If the line is broken, you may cross it to pass another vehicle, to change lanes, or to turn.

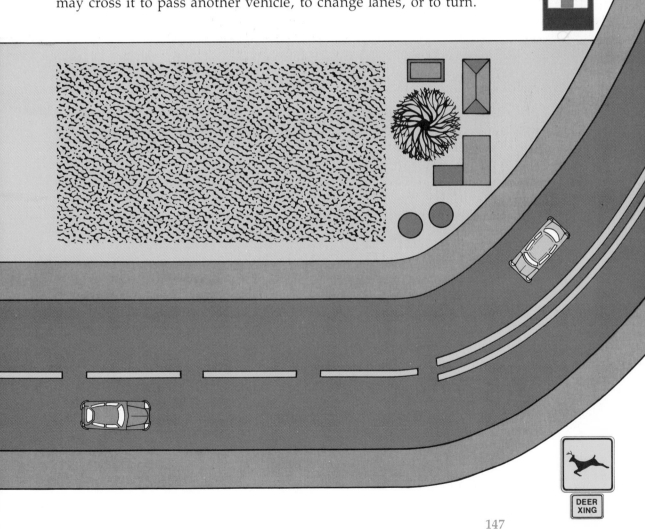

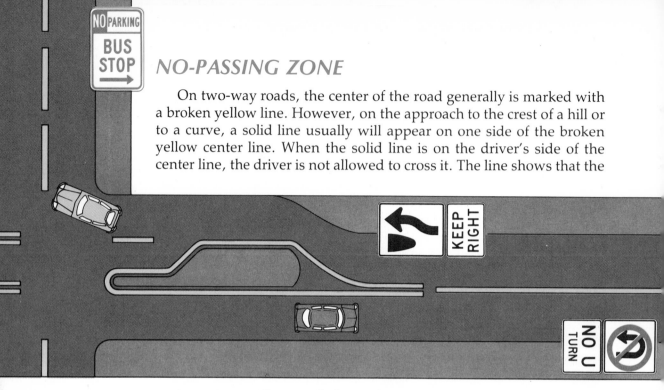

NO-PASSING ZONE

On two-way roads, the center of the road generally is marked with a broken yellow line. However, on the approach to the crest of a hill or to a curve, a solid line usually will appear on one side of the broken yellow center line. When the solid line is on the driver's side of the center line, the driver is not allowed to cross it. The line shows that the

car is coming to a potentially hazardous spot or that the field of vision is limited. Drivers whose cars are traveling with the broken line on the side near them may pass with caution. If there is a double solid yellow line, passing is not allowed in either direction.

Many highways have solid white *edge lines*. These are used to mark the outside edge of the outermost lanes. Edge lines help drivers stay in position in the lane, particularly when visibility is poor.

SPECIAL PAVEMENT MARKINGS

Traffic regulations are sometimes painted on the surface of the road. Examples are: LEFT TURN ONLY, RIGHT TURN ONLY, and THRU TRAFFIC. With these words, there may also be painted arrows, signs, or signals. The letters RR painted on the surface of a road are often used along with other signs and signals to warn drivers of a railroad crossing.

Heavy white lines are used with stop signs or traffic lights to show where vehicles should stop. They also mark pedestrian crosswalks.

Diagonal lines, or "zebra" lines, are often used to mark fixed obstructions, such as traffic islands and lane barriers. Once in a while, they are used to mark no-passing zones. Drivers should not drive or park in places marked with diagonal lines.

TO CONSIDER

1. Explain how traffic signs, signals, and roadway markings are useful to drivers and pedestrians.

2. What are two clues that can help drivers know what a sign means before getting close enough to see the words or symbols on it?

3. What are the shapes and colors of stop and yield signs? How must drivers respond to each?

4. Who has the right-of-way at an intersection where all the streets have stop signs?

5. What are some of the good things about international traffic signs? Do these signs have any bad points?

6. Describe the purpose of red, green, and yellow arrows.

7. What are some clues that warn you of a no-passing zone on a two-way road?

PROJECTS

1. Look for traffic signs, signals, and roadway markings in your community that you think may be hazardous. You may find, for example, a curve warning sign which is covered by shrubs, a posted speed limit which seems too high for safe driving, or faded roadway markings. Photograph them and show the slides to the class.

2. Watch traffic at an intersection that has a traffic light. How many drivers go through the intersection when the light is yellow? How often do waiting drivers "jump" the light by moving into the intersection before the light turns from red to green? What hazards do these drivers cause for other drivers? Tell your class what you find.

COPING WITH HIGHWAY AND ENVIRONMENTAL FACTORS

6 UNIT

Unit VI describes those often-changing factors that can affect the way you drive. It tells you how to stay aware of these factors in order to make safe driving decisions.

Chapter 14, "Traction," explains
• some things a driver should know about traction.
• some ways to identify things that affect traction.
• how to adjust to uphill and downhill driving.

Chapter 15, "Visibility and Other Highway Conditions," discusses
• how to adjust for weather conditions that reduce visibility.
• how to recognize environmental conditions that reduce visibility.
• how to sort out things with collision potential.
• how to handle common on- and off-road hazards.

CHAPTER 14

TRACTION

Vehicle control depends in part on friction. *Friction* is the resistance between the moving tires of your vehicle and the road surface. The friction of an object on a surface is called *traction*. Tires are designed to have as much traction as they can. The greater the traction, the less chance that your tires will skid. Once a skid begins, you lose much of your control of your vehicle. There are a number of factors having to do with traction that you must be aware of:

1. The amount of traction is not constant. It varies with the type and condition of the road surface. It also varies with the way a tire is made and with the depth of its tread. The *tread* of a tire is the part which comes into contact with the road surface. It has a pattern of grooves or ridges.
2. We make our best judgments of traction on dry, paved roads because we are used to driving on this kind of surface.
3. Speeding up, turning a corner, and slowing down all put stress on your tires and cut down on their traction. Judging how much traction you may have is harder at those times. Driving

straight ahead on a level, dry, clean, hard, paved surface provides the best traction. Any change from this ideal means that drivers must adjust their speed to allow for the reduced amount of traction.

REDUCED TRACTION

Two kinds of highway conditions cause reduced traction. The first has to do with the type and condition of the driving surface. There is little difference between hard-surface concrete and asphalt roads. Variations in traction can be great on tar and gravel, sand, or plain gravel, though. The same is true if the pavement is worn or broken. The second highway condition that reduces traction has to do with things on the surface of the road. If the road is covered by loose dirt and small stones, control will be much harder to maintain. It is also hard to keep control if a paved road is covered with gravel or is wet.

There is a way in which you can test the traction you may have. First, check to see that you have room and that there are no other highway users around you. At a low speed (25 to 30 km/h, 15 to 20 mph), press the brake pedal down fast to lock the brakes. Before you lose control, release the brake pedal. Your car's response should give you some idea of the skid conditions without placing you in danger.

Proper inflation and good treads help tires hug the road. The tire below is in good condition. The tread is good, and there are no cuts or scrapes on the tire. Check the condition of your tires often.

Traction can be influenced by many factors.		
1. Bumps and holes	4. Loose dirt or gravel	7. Water, snow, or ice
2. Worn tires	5. Curves	8. Road contours
3. Oversteering	6. Overbraking	9. Overaccelerating

FACTORS AFFECTING TRACTION

Things on the road lessen the contact between the tires and the road. The most common cause of reduced contact is bad weather.

RAIN

Most drivers think they have more control than they do when the road is wet. As a result, the number of accidents goes up when it rains. Wet surfaces give less traction than dry surfaces because there is less contact between the tires and the road. There are two types of dangers on wet roads:

1. Roads are very slippery for 10 to 15 minutes after it starts to rain. This is caused by the mixture of water, dirt, rubber, dust, and oil that builds up on the road. The mixture, which creates a very slick surface, is soon splashed or washed away.

Driving through large amounts of water on worn tires can cause your car to hydroplane. When you drive in rain or through puddles, drive slowly. Scan the road for obstacles. Accelerate, brake, and make steering changes gradually. Drive in the tracks of vehicles ahead of you.

Loose dirt, pebbles, sand, and gravel on the road reduce traction. If you drive too fast or if you turn or stop too suddenly on this type of surface, your car could go into a skid.

2. Roads with deep water (caused by very heavy rains or poor drainage) can also be a danger. Water on the roadway, combined with tires that are worn or do not have enough air in them, can cause your car's front wheels to *hydroplane* (ride on top of a film of water) *even* when you are going at moderate speeds. This means that all direct contact between the road and the tires is lost. You can reduce the danger of driving on these two kinds of wet roads: first, reduce your speed; second, drive in the tracks of the vehicle ahead of you. The vehicle ahead "wipes" the water off the road for a few seconds and so improves your traction.

SNOW AND ICE

Snow and ice make roads very dangerous. The roads get even more dangerous as the snow and ice melt. (Wet ice is more slippery than ice that is dry.) Any change in speed or direction on a slick road may well result in a skid. The sharper the change, the more likely the skid.

Snow tires increase your traction in snow, particularly if the snow is dry. Tire chains increase your car's traction best on icy surfaces.

The wisest action to take in case of either deep water or ice on the road is to stop driving. Gradually reduce your speed, and leave the road as soon as you can find a safe place to stop.

Roads covered with snow, ice, and melting ice are extremely dangerous. The roads are slippery and your car can easily go into a skid. Use snow tires or tire chains. Drive very slowly. Do not accelerate or brake suddenly.

OTHER ROAD CONDITIONS

There are other road-surface conditions that may cut down on traction. Oil from vehicles, sand, and gravel can cause great problems. In the fall of the year, wet leaves are a common hazard. Metal surfaces and wooden planks, such as those on some bridges or in construction areas, can cause skidding, particularly when they are wet. Bumps or holes in the road that cause the car to bounce will reduce traction.

The contour, or slope, of the road's surface also plays an important role in the ability of a car to make a turn. When turning at higher speeds, you need more traction to keep your car from skidding toward the outside of the curve. That is why curves on a well-designed road are *banked* (sloped up toward the outside of the turn). When you make a turn on a banked curve, your car tilts down toward the inside. This tilt improves tracking. However, not all roads give you this advantage. Some roads are *crowned*. They are higher in the center than at the edges. Such roads will aid you in a turn to the right because on those turns the lane tilts up toward the center of the road. Left turns can be dangerous, though. The slope then goes down toward the outside edge of the road.

HILLS

When you drive uphill, it is hard to pick up speed quickly in order to avoid a hazard. It is also hard to pass another car even if the lane is

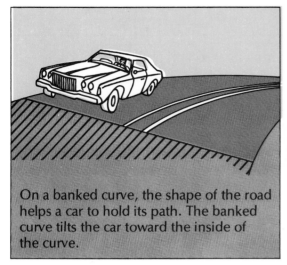

On a banked curve, the shape of the road helps a car to hold its path. The banked curve tilts the car toward the inside of the curve.

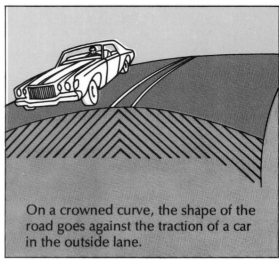

On a crowned curve, the shape of the road goes against the traction of a car in the outside lane.

The slope of the roadway will influence traction.

clear. Some cars might not have the power to complete a passing maneuver. Yet, one thing is easier going uphill—stopping a car.

Downhill driving also requires special attention. Your car will begin to pick up speed. It will be easier to pass another car, but it will also be harder to stop. So put more space between your car and those in front of you when you start downhill. Take your foot off the gas pedal. Brake from time to time to keep a safe speed. If your car has a standard shift and the hill is steep, you could shift into *second* gear. This would help to slow the car.

It is easy to stop on an uphill grade, but your car will accelerate more slowly. This could mean trouble if you need to pick up speed to avoid a hazard. Always leave extra space around your car. It is easy to accelerate but more difficult to stop when you drive downhill. Leave more space between your car and the car in front of you. Brake often.

TO CONSIDER

1. Describe those road conditions which give the best traction.

2. How can you safely test how much traction you have on a slippery surface?

3. What kinds of road conditions can reduce traction?

4. Explain why road surfaces are very slick just after a rain begins. What is hydroplaning?

5. Why do wet leaves, bumps, gravel, and sand reduce traction?

6. How are some roads designed to improve traction?

7. How does driving uphill differ from driving downhill?

8. How can you reduce the danger of driving on wet roads?

9. What are some steps you can take to improve traction on snow and ice?

PROJECTS

1. Ask local traffic authorities if the number of accidents increases when weather conditions reduce traction. Ask them if collisions are more severe or less severe when traction is poor.

2. Make a photo display of hazardous low-traction areas in your community. Label each photo and list the potential hazard.

3. Contact a tire dealer or a manufacturer of tire chains. Find out what the difference is between chains and snow tires. What are the good and bad points of each? When are snow tires or tire chains most useful? How do they compare with regular tires? Prepare a wall chart comparing all three.

4. Inspect a major intersection in your community (taking care not to endanger yourself when traffic is present). Observe the road surface closely. Make a list of any substances present on the roadway that could reduce traction (such as ice, oil, wet leaves, sand, debris, etc.). Then watch vehicles in the intersection. Do any of them have difficulty with traction? If so, why? Prepare a report for your class.

CHAPTER **15**

VISIBILITY AND OTHER HIGHWAY CONDITIONS

You cannot control all the things that can block or limit visibility. But you can be aware of them and adjust your speed and road position to reduce the risks.

ATMOSPHERIC CONDITIONS

NIGHTTIME OR DARKNESS

It is always hard to see at night. Clean, properly aimed headlights do help you to see straight ahead. But they are little help in lighting off-road areas or much of your path as you turn.

You must switch your headlights to low beam when you meet or follow other vehicles. Low beams cut down the glare of your lights. Do not stare at the headlights of approaching vehicles. If a vehicle comes

Fog reduces visibility. Use the defroster/defogger to clear the windows. Use the windshield wipers. Reduce speed. Leave extra space around your car.

toward you with high-beam headlights on, signal the other driver to switch to low beams by flashing your headlights from low to high and back to low quickly.

FOG AND SMOG

Fog and smog can be so *dense* (thick) that they make it hard to see even the front of your car's hood. It is best to reduce your speed.

If you drive in fog at night, use your headlights on low beam. If you use high beams, the water in the fog will reflect your bright headlights back into your eyes.

Headlights do not completely light up the road ahead. This is especially true on curves.

If you drive in a fog at night, use low beams. The water in fog reflects back into your eyes when you use high beams in fog. In the photo above, note how the low-beam lights of the car ahead reflect downward on the road.

SNOW AND RAIN

Snow and rain can reduce traction and visibility. You may be forced to pull off the road. If you do pull off, move well away from the road and turn on your four-way warning lights.

Falling snow that sticks to the car windows may block your vision. During a heavy, wet snow, even the wipers may not be able to keep the windshield clear.

SUN GLARE

At sunrise and sunset, there is a strong glare from the sun. If you are driving toward the sun, it may be very hard to see. The glare can be worse if your car's windshield is dirty or scratched. Sun visors or

Snow reduces your ability to see at a distance. Use your windshield wipers to clear away falling snow. If the wiper blades ice up, pull off the road and clean them.

If you drive toward the sun at sunrise or sunset, you will face a strong sun glare. If your window is dirty or scratched, the glare is worse. Reduce speed, wear sunglasses, and use sun visors.

Never pass on a hill. Be prepared for hazards that may be out of sight over the crest of a hill. Vehicles, animals, pedestrians, or other obstacles may be in your intended path of travel. Select a speed and position that will give you a way out in case there is a hazard ahead.

sunglasses can help. When there is sun glare, you may not see the brake lights of a car that is slowing down, so you should reduce your speed.

ENVIRONMENTAL CONDITIONS

Things often found on or near the road can also limit what you see by hiding all or part of something. This could cause a wreck.

HILLCRESTS

As you come to the top of a hill, your vision will be temporarily limited. The steeper the grade of the hill, the less you will be able to see. To be better prepared, choose a speed and position that will let you respond to hazards that may be just over the crest.

OBJECTS ADJACENT TO THE ROAD

Objects of almost any size may hide important things from your view. A tree trunk may hide an adult. Sign boards or buildings could block a large vehicle.

BUSHES AND SHRUBBERY

Drivers often do not take note of shrubbery because it is not on their pathway. Bushes or shrubbery could hide vehicles that may close in on your path of travel.

162

Leave more space between your car and large vehicles. They limit your vision and can hide possible hazards.

BLIND TURNS

On some turns, the driver's vision along the path of travel is blocked. You may be able to see only 2 seconds ahead. Bushes, walls, or other things along the inside of the turn keep you from seeing farther. Drive cautiously.

OTHER VEHICLES

Almost any other vehicle can limit your field of vision, especially a truck, bus, or van. The larger the vehicle, the more area it hides. In general, moving vehicles do not limit a driver's field of vision as much as parked ones do. Parked vehicles can keep you from seeing persons about to open a car door and step out. They can also hide cars or pedestrians about to move into your path.

VISUAL OBSTRUCTIONS INSIDE A VEHICLE

Things inside your car can cut down your field of vision, too. Passengers may partly block your view in the rear-view mirror. Door posts and roof supports also limit what you can see. At some angles, they can hide other vehicles from your view. Packages piled on the rear seat, clothing hung on a rod, and an open trunk with the lid up can also limit vision.

ON-ROAD HAZARDS

There are many things with which you could collide on any road: bumps, bottles, boxes, tree branches, parts of vehicles, and so on. As

As you drive, search the road for objects with which you could collide.

you watch the road while driving, learn to spot anything that has collision potential. You must be able to judge not only the dangers involved in hitting something in the road but also the dangers involved in trying to avoid it.

OFF-ROAD OBJECTS AND HAZARDS

Most of the things that cause hazards on the road (such as holes, bumps, or litter) also are in off-road areas. Some common off-road hazards are light poles, sign posts, fire hydrants, trees, bushes, fences, ditches, and embankments.

Fixed objects off the road are not as hazardous as those that are on the road. However, you must not ignore them. *Scan* (make a wide search of) conditions off the road ahead to get important information about the shoulder of the road. *Scanning* ahead and *planning a safe escape route* will reduce hazards if you must leave the road in a hurry. The right information about off-road areas will help you to recover smoothly if you are forced to steer onto the shoulder of the road.

Objects near the road are a problem not only because drivers might hit them when leaving the road. Sometimes, off-road objects make drivers nervous. They feel threatened by light poles, trees, signs, and bridge railings. Such drivers may move too close to the middle of the road, thus placing themselves on a collision course with oncoming drivers.

Scan the shoulder of the road ahead. This will help you to avoid hazards if you have to leave the road quickly.

TO CONSIDER

1. How does reduced visibility cut down on your ability to avoid collisions?

2. If you decide to pull off the road and stop because of heavy rain or fog, what can you do to make your car more visible?

3. What steps can you take to compensate for sun glare?

4. Describe three situations in which visibility would be limited by fixed objects or geography.

5. How can you reduce visual obstructions inside your car?

6. If a car ahead of you suddenly swerves for no apparent reason, what should you do?

7. Explain why you must be aware of fixed objects on the shoulder of the road.

8. What steps can you take to improve your visibility at night?

9. Why is it better to use your headlights on low beam in fog rather than on high beam?

10. How can visibility be limited by other vehicles?

11. How can you position your car to cut down the risk of a collision?

PROJECTS

1. Observe traffic at night. Do drivers cooperate with each other by switching on low-beam headlights when they meet, pass, or follow other vehicles? What percentage of drivers cooperate in each case? How many drivers have burned-out or poorly aimed headlights? Report your findings to the class.

2. When you ride with a family member or a friend, make a list of the objects on a 5-mile stretch of road and road shoulder. Describe each object and discuss the kind of hazard—if any—that it is likely to cause.

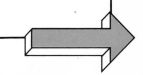

OPERATING YOUR VEHICLE

UNIT

This unit will help you learn about your car—how to handle it and how to keep it in good condition.

Chapter 16, "Vehicle Performance," explains
• what you should know about the major systems that make your car run.

Chapter 17, "Vehicle Maintenance," tells
• how to recognize changes in the condition of your car.
• how to check for the causes of those changes.

Chapter 18, "Vehicle Performance and Decision Making," discusses
• how to judge your car's performance.
• how to make good time-space decisions.

Chapter 19, "Selecting, Operating, and Insuring Your Car," describes
• how to buy a new or used car.
• how to drive in a way that saves fuel.
• how to insure your car for your needs.

VEHICLE PERFORMANCE

Several major systems in your car provide its power and give you control over its movement. They are the power train, the fuel system, the electrical system, the ignition system, the exhaust system, the lubricating and cooling systems, the suspension and steering systems, and the braking system.

THE POWER TRAIN

In most cars, the engine sends power to only two of the four wheels. These wheels, most often the two in the rear, are called the *drive wheels*. The power is sent to the *clutch* and *transmission*. (It is the clutch and transmission that allow the driver to change gears.) The transmission is connected by the driveshaft to the *differential, rear axles,* and *rear wheels*. The differential does two things:

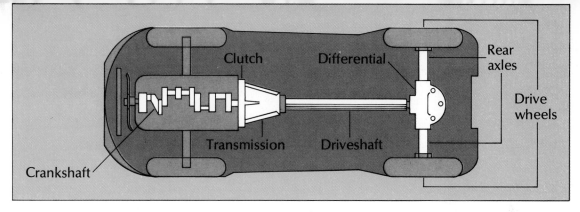

The power train delivers power from the engine to the drive wheels.

1. It changes by 90 degrees the direction of the power (rotation) supplied by the driveshaft. This power is used to turn the drive-wheel axles.
2. It lets each of the drive wheels turn at a different rate of speed. This enables a car to turn a corner.

THE ENGINE

The *engine* produces the car's power by exploding an air-fuel mixture within its cylinders. The amount of power produced is determined by

1. the number and size of the cylinders.
2. the quality and quantity of the air-fuel mixture.
3. how much pressure the mixture is placed under.
4. the timing of the spark from the spark plug, which ignites the air-fuel mixture and causes it to explode.

The engine operation starts with the *ignition switch*. When you turn the key in the ignition switch to *start*, power is drawn from the battery

The differential sends power from the driveshaft to each of the drive-wheel axles. It also allows each of the drive wheels to turn at a different rate of speed.

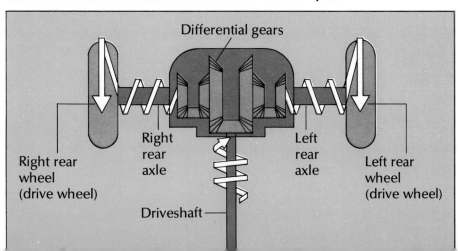

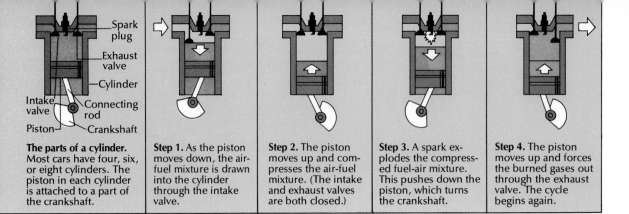

The parts of a cylinder. Most cars have four, six, or eight cylinders. The piston in each cylinder is attached to a part of the crankshaft.

Step 1. As the piston moves down, the air-fuel mixture is drawn into the cylinder through the intake valve.

Step 2. The piston moves up and compresses the air-fuel mixture. (The intake and exhaust valves are both closed.)

Step 3. A spark explodes the compressed fuel-air mixture. This pushes down the piston, which turns the crankshaft.

Step 4. The piston moves up and forces the burned gases out through the exhaust valve. The cycle begins again.

The most common type of internal combustion engine is the four-stroke piston engine. In a four-step cycle, the controlled explosion of an air-fuel mixture pushes the pistons up and down. The pistons, then, move the crankshaft.

to the electric starter motor. This motor has a gear which turns the flywheel of the engine. When the flywheel turns, it turns the crankshaft, which causes the pistons to move up and down in the cylinders. It also causes the intake and exhaust valves to open and close. The *four-step* (or stroke) *cycle* of each *piston* gives your car its power.

1. When the piston goes down, a vacuum is created. This draws the air-fuel mixture through the intake valve into the cylinder. The exhaust valve is closed during this downward motion. When the piston gets down as far as it can go, the intake valve closes, too.

2. The piston then starts to move upward in the cylinder, pushing the air-fuel mixture into about one-tenth of the space it had before. The *spark plug* (there is one for each cylinder) is then electrically charged. This sets off a spark which causes the compressed air-fuel mixture to explode.

3. This explosion drives the piston back down. (All of this happens quickly. The speed of the engine depends on the number of explosions per minute.)

4. The exhaust valve now opens, and the piston rises, forcing the burned gases out.

This up-and-down motion of the pistons keeps the crankshaft turning. This power, sent from the crankshaft to the rear axle, makes the rear wheels move.

THE FUEL SYSTEM

The *fuel system* is made up of the fuel tank, the fuel pump, the carburetor, and the intake manifold. The pump forces the fuel from the tank to the carburetor. There the fuel is mixed with air and then drawn

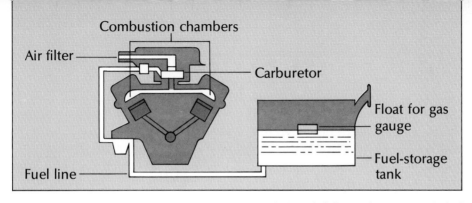

The fuel system has a twofold purpose. It stores fuel and delivers the correct air-fuel mixture to the engine.

into the intake manifold. From here, the air-fuel mixture enters the engine cylinder through the intake valves.

THE ELECTRICAL SYSTEM

The *electrical system* begins with an energy source: generally a 12-volt battery. There is also an alternator or a generator, a voltage regulator, and the wires that carry the electricity throughout the car.

The battery provides the power needed to start the engine. It also allows you to operate equipment, such as the lights and radio, for a short time when the engine is not running.

After the engine is started, the starter motor disengages when you release the ignition key. The alternator or generator provides electricity to keep the engine running, recharge the battery, and operate equipment. The *voltage regulator* controls the amount of electricity generated and the rate at which the battery is recharged. If the voltage regulator fails, the battery could receive too much electric charge and be damaged, or not be recharged at all.

The electrical system supplies the energy to start the car. It also distributes the electrical charges to each of the cylinders.

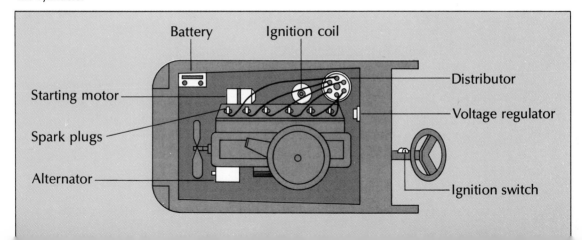

THE IGNITION SYSTEM

The *ignition system* is made up of an ignition switch, a starter motor, an ignition coil, points, a condenser, a distributor, ignition wires, and spark plugs. Many new cars are equipped with an electronic ignition system. Such a system does not have points. Instead, a magnetic pickup device in the distributor and an electronic switch start and stop the flow of electric current.

SPARK PLUG

There is a *spark plug* for each cylinder. The part of the spark plug in the cylinder is made up of a *metal tip* (electrode) and a short space (gap) below a *metal prong* (ground). At just the right moment, a high electric voltage (increased by the ignition coil or the electronic ignition system) is sent from the distributor to the electrode of the spark plug. A spark jumps the gap between the electrode and the ground prong. The spark causes the air-fuel mixture in the cylinder to explode.

The battery generally supplies electric current at 12 volts to the system. But a high voltage is needed to ignite the air-fuel mixture—18,000 volts in a car with an ignition coil system and 30,000 volts in a car with an electronic ignition. Whichever ignition system a car has, the purposes here are the same. These purposes are

1. to increase the voltage from 12 volts to the needed voltage.
2. to bring the electric charge to the proper spark plug at just the right time.

This is done through the use of: (1) an *ignition coil* (transformer), points, a condenser, and a *distributor* (a rotating switch) or (2) an electronic ignition and a distributor.

THE EXHAUST SYSTEM

The exhaust system serves two purposes:

1. It carries off water vapor, unburned fuel, and harmful gases, such as carbon monoxide, nitrous oxides, and lead oxides.
2. It reduces the amount of the sound coming to the outside from the explosions within the cylinders.

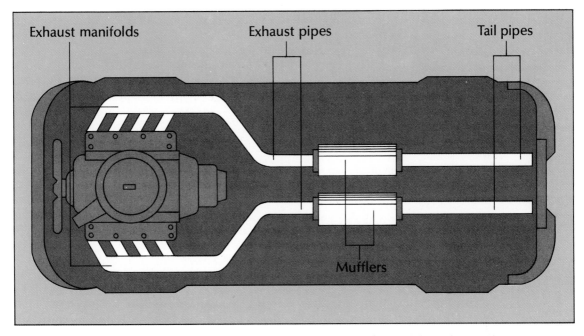

Exhaust manifolds   Exhaust pipes   Tail pipes

Mufflers

The exhaust system carries off unburned gases from the engine and reduces engine noise. It should be checked often for holes and worn fittings.

The *exhaust manifold* is a collecting system for the unburned gases as they exit from the cylinder. The exhaust pipe carries the gases to the muffler. The *muffler* helps to reduce the noise. The *tail pipe* carries the gases to the rear and away from the car.

EXHAUST EMISSION-CONTROL SYSTEM

Unburned fuel and other gases produced by the explosions in the cylinders collect in the engine crankcase. The *positive crankcase ventilation (PCV) system* was developed to reduce this problem. The PCV system recycles gases in the crankcase back into the cylinders to be burned again.

Since 1975, cars made in the United States have been equipped with *catalytic converters.* These devices reduce the amount of harmful gases that goes into the air from the tail pipe. The use of leaded gasoline in the engine will destroy the catalytic converter. Other devices collect or control gasoline vapors from the fuel tank and carburetor.

Proper adjustment of an engine's timing and its carburetor will result in more efficient use of fuel. *Air-injection pumps* and *high-temperature thermostats* save even more fuel and reduce air pollution.

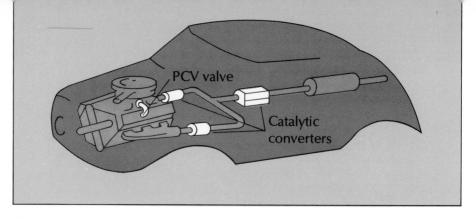

The PCV system draws vapors from the crankcase back into the combustion chamber for reburning. Catalytic converters reduce the amount of harmful gases in the exhaust.

THE LUBRICATING AND COOLING SYSTEMS

Many parts of an engine move very fast and rub against each other, creating *friction*. Friction produces heat. This heat and the heat produced by the air-fuel explosions produce very high engine temperatures. The temperatures may be greater than 2200 degrees Celsius (4000 degrees Fahrenheit). If not cooled, the engine would soon weld itself into a solid chunk of steel. The lubricating and cooling systems deal with this heat.

THE LUBRICATING SYSTEM

The *lubricating system* reduces heat by coating the engine's parts with oil. Oil reduces friction and wear between moving parts. The oil also helps seal the joint between the piston rings and cylinder walls. It absorbs shock from the bearings, cleans internal engine surfaces, and prevents rust and corrosion.

Oil is stored in the oil pan attached to the bottom of the engine. An oil pump, operated by the engine, pumps oil from the oil pan to the moving parts of the engine. Other parts of the engine are lubricated by having oil splashed on them by the crankshaft and connecting rods.

THE COOLING SYSTEM

The *cooling system* gets rid of engine heat. In cars with air-cooled engines, this is done by forcing air over metal cooling vanes that surround the cylinders.

The more common system is the so-called water-cooled engine. Few engines today are actually cooled by water. Instead, cars use a *coolant* (a special liquid that can withstand very high or very low temperatures). This liquid moves around the *water jacket* (passageway) that surrounds each of the cylinders, and absorbs heat.

Hoses connect the engine to the radiator. A pump forces the liquid from the engine to the radiator, where it flows through a network of tiny pipes. As the liquid circulates through the radiator, a fan driven by a belt forces air through the radiator to cool the liquid. A thermostat in the system acts as a gate to control the flow of liquid and to keep the best operating temperature. Then, the cooled liquid is circulated again to the engine.

If the cooling system fails, the engine will overheat. In very cold weather, the liquid will freeze if there is not enough antifreeze in it. *Antifreeze* lowers the freezing point of engine coolant. Frozen coolant cannot flow into the engine, and so the engine gets hot.

A temperature gauge or warning light on the dashboard gives information about engine temperature. If the light goes on or the gauge reads *hot,* stop the car in a safe place and turn off the engine. Great damage can occur if you drive with an overheated engine. Do not remove the radiator cap from an engine that is hot. The boiling water may rush out and cause serious burns. Let the engine cool and then check for the problem.

The lubricating system delivers oil to the engine. Oil is pumped directly to some parts of the car and splashed onto others.

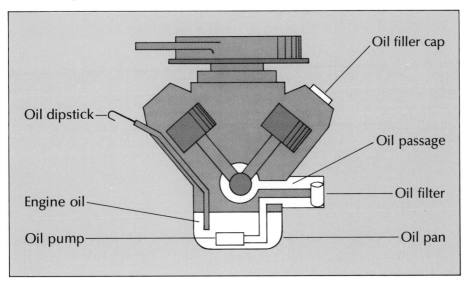

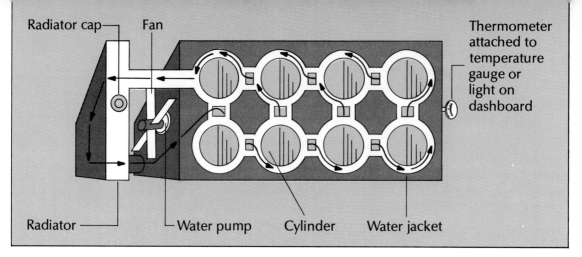

The cooling system circulates a coolant around the engine. The coolant draws off the extra heat that builds up around the cylinders.

THE SUSPENSION AND STEERING SYSTEMS

You change the direction a car is going by turning the steering wheel. To respond properly to steering corrections, all the wheels must maintain contact with the roadway. Bouncing reduces the road contact. However, a good *suspension system*, made up of springs and shock absorbers, reduces the effect of bumps and provides better contact between the tires and the road.

SPRINGS AND SHOCK ABSORBERS

Springs and shock absorbers connect the car's frame to the wheels. *Springs* "soften" the effect of bumps. If a car had only springs, it would keep bouncing after going over a bump and would lose traction.

Shock absorbers are mounted between the frame and axle near each wheel. They act as a "cushion" for the car's frame, and they control bouncing. This produces a smoother ride. The result is better steering and braking control.

STEERING CONTROL

The steering system enables the driver to turn the front wheels. The steering wheel is connected by a steering shaft and movable rods to the front wheels.

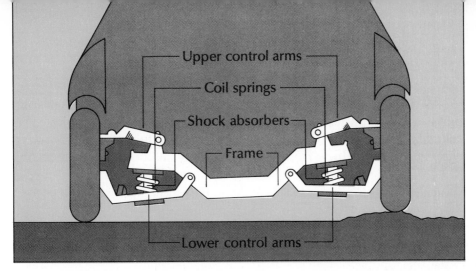

Upper control arms

Coil springs

Shock absorbers

Frame

Lower control arms

The suspension system is made up of springs and shock absorbers. They connect the car's frame to its wheels. They also reduce the hard contact of bumps and turns on passengers.

To maintain their movement, the wheels must be held in an upright position. They must also be able to move up and down even when they are turned. Control arms hold the front wheels upright. Upper and lower control arms are hinged with ball joints to allow the wheels to move up and down over bumps while the vehicle is moving.

A failure in any part of the steering or suspension systems will drastically affect your ability to control a vehicle.

The steering system controls the direction of the front wheels. Gears and rods carry the movement from the steering wheel to the front wheels.

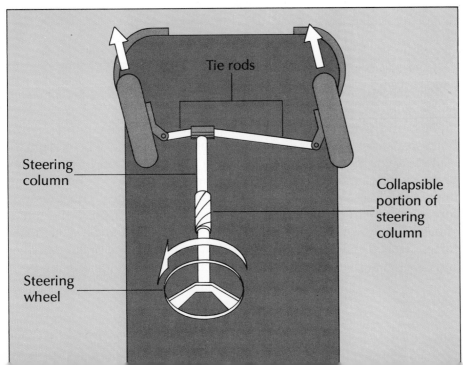

Tie rods

Steering column

Collapsible portion of steering column

Steering wheel

THE BRAKE SYSTEMS

All passenger vehicles have at least two brake systems—a hydraulic brake system and the mechanically operated parking brake. The *hydraulic brake system* brings the moving vehicle to a stop. The *parking brake* keeps the vehicle from moving after it has been stopped.

The hydraulic brake system supplies stopping power to all four wheels. The parking brake works only on the rear wheels.

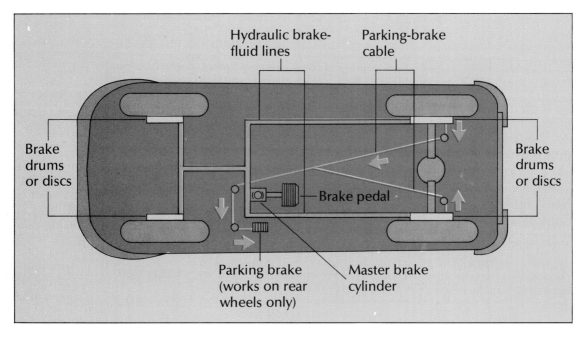

Hydraulic brake-fluid lines

Parking-brake cable

Brake drums or discs

Brake drums or discs

Brake pedal

Parking brake (works on rear wheels only)

Master brake cylinder

THE HYDRAULIC BRAKE SYSTEM

The hydraulic brake system is made up of the brake pedal, a master brake cylinder, brake-fluid lines, wheel cylinders, brake shoes and linings, and wheel drums. (Cars with disc brakes are equipped with brake pads instead of brake linings, brake shoes, and wheel drums.)

When you push down on the brake pedal, a piston in the master brake cylinder moves forward. This movement forces fluid into the brake-fluid lines, which builds up pressure in the lines. This pressure forces pistons in the wheel cylinders to move out against the brake shoes. The brake shoes push against the brake linings, which get forced against the wheel drums. With disc brakes, the brake pads get forced against the wheel discs. The friction that develops, using both kinds of brakes, slows the car. Letting up on the brake pedal takes the pressure off the wheel drum or discs. The pistons in the wheel cylinders then force the brake fluid back into the master brake cylinder.

Many cars are equipped with power brakes. The power assist reduces the force you must use on the brake pedal. Power brakes do not shorten or increase stopping distance.

THE PARKING BRAKE

The parking brake is operated by a foot pedal or a hand lever. The pedal or lever is attached to a cable that is connected to the rear brake shoes.

The main purpose of the parking brake is to hold the vehicle in place after it has stopped. You can try to stop a vehicle by using the parking brake. But, you should do so only under unusual conditions (such as hydraulic brake-system failure).

In the hydraulic brake system, when you press down on the brake pedal, you force the brake shoes and brake lining out against the wheel drum. This causes friction, which slows down the wheel.

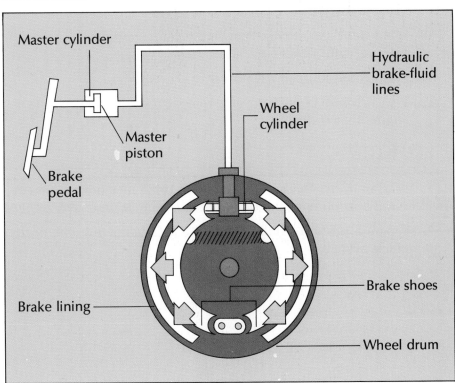

TO CONSIDER

1. Describe the operation of the systems that make your car run.

2. Why is it useful for a driver to know how the different parts of the car work?

3. How is the up-and-down motion of the pistons changed to the rotary motion of the driveshaft?

4. How is the rotary motion of the driveshaft transmitted to the drive-wheel axle?

5. Name two important functions of the exhaust system.

6. What is the purpose of the engine oil?

7. What is the function of springs and shock absorbers, in addition to passenger comfort?

8. What are the differences between the hydraulic brake system and the parking brake?

9. What is the purpose of the cooling system?

10. What steps should you take if your car's temperature gauge or warning light reads *hot*?

11. What could happen if your car overheats?

12. Why is it very important *not* to remove the radiator cap from an engine that is hot?

PROJECTS

1. Make an under-the-hood check of your family's or school's car. Identify as many of the parts of the engine as you can.

2. Prepare a poster or bulletin-board display showing one of the vehicle systems and how it works.

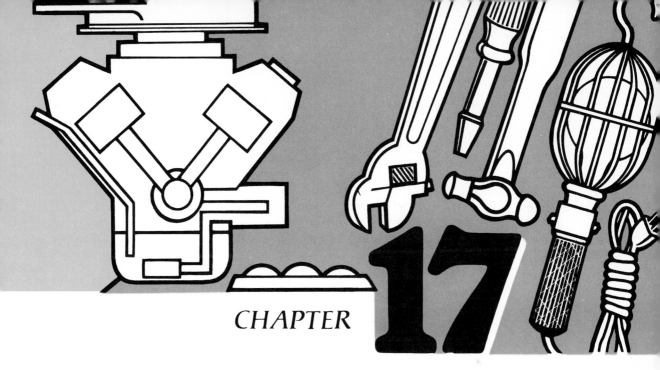

VEHICLE MAINTENANCE

MAKING YOUR OWN INSPECTION

There are a number of routine checks you should make inside and outside your car. Your owner's manual has the information you need to make these checks. If you do not have an owner's manual, get one from a dealer or order one from the company that built your car.

OUTSIDE THE VEHICLE

Always make these checks before you get in your car:

1. Check under the car for leaking oil or radiator fluid.

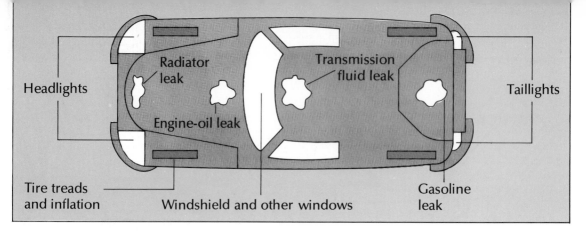

You should make these routine outside checks of your car. Make sure that the car is in proper working order and has not been damaged.

2. Check for damaged windows, windshields, mirrors, or lights.
3. Check for burned-out or broken headlights, brake and signal lights, and side warning lights.
4. Check tire inflation, and look for tire damage or tire wear.
5. Check for damage to the car body and trim.

UNDER THE HOOD

The following checks should be made at least once a month and before long trips. Some of these checks should be made each time you stop to buy gasoline.

1. Check the amount of fluid in the radiator, the battery, and the windshield-washer fluid tank. (Make sure the fluid in the radiator is cool before you remove the radiator cap.)
2. Check the engine oil, power steering, and master-brake cylinder reservoirs.
3. Check the fan belt and the belts that run the power steering, power brake, and air-conditioning units. They may need adjustment. Replace any frayed or cracked belt.
4. Check all hoses and hose connections for leaks.
5. Check for loose, broken, or disconnected wires. Check also for cracked insulation on wires.
6. Check the transmission fluid. (This test must be made with the engine running and the gear selector in park. You will have to run the engine for a few moments to give the transmission fluid time to warm up.)

182

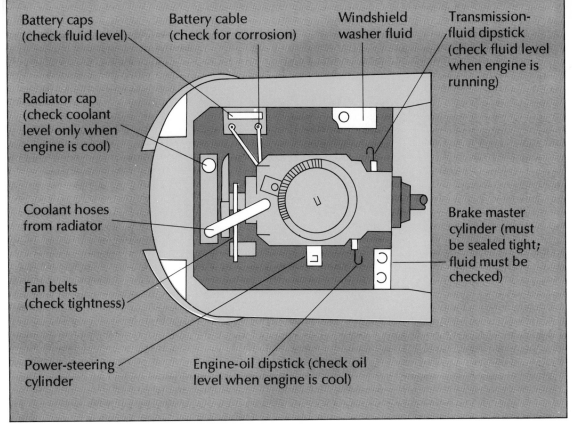

Battery caps
(check fluid level)

Battery cable
(check for corrosion)

Windshield
washer fluid

Transmission-
fluid dipstick
(check fluid level
when engine is
running)

Radiator cap
(check coolant
level only when
engine is cool)

Coolant hoses
from radiator

Brake master
cylinder (must
be sealed tight;
fluid must be
checked)

Fan belts
(check tightness)

Power-steering
cylinder

Engine-oil dipstick (check oil
level when engine is cool)

You or a service station attendant should make these under-the-hood checks each time you buy gasoline.

VEHICLE SYSTEMS MAINTENANCE

Some kinds of maintenance, such as oil changes and grease jobs, are pretty much the same in most vehicles. However, the schedule of services is different for various cars. The garage or mechanic you choose to service your car is very important. This is especially true if you do not know much about how a car runs. If you do not know a good mechanic or service station, ask your family or friends. Certification by national agencies can also serve as a guide. Among such agencies are the American Automobile Association, Approved Auto Repair Service, and the National Institute of Automotive Service Excellence.

When you bring your car in for service or repairs, give the mechanic any information you can about the car's performance. Do not tell the mechanic how to fix it. Get a written estimate of the cost. Tell the mechanic to call before any work is done that will be more than the estimate. Ask that any parts that are replaced be returned to you or held for you to look at.

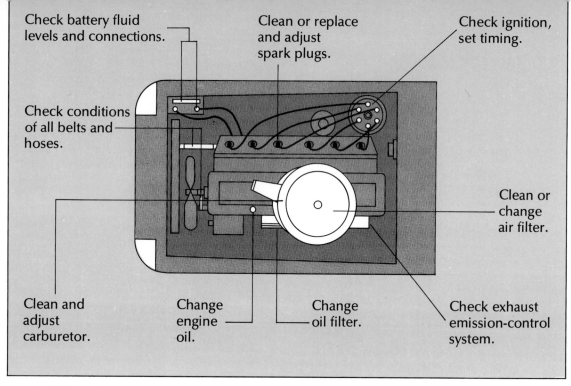

Check battery fluid levels and connections.

Clean or replace and adjust spark plugs.

Check ignition, set timing.

Check conditions of all belts and hoses.

Clean or change air filter.

Clean and adjust carburetor.

Change engine oil.

Change oil filter.

Check exhaust emission-control system.

You should have the mechanic check these items each time you have your car's engine tuned.

THE INTERNAL COMBUSTION ENGINE

The heart of your car is its engine. The engine is among those things that need the most frequent adjustment and maintenance. A car driven 19,000 kilometers (12,000 miles) per year generally should need no more than one major and one minor tune-up in a 12-month period. An engine tune-up includes changing the oil and/or oil filter; checking the carburetor adjustment; cleaning and either *gapping* or changing the spark plugs and air filter; checking the alternator, battery, and voltage regulator; and checking the ignition wires and timing. Various drive belts and hoses must be checked for wear. The fluid level in the radiator should also be checked. The battery terminals may need cleaning. Pollution-control devices must be checked or replaced. Any parts that are replaced must meet the carmaker's specifications for the car you have.

The frequency of engine tune-ups, oil changes, and grease jobs will depend on the kind of driving you do. For instance, stop-and-go city traffic is harder on a car than steady highway driving. The air filter must be changed more frequently in places where there is a lot of dust. Check your owner's manual for information on your car.

If an engine needs major repairs, it may run unevenly after a tune-up. An engine compression check may be needed. A *compression check* can spot such problems as burned or badly seated intake or exhaust valves, worn piston rings, or damaged cylinder walls. These problems require a major overhaul of the engine.

OTHER PARTS OF THE POWER TRAIN

The fluid level in both automatic and manual transmissions must be checked at least every 10,000 kilometers (6000 miles). So should the fluid level in the rear-axle housing. Automatic transmission fluid should be changed every 40,000 kilometers (24,000 miles) or as indicated in your owner's manual.

Universal joints connect the drive shaft to the transmission and *differential.* If these joints are not sealed units, they should be greased every 10,000 to 13,000 kilometers (6000 to 8000 miles). If the universal joints are sealed units, they should be checked for signs of leaks or damage. If there are such signs, the units should be replaced.

THE SUSPENSION AND STEERING SYSTEMS

Sudden failure of the suspension or steering systems is rare. Most of the problems are the result of wear. They usually develop gradually. You should have these systems checked and serviced every 6 months.

The suspension and steering systems are most easily checked when your car is up on a hoist for servicing. Shock absorbers should be

Be alert for signs of wear in the steering and suspension system.

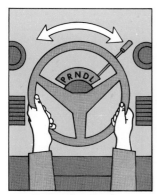

Free play in the
steering wheel

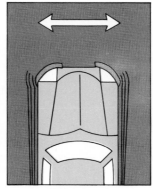

Front-end
wobble

Excessive
bouncing

checked for leaks and for the condition of the fasteners. Some carmakers recommend that tie-rod fittings and ball joints be greased every 6500 to 10,000 kilometers (4000 to 6000 miles) or 4 to 6 months. Other makers suggest that they be serviced every 40,000 to 58,000 kilometers (25,000 to 36,000 miles). If any part shows signs of wear or looseness, it should be replaced.

Your tires can also tell you something about the condition of the steering and suspension systems. Heavy tread wear on one side of one or both front tires shows that there is need for front-end alignment. Flat spots in the tire tread show that the tires need to be balanced.

As you drive, you may notice that there is *play* in the steering wheel. (It can be turned quite a bit before the wheels move.) Five centimeters (2 inches) or more of play in a manual system indicate a problem. Any play in a power-steering system is serious and should be checked right away. Other signs of trouble are front-end shimmy or wobbling and a pulling to the right or to the left as you drive. Pulling to the right or to the left can also mean that one or more tires are soft. Any of these signs may mean that the front end needs to be aligned or that the wheels need to be balanced.

SELECTING SHOCK ABSORBERS

Shock absorbers wear out gradually. If your car bounces more than once after going over a small bump, the shock absorbers are wearing. If the vehicle sways or leans on a turn or curve, the shocks are worn. You can check your shock absorbers by pushing down hard on the trunk or hood a few times to make the car bounce. If the car bounces more than once after you stop pushing, the shocks should be replaced.

Shock absorbers should be checked for leaks and for the condition of the fasteners.

The photo on the right shows a tire that has scrapes and cuts. Its worn condition could cause a blowout. Driving on worn tires could be very dangerous.

Heavy-duty shock absorbers are available for special use. Under normal conditions, they usually give a harder ride. But they improve handling and support bigger loads. Some shock absorbers made for rear wheels can be adjusted. The adjustment is made by adding or reducing air pressure in the shocks. These shock absorbers give more support for the added weight of a trailer or a heavy load.

THE WHEEL BEARINGS

Wheels should be pulled off and the bearings checked every 30,000 to 50,000 kilometers (20,000 to 30,000 miles). The front-wheel bearings should be repacked with grease, and the grease seals should be replaced. The rear-wheel grease seals should be inspected for leaks. Grease seals that leak can result in poorly lubricated wheel bearings or greasy wheel drums and brake linings. These conditions can cause costly damage and can be dangerous.

Below are signs of wear in the brake system. Have your car's brake system checked immediately at the first sign of wear.

Sudden "Grabbing"

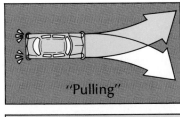

"Pulling"

"Squeal" or "Chatter"

"Soft" pedal

THE BRAKE SYSTEM

When you press down on the brake pedal, you should feel firm resistance and your vehicle should come to a smooth, straight stop. The first sign of brake trouble may be that you have to press down farther than usual before the car begins to stop. Your car may pull to one side. The brakes may suddenly "grab" as you press down. If the brakes squeal or pull unevenly, they should be checked right away.

187

The level of fluid in the master brake cylinder should be checked every time the engine is tuned. In cars that have disc brakes, the fluid level may go down slightly as the brake pads wear down. If there is continued loss of fluid, have the whole system inspected for leaks.

Brake linings should generally be checked at 25,000 and 40,000 kilometers (15,000 and 25,000 miles) and then every 8000 kilometers (5000 miles). If you make quick stops and brake hard, the brake linings will wear out faster. So more frequent checking and repair may be needed. It is very important that worn brake linings be changed before they wear through the brake shoes. Otherwise, wheel discs or drums can be damaged and may have to be replaced. Also, driving with worn brake linings is dangerous.

THE TIRES

The general construction of tires, their tread depth, and their inflation all are important to vehicle control. If the tires on your car do not give enough traction, you are in trouble.

INSPECTING YOUR TIRES

Check for cuts or blisters on the sidewalls and treads of your tires. Check, too, for nails, glass, or metal stuck anywhere in the tires. Your tires should not be *overinflated* (too much air pressure) or *underinflated* (too little air pressure). Either could cause serious driving problems.

Inspect the condition of your tires frequently.

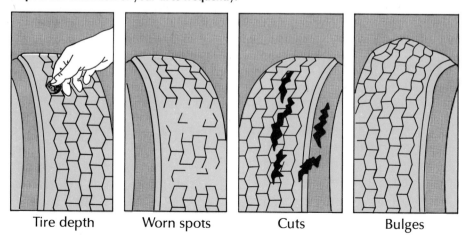

| Tire depth | Worn spots | Cuts | Bulges |

Tread depth can be critical in certain situations. The minimum legal tread depth is 1.6 millimeters (2/32 inch). Although that may be enough tread on a smooth, dry surface, it may be dangerous on a wet surface. The depth of a tread can be seen by the tread-wear indicator bar that is built into the tire.

TIRE INFLATION

Tires inflated to the pressure recommended for long-distance, high-speed driving improve vehicle control. Pressure should never be allowed to fall below the carmakers' and tiremakers' suggested minimum. Underinflation causes increased flexing of the sidewalls. This flexing produces heat and reduces vehicle control. The flexing of the sidewalls also increases the chance of tire failure. Higher tire pressure will give you a ride that is not as smooth as that of a softer tire, but it will give more traction. Tires should not be inflated above the maximum that is recommended by the manufacturer. When a tire is over-inflated, the center of its tread wears out quickly. Use a tire pressure gauge to check if your tires have the proper air pressure.

TIRE ROTATION

Tires do not usually wear at the same rate. To even out the wear, tires should be rotated. Their positions on the car should be switched from front to rear and in some cases left to right. It is generally recommended that tires be rotated every 6000 to 10,000 kilometers (4000 to 6000 miles). Keep these two things in mind:

1. Tire rotation plans differ, depending on the tire's construction. Check your owner's manual for the right plan for your tires.
2. Tire rotation should not be used as a substitute for front-end alignment, wheel balancing, or new shock absorbers. Uneven tread wear on the front tires means that your steering or suspension system needs attention.

THE EXHAUST SYSTEM

How long the exhaust system of your car will last depends on the conditions under which your car is driven. Stop-and-go, short-trip driving is hard on it. On short trips, acid and water collect in the system and corrode the metal. On long trips, heat and evaporation get rid of the acid and moisture.

The purpose of the tail pipe is to carry off poisonous gases from the car. It is important that you have the tail pipe inspected every time your car is serviced.

It is very dangerous to drive a vehicle with an exhaust leak or with a broken tail pipe. These defects allow exhaust gases to be trapped beneath the vehicle, even when the vehicle is moving. If there are any holes in the floor or wheel wells, the gases can be drawn up into the passenger compartment. The most dangerous of these gases, carbon monoxide, has no odor, color, or taste. Small amounts of carbon monoxide make you sleepy or give you a headache at first. If you breathe too much of this deadly gas, it will kill you.

To guard against such problems, the exhaust system should be inspected, from the exhaust manifold to the tail pipe, every time the car is serviced. Points that need special attention are the connections at either end of the muffler, the muffler itself, and the tail pipe. Two places on the tail pipe require special attention. These places are

1. the last 5 centimeters (2 inches) of pipe that carry the exhaust gases out from beneath the vehicle.
2. the section of pipe that bends up over the rear axle.

There are times when the danger of carbon monoxide poisoning becomes a special hazard. These actions should be avoided:

1. Driving with the rear window of a station wagon open or driving with the trunk lid up.
2. Running a car's engine in a closed garage.
3. Sitting in a parked car with the windows closed, the engine running, and the heater turned on.

Leaks in the exhaust system or a rusted-off tail pipe are very dangerous. They can spread poisonous gases into the passenger section.

THE LIGHTING SYSTEM

The lenses of your headlights must be kept clean. Even a fine film will reduce the amount of light they provide. Check also for *headlight alignment*. (Headlight alignment means directing the high and low beams to cover specific areas of the path ahead.) If your high-beam headlights do not seem to light up the roadway far enough ahead, they may need alignment. Your first sign of poor headlight alignment may come from other drivers. At night, oncoming drivers may flash their headlights from high to low beams as they drive toward you. If your headlights are on low beam, they may be poorly aligned and are blinding the other driver. The same is true if the driver in front of you reaches up to adjust the rear-view mirror as you drive closer. Another possible cause of poor headlight alignment is too heavy a load in the trunk of your car.

Check your car's signal indicators, brake lights, and headlights. Your visual lead can be greatly reduced if the lights are not aligned correctly. Also check for broken, dirty, or burned-out lights.

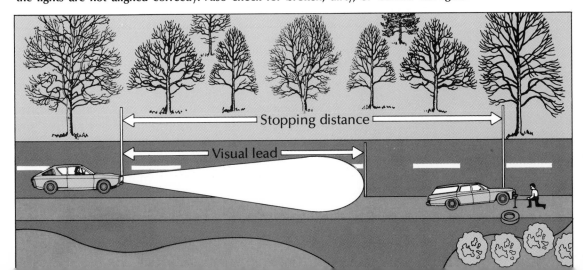

TO CONSIDER

1. Describe the outside and under-the-hood checks you should make before driving your car.

2. What are some of the signs of trouble in the suspension and steering systems?

3. What are some signs of trouble in the braking system?

4. Explain why proper tire inflation is essential.

5. What should you look for when you check your vehicle's tires?

6. What are some of the characteristics of carbon monoxide? What are the effects of breathing it?

7. What are some problems you should check for in the vehicle lighting system?

8. Why is a complete program of vehicle maintenance important?

9. Why is it important for the exhaust system of your car to work properly?

10. What steps must be taken before you can check the transmission fluid level?

11. Explain what occurs during a complete engine tune-up. What determines how often you need a tune-up? List three problems that can require a major overhaul of an engine.

12. What test can you use to see if your shock absorbers need to be replaced?

13. How often should brake linings be checked?

PROJECTS

1. Visit a local service station or diagnostic center and note the way it operates. Ask the owner what kinds of maintenance are most often neglected by car owners. Report to your class.

2. Make a list of the mechanical defects you would recognize after reading this chapter. Which defects are the most dangerous and which would result in the most costly problems if neglected? Study the owner's manual of your school's or your family's car. Has your school or family followed the maintenance suggestions made in the manual?

CHAPTER 18

VEHICLE PERFORMANCE AND DECISION MAKING

ACCELERATION

To make good time-space decisions, you must be able to tell how well vehicles perform in at least three areas.

193

1. Acceleration and speed.
2. Directional control and cornering.
3. Braking and deceleration.

If you understand these factors, you should be able to predict with some accuracy what you can expect from your car and from other drivers.

Acceleration, or pickup, is an increase in speed. The time it takes to accelerate from a stop or from one speed to another is called the *rate of acceleration.* Pickup depends on engine power, transmission and differential gear ratios, friction between the drive wheels and the road surface, and the weight the engine is pulling.

The ability of cars to maintain a given speed varies. For example, a subcompact car may not be able to hold its speed on a hill. Its acceleration may be limited by its small engine.

Large passenger cars, especially those that have high-horsepower six- or eight-cylinder engines, generally have good acceleration and can hold their speed. Other large vehicles, however, do not. For example, tractor-trailer rigs and interstate buses have huge engines. But they accelerate very slowly.

Generally, it is best to accelerate gradually to a desired speed. Beginning drivers, especially, sometimes make errors when they increase speed quickly.

Trucks, tractor-trailer rigs, and buses have huge engines. But they cannot accelerate quickly. If you are coming up behind a truck and are moving at a faster rate of speed, allow yourself time to slow down. Prepare to pass when it is safe to do so. Follow at the proper distance and speed until you can pass safely.

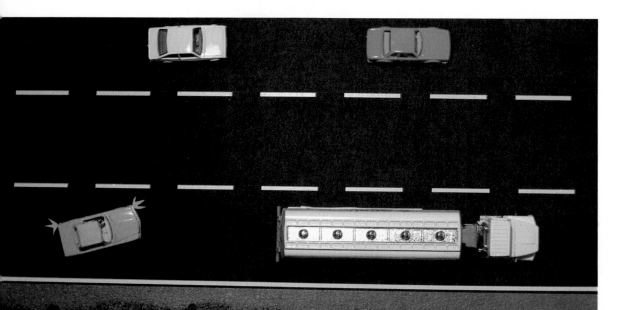

ACCELERATION RATE VARIES

The rate of acceleration varies with speed. As the speed of a vehicle increases, the rate of acceleration decreases. Therefore, it takes more time to accelerate from 70 to 90 km/h (45 to 55 mph) than from 30 to 50 km/h (20 to 30 mph).

The acceleration rate is influenced by the gear ratios of the transmission and the differential. A high drive-train gear ratio (in low gear) provides more power. This results in a higher rate of acceleration and slower speeds. Vehicles with low drive-train gear ratios (in high gear) have less power. They can give better gas mileage, however.

In a vehicle with a manual transmission, the acceleration rate can be increased by shifting down from *third* or *fourth* gear to a lower gear. In a vehicle with an automatic transmission, the extra power is provided by a *passing gear*. Pressing the accelerator suddenly to the floor causes a downshift to a lower gear. This gives the vehicle a more rapid rate of acceleration.

SPEED

Speed is most directly controlled by the amount of gasoline your engine gets. Speed is stated in kilometers per hour (km/h) or miles per hour (mph). We usually state speeds in terms of averages. If it takes 1 hour to go 50 kilometers (30 miles), the average speed is 50 kilometers (30 miles) per hour. In driving the 50 kilometers (30 miles), your speed may vary from 0 to 90 kilometers (55 miles) per hour.

MONITORING YOUR SPEED

It is difficult, especially for new drivers, to estimate speed accurately. It is important, therefore, to learn to check your speedometer. The *speedometer* tells you, within a few kilometers, about how fast you are traveling. However, remember that tire size, tire inflation, and

The speedometer shows how fast a vehicle is traveling. Quickly glance at your speedometer from time to time to check your speed.

amount of tread can cause speedometer readings to vary as much as 5 percent. With experience, you should become more aware of your speed without looking at the speedometer. For instance, as speed varies, you will notice a difference in the car's vibrations. You will also notice a difference in the level of sound from the tires, the wind, and the engine.

It is more difficult to estimate your speed after a large change in speed. If you have been driving at 30 to 50 km/h (20 to 30 mph) and suddenly accelerate to 70 km/h (45 mph), you will feel as if you are moving much faster. On the other hand, if you have been traveling at highway speeds and suddenly enter a 40 km/h (25 mph) zone, you are likely to slow down less than you should because you are used to higher speeds. The only way to prevent yourself from speeding in this case is to check your speedometer.

DIRECTIONAL CONTROL AND CORNERING ABILITY

How well you are able to control your car's direction depends on the car's directional control and cornering ability.

DIRECTIONAL CONTROL

The ability of a car to hold to a straight line is called *directional control.* If your car has good directional control, very little correction should be needed to keep it moving in the direction in which you steer

A vehicle that has good cornering ability holds turns well. It does not oversteer or understeer.

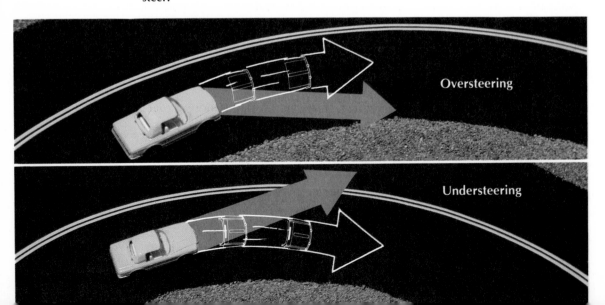

Oversteering

Understeering

it. Road contour, traction, and wind may call for steering corrections. But a vehicle with good directional control does not change direction by itself.

When you are driving straight ahead, the rear wheels should track in line behind the front wheels. If you see a vehicle that is *not* tracking this way (for example, a vehicle with a bent frame or one that sags to one side), be alert. If the vehicle does not track as it should, its directional control will be less precise. It will need more room to make any maneuver.

CORNERING ABILITY

The ability of a vehicle to be steered around a turn without going out of control is called *cornering ability*. When it makes a turn at a moderate speed, a vehicle should not roll or sway. One that rolls or sways is hard to control.

Some vehicles oversteer or understeer on turns. That is, they move away from the path of travel. *Oversteering* means that the front of the car moves to the inside of a turn while the rear end slides out. *Understeering* is just the opposite. The front end plows straight ahead.

For most drivers, oversteering is the more dangerous. To correct for oversteering, you must, during the turn, move the steering wheel in the direction opposite to the desired path of travel. Understeering, by contrast, is easily corrected unless it is severe or made worse by high speed. You reduce your speed and turn the steering wheel more in the desired direction.

The steering systems of various vehicles respond differently. The most obvious differences are between vehicles with *power steering* and those without it. In full-size passenger cars that have large engines and air conditioning, power steering is usually a must. Without it, it would be very hard for many drivers to turn corners or to parallel park. When it works well, power steering needs much less effort than manual steering. It also makes the vehicle respond quickly to movements of the steering wheel. In addition, it reduces the chance that the steering wheel will be jerked from the driver's hands if one of the front wheels should strike the curb or a large object on the road.

There are some hazards in changing from manual steering to power steering. Experienced drivers usually know of certain road-surface conditions from the vibrations they receive through the steering wheel. With power steering, much of this information gets lost. A second hazard is the possible failure of the power-steering unit. The most frequent cause of failure is a stalled engine. If power steering fails, the effort required to turn the steering wheel must be greatly increased.

If your car is overloaded, you will lose directional and cornering ability. By overloading your vehicle, you will also increase the chance of a rear-end skid on sharp curves or turns.

FACTORS INFLUENCING DIRECTIONAL CONTROL AND CORNERING

A problem with the suspension, steering, or tires decreases your ability to control a vehicle. Even under good roadway conditions, soft tires or tires out of balance affect vehicle handling. Worn shock absorbers or poor front-end alignment adds to the problem. A vehicle that is overloaded or loaded badly also has poor handling ability.

There are clues you can look for to tell you something about the directional control and cornering ability of the vehicles around you:

1. Vehicles that sag to one side or to the front or rear may have worn shock absorbers or broken springs.
2. Vehicles that are overloaded have an increased chance of skidding on sharp curves or turns. One sign of overload is that the back end of the vehicle is lower than normal.
3. Heavy loads in a roof luggage carrier, especially when they are placed at the rear of the vehicle, will affect directional control. Also, vans or cars with full luggage racks are more seriously affected by winds.
4. Wheels that shimmy, wobble, or bounce indicate a tire, steering, or suspension-system defect. Any of these makes a vehicle harder to handle.
5. Cars with raised or "raked" rear ends usually corner poorly. Their exposed fuel tank is also a hazard. It increases the chance of fire in a rear-end collision.
6. Vehicles pulling other vehicles or trailers almost always suffer some loss of directional control. They also lose some cornering ability and acceleration.

7. Most motorcycles driven at highway speeds need as much room as cars do to carry out lane-change and passing maneuvers. Motorcycles are highly maneuverable only when they are well controlled and driven at slow speeds.

BRAKING AND DECELERATION

Many factors influence stopping time and distance. Among them are the road surface, speed, and the condition of a car's brakes and suspension system. But too few drivers realize how big a role perception, reaction time, and braking time play.

To bring a vehicle to a stop, a driver must do three things:

1. Become aware of a need to stop.
2. React by releasing the gas pedal and moving a foot to the brake pedal.
3. Press the brake pedal, and brake the vehicle to a stop.

Each of these actions takes time: time to see (and decide), time to react, and time to brake. Time means distance. All drivers should be aware of the relationship between speed and braking distance.

1. The braking-distance increase equals the square of the increase in speed. So if the speed of a vehicle is doubled, its braking distance is four times as great.
2. The time needed to stop increases from approximately 2 seconds at 50 km/h (30 mph) to nearly 4 seconds at 90 km/h (55

When you are leaving an expressway, begin to slow down in advance of the exit ramp. In this way, you will not have to brake hard or suddenly when you enter the ramp. By slowing down gradually, you save wear and tear on the brake linings.

Cars with raised rear ends have poor cornering ability. Raised rear ends are also very hazardous. In such cars, the fuel tank is exposed. This increases the chance of an explosion in rear-end collisions.

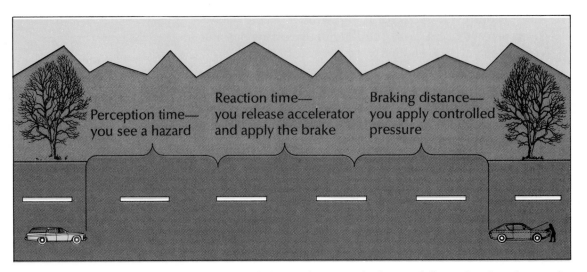

Perception time—
you see a hazard

Reaction time—
you release accelerator
and apply the brake

Braking distance—
you apply controlled
pressure

The total time that passes before a driver can brake to a full stop involves three major things. First, a driver must perceive (become aware of) a hazard. Next, the driver must react to what is seen or heard. Finally, the driver brakes to a stop.

mph). But 2 to 4 seconds' time offers little room for error when the time you need to identify a hazardous situation is not known. You should try to plan your immediate path of travel at least 4 seconds ahead.

BRAKING TO A STOP

Controlled stopping is a result of friction between the brake linings and wheel drums or wheel discs and pads. This friction slows the rotation of the wheels and tires and increases the friction between the tires and the road.

There are a number of factors that affect the distance needed to stop after the brakes are applied. Among these are the area of the braking surface (the drum and brake linings) and the vehicle's size, weight, height, and load. The tire size, tread, and inflation, and the type of road surface also affect stopping distance.

Maximum braking occurs just before the tires start to slide on a roadway surface. At this point, the friction from the brakes and the friction between the tires and the road are nearly equal. More pressure on the brake pedal locks the wheels and causes them to skid. Locked wheels do not increase braking force. In fact, the heat that comes from the friction between the tires and the road surface melts the rubber. This lengthens the stopping distance a bit.

TO CONSIDER

1. Explain why you should judge the performance capabilities of other vehicles on the road.

2. What are the factors that affect a vehicle's directional control and cornering ability?

3. What factors affect a vehicle's braking ability?

4. Explain why the total stopping-time distance equals the perception-time, reaction-time, and braking-time distances.

5. Discuss how your car's performance capability should affect your driving decisions.

6. Why does the ability to accelerate vary among different vehicles?

7. What is the purpose of the passing gear?

8. What factors can make you aware of your car's speed without looking at the speedometer?

9. What is the difference between oversteering and understeering? Why is oversteering more dangerous for most drivers?

10. When a car's rear end has been raised, what hazards are created?

11. What factors influence stopping time and distance?

12. What happens when too much pressure on the brake pedal locks the wheels?

PROJECTS

1. Interview several experienced drivers. In what kinds of situations do they adjust their speed and position according to the performance capabilities of other vehicles? Report your findings to your class.

2. Sit a safe distance from a curve in a busy road near your home. Take note of the way cars with directional-control problems make the turn. Report to your class.

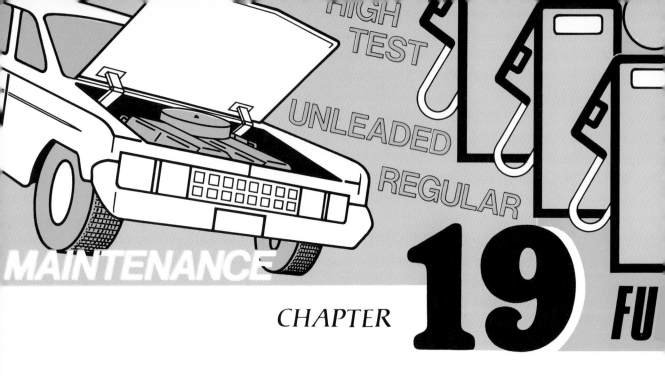

CHAPTER **19**

SELECTING, OPERATING, AND INSURING YOUR CAR

    Buying a car is one of the most expensive purchases most people make. Operating expenses such as gasoline, oil, maintenance, insurance, license and registration fees, and taxes all add to the expense of car ownership. These expenses may vary. The type of car you buy, where you live, and your driving record affect the cost of operating a car. Whether you use your car for work or for pleasure, the number of miles you drive each year and the number of years you keep your car also affect the cost of operating it.

DETERMINING YOUR TRANSPORTATION NEEDS

Before you choose a car to buy, learn what your transportation needs are. Find out whether or not public transportation is available to fill all or part of your needs. If there is no, or limited, public transportation available, then find out what size and type of vehicle you need. Ask yourself how many kilometers (miles) you will travel each day, month, or year. How many people will drive the car? How many passengers will you usually carry? If the need should arise, how heavy a load or how many large packages will you have to carry?

SELECTING A CAR

Once you are ready to select your car, remember that cars are grouped by size and *class* (vans, station wagons, sedans). In cars of different sizes, you will find large differences in *gas mileage*. A car's gas mileage is the average number of kilometers (or miles) it can travel on a liter (or gallon) of gasoline. You can also find large differences in mileage among cars of the same class. One small car may travel as little as 7.5 kilometers per liter (18 miles per gallon). Another may get 12 kilometers per liter (28 miles per gallon).

When you buy a car, you should consider ordering equipment that will work to help your car use as little fuel as possible. You should also consider the following:

1. *The weight of the vehicle.* In general, the less a vehicle weighs, the better gas mileage the vehicle will deliver. If the engine has to pull less weight, it does not have to work as hard. However, just because a car looks smaller does not mean it will weigh less than a car that appears larger.
2. *The design of the vehicle.* The design of a vehicle will influence its gas mileage. If a vehicle is streamlined, the engine will not have to work as hard to overcome air resistance. A vehicle with less air resistance will generally require less energy to move.

For instance, vans usually have a large, square front. As a result, they have greater resistance to air movement. Because of their design, vans require more power to move. Hence, more gasoline is burned to provide that power.

3. *The type of engine.* The engine you select is very important. With the national speed limit of 90 km/h (55 mph), there is little need for a large V-8 engine unless you will be driving up steep hills or pulling a trailer. In fact, a four- or six-cylinder engine will meet the needs of most people. Between 55 and 90 km/h (35 and 55 mph), a compact car with a large V-8 engine will usually use more gas than a car with a four- or six-cylinder engine. In fact, some standard-size cars with six-cylinder engines get better gas mileage than smaller cars with eight-cylinder engines.

4. *The type of transmission.* In most cases, a stick shift will provide better gas mileage than an automatic transmission. A stick-shift car with a four- or five-speed transmission provides the best gas mileage. For most drivers, the greater ease of driving a car with an automatic transmission is a convenience they do not want to give up. Remember, some automatic transmissions are more efficient (use less gasoline) than others. A three-speed automatic transmission is more efficient than a two-speed transmission. An automatic transmission with a torque converter is also usually more efficient. A *torque converter* is designed to reduce slippage in your automatic transmission. This, in turn, improves your gas mileage.

5. *The drive train.* The rear-axle gear ratio is important in fuel economy. This ratio represents the number of times the drive shaft must revolve in order to turn the drive wheels once. The higher this ratio, the poorer the fuel economy. The lower the ratio, the better the fuel economy.

6. *The power options.* Adding any type of power equipment to your car will generally cause it to use more gasoline. It takes energy to operate power equipment. Extra equipment also means extra weight.

On a medium-size car with a medium-size engine, power equipment will generally not cause a large drop in gas mileage. However, on a small car with a small engine, extra equipment can cause a rather large drop in gasoline mileage. For instance, it is true that adding an air

When you are looking for a new car, try to find one that will help you save on fuel. Read the chapter to learn about other things to consider before buying a car.

conditioner adds weight, and weight reduces gasoline mileage. However, adding an air conditioner does not always mean a big drop in kilometers per liter (miles per gallon) either. For example, in hot weather you may have to drive with the car windows down, which causes a sharp increase in wind resistance. With some cars, wind resistance increases gasoline usage as much or more than driving with the air conditioner on. However, when using an air conditioner, keep the car cool, not cold. Dress lightly so that less cooling is required.

Other power equipment, such as power steering, may be necessary for some drivers. While it may add weight to a vehicle, the ease of steering is such that many drivers will prefer to order it. Also, keep in mind that if you buy a small car with a fuel-saving engine and drive train, you will use less fuel and reduce operating costs.

When Purchasing a Used Car, Check:

☐ 1. The condition of paint. (New paint may indicate collision damage.)

☐ 2. For rust. (Examine lower edges behind bumpers, rocker panels, below the doors, door sills, floors, and inside the trunk. A car with rusted-out areas should be rejected unless you know how to make or can afford repairs.)

☐ 3. For worn tires including the spare. (Uneven wear on any tire may indicate front-end problems.)

☐ 4. The tail pipe. (A light gray color indicates proper combustion. A heavy sooty appearance could mean excessive piston-ring wear.)

☐ 5. The radiator. (Remove the radiator cap. Is the coolant clean? Does the cap have rust caked on it? Are there signs of leaks on the back of the radiator?)

☐ 6. The transmission. (Pull out the transmission dipstick and sniff it. A burnt smell may mean an overheated transmission and trouble. Feel the oil on the crankcase dipstick. If it's gritty, there may be dirt in the engine.)

☐ 7. The service stickers. (These will determine the frequency of tune-ups and oil changes.)

☐ 8. All windows and door locks for ease of operation.

☐ 9. The brake pedal. (Step down on and hold the brake pedal with a steady pressure for 1 minute. If the pedal sinks down to the floor, brake pedal needs repairing.)

☐ 10. The engine. (Start engine and listen for loud or unusual noises when the engine starts and while the starter is working. Make sure that all dash gauges and warning lights—oil pressure, generator, temperature gauge—go on and off when the engine starts.)

☐ 11. The headlights, taillights, brake lights, and turn indicators.

☐ 12. The steering wheel. (Take a test drive. A shaky steering wheel and wobbly ride may mean bad ball joints, misaligned front wheels, or the need for wheel balancing. Make several sharp turns at low speed. The steering shouldn't stiffen up. If there is power steering, no squeaks or sudden increase of steering effort should occur.)

☐ 13. For slamming sound or lurching as the car starts. (An automatic transmission should take hold promptly when put in gear.)

☐ 14. Piston rings. (On long downhill grade or in a flat area, slow from 80 km/h (50 mph) to about 24 km/h (15 mph) without using the brakes. Then step hard on the accelerator. If there is blue exhaust smoke, the car may need new piston rings or an engine overhaul.)

SHOPPING FOR A CAR

Once you have decided upon the type and size car you need, get ready to shop. Compare different makes (manufacturer's brands) of cars and prices. All makes of cars within a class will not sit, feel, ride, or drive the same. Check with family and friends for their comments about various dealers. Visit different car dealers to compare their prices. Find out which dealers provide the best service. Talk with mechanics certified by the National Institute for Automotive Service Excellence, and participate in programs such as the American Automobile Association's Approved Automotive Repair Program.

If you decide to buy a *used* car, your choices of where to buy are greater. You can buy from a private owner, a used-car dealer, or the used-car section of a new-car dealership. When you buy from a private

Think of reasons why this used car may or may not be a good choice for a buyer. What would you look for when selecting a used car?

owner, the purchase price is often less. However, if something goes wrong with the car, you have to pay for all repairs. In the long run, repairs can be more expensive than the purchase price.

Many used car dealers have a large selection of cars available. Some have their own repair facilities. Some offer a limited guarantee on the engine or drive train or both. Others sell their cars in the condition in which they were purchased. In such a case, the buyer takes all responsibility if anything goes wrong with the car.

You will find a wide variety of cars for sale in a used-car lot.

For the best selection of newer used cars, it is better to go to a new-car dealership. Those dealers have their own repair facilities and trained mechanics. Cars from those dealers may cost somewhat more. However, their cars are generally reconditioned before they are sold. They also usually come with a 30- to 90-day *or* 1600- to 4800-kilometer (1000 to 3000 mile) limited guarantee.

Before you decide to buy any used car, you should check it over carefully. If your knowledge of cars is limited, you should get someone to help you.

DRIVING IN A FUEL-EFFICIENT MANNER

Fuel efficiency refers to methods used to cut down on the burning of gasoline. There are many things you can do to reduce gasoline consumption and operating costs after you buy your car. Included among these are trip planning, good driving practices, proper maintenance, and proper loading.

PLAN YOUR TRIPS

Most people drive many more miles per week, month, and year than is necessary. These miles could be reduced by simple trip planning. Too many drivers think of trip planning only in terms of vacations or long-distance driving. They do not apply trip planning to everyday use of the car.

A number of short trips that add up to 50 kilometers (30 miles) a day take much more gasoline than one trip covering 50 kilometers (30 miles). The reason for this difference is that the engine does not have time to warm up. Starting and stopping your car reduces gas mileage. The way to correct loss of gas mileage is to plan ahead.

USE THE TELEPHONE

If you need an item that may be hard to find, use the telephone. Check to find out which stores have the item in stock. By gathering this information in advance, you can make one trip with fewer stops. Such action saves both time and fuel.

CARPOOLING

Carpooling can save you gasoline and money, even if you ride in a carpool only one or two days a week. It takes time to pick up and drop off passengers. It's irritating when people are late or someone's car won't start. However, the money and gasoline you save can be worth the sacrifice.

These people have parked their cars and will travel to their destination in one vehicle. Carpooling saves money and gas.

DON'T WASTE GAS IDLING

The way you drive makes a big difference in your transportation cost. Many drivers believe that they should let the engine *idle* (run while not in gear) for several minutes before moving their car in the morning. This is not true. Allow your engine to idle for no more than 30 seconds, even in cold weather. Start moving quickly. Then drive at a moderate speed for the first 5 to 10 minutes. During the first few minutes, you can improve your gas mileage if you don't drive too slowly. Accelerate smoothly but briskly to reach driving speed. The more time you spend getting up to travel speed, the more gasoline your engine will use. Do not push the gas pedal to the floor, however. Doing so causes you to use large amounts of gasoline and may damage a cold engine.

ANTICIPATING

Driving at a smooth pace is one of the most important driving techniques you can develop. A 12-second visual lead will enable you to anticipate changes in the traffic around you. A 2-second following distance will allow you to make your moves smoothly. If you apply these principles when you drive, you will reduce the need to brake or to accelerate suddenly. By reducing the number of changes you make in speed, you use less gasoline.

Tailgating takes extra gas because you constantly change your speed. This is even more of a problem if the vehicle ahead is a truck or a van which limits your area of vision. When driving on hills, accelerate as you approach a hill. Don't wait until you're halfway up and then accelerate. As you drive down hills, ease off on the gas. Let gravity help pull you down.

MAINTENANCE

Maintenance is critical to the safe performance of your vehicle. It is also critical to fuel economy. A properly tuned engine helps you to get maximum gas mileage. There are different ways of determining when your car needs attention. One way is to follow the manufacturer's recommendations. Another is to keep track of the gasoline you buy. Every time you buy gas, fill the tank and record the kilometers (miles) on the odometer. You can then check your gas mileage by dividing the number of miles traveled between fill-ups by the number of liters (gallons) of gasoline you buy. By recording this information every time you buy gas, you will be able to tell when your kilometers per liter (miles per gallon) start to drop. If you have been driving the same as usual and under normal conditions, a drop in gas mileage indicates that some part of the car needs attention.

TIRE PRESSURE

Tire pressure is very important to good gas mileage. Often, people drive with *underinflated* (not enough air) tires. When tires are soft, they are more resistant to movement. This resistance reduces gas mileage. In fact, for each 0.90 kilograms (2 pounds) that your tires are underinflated, you will use about 1 percent more gasoline.

To provide maximum riding comfort, your owner's manual will generally tell you to inflate your tires from 10 to 11 kilograms (24 to 28 pounds) of pressure. For better handling and added tire life, an increase of about 2 kilograms (4 pounds)—but not to exceed 14 kilograms (32 pounds) of total pressure—will decrease rolling resistance. As a result, your gasoline mileage will increase. For each additional 0.90 kilograms (2 pounds) of tire pressure, you will gain about 1 percent in your gas mileage.

CHECKING UNDER THE HOOD

When you check under the hood to determine the safe operation of your car, remember to check the alternator and fan drive belts. Also check the water level in the battery, the radiator coolant, the engine oil, and the battery terminals for corrosion. Any one of these items may contribute very little by itself. Together, however, they aid in gasoline savings by making certain of efficient engine operation.

LOADING YOUR VEHICLE

Objects in the trunk add to the weight of the car. Added weight means less gas mileage. Therefore, keep only those items necessary for repair or operation of your car in the trunk. When you are on a trip, keep your luggage in the trunk instead of on car-top carriers and luggage racks. Luggage on carriers and racks increases air resistance, which reduces gas mileage.

FINANCING THE PURCHASE OF YOUR CAR

Few people pay cash for a new or late-model used car. Most people finance their purchase by obtaining a loan. Loans are usually obtained from a bank, credit union, finance company, or a special financing arrangement with the car dealer. If you must borrow money to buy a car, use as much care in obtaining a loan as you do in selecting a car. Different loan agencies have different rules for lending money. The interest they charge you to borrow money is also different. The amount of money a loan company will allow you to borrow is based on the value of the car. The amount of time you will have to repay the loan will depend on whether you are buying a used or new car. The amount you have to pay each month will depend on

1. the amount of money you borrow to pay for the car.
2. the interest on your loan.
3. whether your car's insurance costs are included in your monthly payment.

BUYING INSURANCE FOR YOUR CAR

The purpose of buying insurance is to protect you against a large financial loss. One type of automobile insurance protects you against damage to your car. Another type protects you financially in case you injure a person or damage the property of other persons.

Shop around for auto insurance just as you shopped for your car. Discuss the number and types of insurance policies with the sales agent.

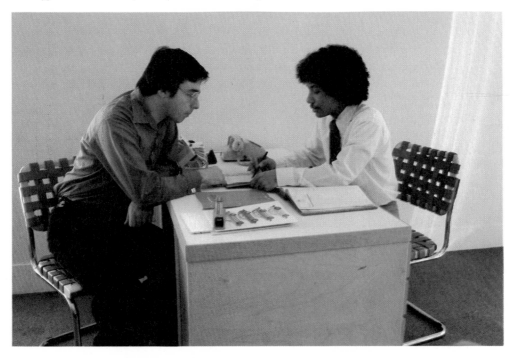

There are many different types of car insurance. There are also many factors that help determine how much your car insurance will cost. Among these are

1. the type of policy (what is covered).
2. your age (young drivers pay more).
3. your driving record (convictions and collisions increase your insurance cost).
4. how far you drive each year (the further you drive, the more the insurance costs).
5. whether or not you drive to work, how far you drive to work, and whether you drive yourself or go in a carpool (carpooling reduces the cost).
6. where you live (rural areas cost less than cities).

The following are the most common types of automobile insurance.

LIABILITY INSURANCE

The purpose of *liability insurance* is to protect you against claims if you are in a collision and are found to be at fault. It provides protection in case you are sued for accident damage. This type of insurance helps you to pay persons who have suffered injury or loss in an accident caused by your actions.

Liability insurance is the most important car-insurance protection you can buy. It protects you and anyone else who has your permission to drive your car. If you were found at fault in a collision and could not pay, the court could force you to sell your property. Your driver's license could be suspended until the money was paid.

In many states, drivers *must prove* that they are insured. This is called *compulsory insurance*. Where there are such laws, drivers have to carry a fixed minimum amount of liability insurance before they can have their cars registered. The purpose is to make sure that claims arising from accidents can be paid.

There are two types of automobile liability insurance:

• *Bodily injury insurance*. This insurance provides financial protection in case you cause the injury or death of another person or persons. You can usually buy this insurance in amounts of $10,000 to $300,000 or more.
• *Property damage liability*. This insurance provides you protection in case you damage the property of other persons. The amount of protection which you can buy again generally ranges from $10,000 to $300,000.

NO-FAULT INSURANCE

No-fault insurance is a system in which your own insurance company pays your losses, up to a certain amount. This does away with the need for finding out who is at fault. In very serious accidents, the injured can still go to court to collect, either from the person who caused the accident or from the insurance company.

MEDICAL PAYMENT INSURANCE

Medical, hospital, or funeral expenses are included in *medical payment insurance*. This insurance pays a fixed amount if you or passengers in your car are injured or killed in a collision. It also pays if you or a member of your family is killed or injured while riding in someone else's car. It would usually pay if you or members of your family are struck as pedestrians, or while riding on a bike, in a bus, or in a taxicab. Medical payment insurance pays regardless of who causes the accident. The amount of payment is determined by the limits of the policy. This amount usually ranges from $1000 to $5000 per person.

COLLISION INSURANCE

Damage to your car caused by a collision is covered by *collision insurance*. Collision insurance covers repairs to your car regardless of who is at fault. It pays for damage even if no one else is involved. For instance, you might be forced to drive off the road and, in doing so, might strike a post. If your car is parked and damaged in a parking lot, collision coverage would pay for the repairs.

Full-coverage collision insurance (a policy which pays the entire amount of the damage) is very expensive. As a result, most persons buy what is called a *deductible policy* (a policy in which you pay a fixed amount and the insurance company pays the rest). With most such policies, you agree to pay the first $50, $100, $250, or $500.

The cost of collision insurance is based on the value of your car. As your car gets older, it becomes worth less money. As a result, at some point you may want to drop collision insurance. This decision should be based on your ability to repair or replace your car if it is in a collision. Many people consider dropping collision insurance when their car is 5 to 7 years old. However, if you are financing the purchase of a car, the finance company may require that you buy collision insurance until the car is paid for.

COMPREHENSIVE INSURANCE COVERAGE

Damage to your car caused by something other than a collision is covered by comprehensive insurance. This type of insurance covers damage caused by fire, theft, flying or falling objects, explosions, natural disasters, riots, or collisions with wild animals. Like collision insurance, comprehensive insurance is available with a deductible. Many insurance policies require a $100 deductible on glass breakage. In such cases, the only way that you can receive full coverage on glass breakage is to agree to pay a higher insurance premium.

UNINSURED MOTORIST INSURANCE

This insurance protects you in case you are injured by a hit-and-run driver or a driver who does not have liability insurance. Uninsured motorist insurance coverage does for you what bodily injury insurance would do if you hurt someone else. Damage to your property is not generally covered by uninsured motorist coverage. If your car is damaged, it would be covered by your own collision insurance.

TO CONSIDER

1. Name the various expenses you must pay to own and operate a new car.

2. What factors should you consider before ordering power equipment for your car?

3. How can you plan your trips so as to use the least fuel?

4. What driving methods can you use to conserve fuel?

5. What maintenance checks will help conserve fuel?

6. Explain the different kinds of automobile insurance plans.

7. What factors should you consider if you are planning to buy a new car?

8. List five factors that influence a vehicle's fuel economy. Which factor do you think is most important, and why?

9. How will using the 12-second visual lead help you to save gas? Why does tailgating use extra gas?

10. What information should you check and compare before borrowing money to pay for a car?

PROJECTS

1. Interview the service manager or a mechanic at a local car dealer or repair station. What maintenance work do they recommend for best fuel economy? In their experience, what are the most common maintenance problems that waste fuel? Write a report of your findings.

2. Begin measuring the fuel economy at each fill-up of the family car or the car of a friend. After determining what the typical fuel economy is, work with the driver of the car to begin a "gas watchers plan." Develop a method to use the car more efficiently. Plan trips in advance. Put into practice fuel-saving techniques while driving. Keep a record of improvements resulting from your efforts, and present a report to the class.

3. Interview a local insurance agent. Ask the agent why insurance rates are so much higher for new drivers under 25 years of age. What are some steps the beginning driver can take to reduce insurance costs?

COOPERATING WITH OTHER HIGHWAY USERS

UNIT

This unit discusses special vehicles, pedestrians, and animals. They, too, can cause hazards within the highway system.

CHAPTER 20, "Small and Large Special Vehicles," tells you

- how to react to bicycles and mopeds.
- what you should know about snowmobile traffic.
- how to drive campers, vans, mobile homes, and cars towing trailers.

CHAPTER 21, "Pedestrians and Animals," discusses

- how to adjust your driving for young and elderly pedestrians.
- where to expect surprise movements from pedestrians.
- how to conduct a ground search for pedestrians and animals.
- how to cope with animals on the highway.

CHAPTER **20**

SMALL AND LARGE SPECIAL VEHICLES

People often use bicycles and mopeds to travel to and from work. But basically, these vehicles are used for leisure-time activities, as are snowmobiles and larger recreational vehicles. There has been a marked increase in the number of bicycles, mopeds, and snowmobiles sold since 1970. There are now over 90 million bicycles, 250,000 mopeds, and 2.2 million snowmobiles in the United States.

With the increased use of these vehicles, there have been more injuries and fatalities. Most of the accidents are a result of errors made by the operators of these vehicles. These errors include lack of experience with the vehicle, failure to see possible hazards, and not being seen by other drivers. Improper use of the vehicle, failure to wear proper clothing, and violations of traffic laws are other errors.

WHO RIDES BICYCLES?

For many years, bicycles were thought of as toys used mostly by children. However, many adults now ride bicycles. Some persons ride them because of the high cost of fuel. Others are concerned about the environment. Still others ride bicycles for their own physical fitness.

Many people, particularly adults, ride bicycles in heavy commuter traffic—sometimes where high speeds are allowed. They also ride in all types of weather and after dark. As a result, bicycle injuries and fatalities among people over 15 years old have risen sharply in the last decade.

There are also more large tricycles in use. These are found mostly in retirement communities. They are used for shopping and recreation. Due to their size, these vehicles are easier to see than standard bicycles. However, they tip over more easily, particularly if they are moving too fast or are turned too quickly.

More adults are using bicycles instead of cars to get from one place to another. Parking areas are now made for bikes as well as for cars.

SCANNING THE ROADWAY AROUND BICYCLISTS

As a driver, you must scan the roadway ahead of a bicyclist. You need to ask yourself if anything will require an adjustment in the bicyclist's position. Railroad crossings, stones, or storm drains may require little or no response from you. But to a bicyclist, they are critical and may call for a major adjustment. Storm drains are a particularly serious hazard. They are usually next to the curb, just where bicyclists ride. The front wheel of a bicycle may slip between the bars of the grating, stopping the bicycle and throwing the rider off. A bicyclist who sees such a drain ahead will steer around it, moving from the curb into the traffic lane. You must allow a bicyclist room and time to respond. Bicycles are more limited in their ability to turn or stop than is generally believed. Will you have to adjust your speed or position?

MOPEDS

The word *moped* comes from the names of two vehicles: a motor-driven cycle and a pedal-driven cycle. The engine on a moped is small (50 cubic centimeters) and produces only 1 to 2 horsepower of energy. (Motorcycles have 70- to 1200-cubic centimeter engines.) Because of their small engine, mopeds can drive about 265 kilometers (165 miles) on 4 liters (a gallon) of gasoline. State speed laws for mopeds vary from 40 to 60 km/h (20 to 40 mph).

Bicyclists are road users, too. Give them room and time.

More people are riding mopeds in fast-moving traffic areas. Why should this rider wear boots, gloves, full-length pants, a helmet, and a jacket?

Mopeds cost less than cars and motorcycles. For this reason, more people are buying them.

It costs much less to buy and operate a moped than a motorcycle or a car. For this reason, the number of mopeds in the United States is growing rapidly. In 1974, there were about 25,000. By the end of 1977, there were about 250,000. Sales of 300,000 or more mopeds per year are projected for the 1980s.

Although mopeds have their advantages, there are some problems connected with their use. There is little data on moped accidents in the United States. But in Europe there are about fifty-one deaths each year for every 100,000 mopeds registered. This number of deaths is less than that for motorcycles. But it is 6 times higher than the death rate for bicycles. Some people believe we can expect a similar rate in the United States if the moped popularity continues.

Since moped owners often use them to get to and from work, mopeds are found on roads with fast-moving traffic. However, mopeds are often unable to keep up with the traffic. Their slow speed causes conflicts, since many cars must suddenly adjust their speed or position. These conflicts can lead to collisions.

Drivers of both mopeds and cars can take certain steps to reduce the chance of collisions. Moped operators can make themselves more visible by (1) wearing reflective clothing, (2) placing reflective devices on their mopeds and making sure that all lights are working well, and (3) traveling as far to the right in their traffic lane as possible. Also, moped riders should stay away from heavily traveled roads until they are good at operating their mopeds. To protect themselves against injury, they should wear helmets, leather gloves, heavy pants, and jackets.

Snowmobiles are hard to stop. If you drive in areas where snowmobiling is popular, reduce your speed. This will allow you to react if a snowmobile crosses your path.

SNOWMOBILES

A snowmobile is a motor-driven vehicle designed for travel on snow or ice. It moves on a revolving belt or tread. It is not generally considered a motor vehicle. Therefore, snowmobiles do not have to be registered with the Department of Motor Vehicles.

There are about 2.2 million snowmobiles in the United States. They are usually not allowed on state highways. But in some parts of the country, local communities allow snowmobiles on certain roads.

Like many other special vehicles, snowmobiles are difficult to see because they are very close to the ground. They are often driven over ground that is covered with light, fluffy snow. This may create a cloud of snow that makes them even harder to see.

Snowmobiles can travel fast for long periods of time. This makes them very dangerous. They are hard to handle and to stop. Snowmobiles are often driven by young children. Therefore, as a driver, you must leave extra time and space to adjust to any maneuver that a snowmobile may make.

RECREATIONAL VEHICLES

Recreational vehicles are those which are used mainly for pleasure. In most states, if you have a license to drive a car, you will also be allowed to drive a van, a motor home, a pickup truck, or a car with a trailer in tow. However, such vehicles handle differently from a car.

DRIVING A RECREATIONAL VEHICLE

The way a recreational vehicle handles depends on its size, height, width, weight, and whether it is loaded or empty. To have the least effect on handling, loads should be kept as low as possible and spread evenly inside the vehicle. Remember that a loaded vehicle takes a greater distance to stop. So, you must begin to brake earlier. A loaded vehicle does not accelerate as rapidly, either. So a greater gap is needed when entering traffic or trying to pass another vehicle.

Vans, mobile homes, and pickup trucks equipped with a camper cap are more affected by crosswinds than is a car. In a strong crosswind, these vehicles may sway. It may be hard to keep them in the proper lane.

Your field of vision in a recreational vehicle may be different from that in a car. You often sit higher. So you can see the traffic ahead better. Visibility to the rear and sides, however, may be blocked by the body of the vehicle. Because of the limited visibility to the rear, it is very important to check carefully behind you before backing up, especially in driveways.

Vans and mobile homes will sometimes sway in strong crosswinds. Therefore, it may be hard for these vehicles to stay in the proper lane.

It is difficult to see along sides and to the rear of large vehicles. Trailers, vans, and mobile homes should be equipped with oversized outside mirrors.

Because of their size, recreational vehicles also block the view of other drivers. You should be especially alert to problems that may be caused when other drivers cannot see possible hazards.

Drivers of camper trucks and mobile homes sometimes forget how high the vehicle is. They may strike overhead obstructions such as the overhang at a gas station or a motel. This is especially true for someone driving such a vehicle for the first time.

DRIVING WITH A TRAILER

Before you buy or rent a trailer, make sure that the vehicle you use to *tow* (to pull) it is properly equipped. For example, make sure that you have the right-sized radiator. If your car has an automatic transmission, you may also need a transmission cooler, heavier springs, special shock absorbers, and the proper tires. Check your owner's manual to see if the equipment on your car matches the requirements made by the car manufacturer. Regardless of the size of the trailer you plan to tow, you must have the proper hitch and safety chains. The trailer must have a lighting system for taillights, signal lights, and brake lights. Oversized outside mirrors may also be needed for visibility to the rear.

The distribution of the load affects the way your car handles. Improper loading may cause the trailer to *fishtail* (weave from side to side). This can cause you to lose control. Too much weight placed in or on the back of the car will cause the front to rise. This will cause steering and braking problems and will also affect headlight alignment. With the added weight on the back of the car, the front tires can *hydroplane* (skim the surface on a wet pavement) at a much lower speed.

Distribution of the load on a trailer is very important. The load should be spread equally across the bed of the trailer. The heaviest items should be placed over the trailer wheels at the bottom of the load. About 60 percent of the total load should be on the front half of the trailer. The rear of your car should support 10 to 15 percent of the trailer load. All items should be packed tightly and tied securely so that they cannot shift when the trailer is moving. The gross weight of the trailer should not exceed the weight capacity stated on the trailer. Finally, you should not place a heavy load in the back seat or trunk of the car. The heaviest passengers, for instance, should sit in the front.

If you have not had experience with a trailer or are using an unfamiliar type of trailer, practice driving it in a vacant lot or on lightly traveled roadways before starting on a long trip. Once you are on the highway, check traffic carefully and signal every move early. Records show that a car pulling a trailer is twice as likely to be in a collision as a car without a trailer. Allow a much greater gap before pulling into traffic or starting to pass, or when anticipating a stop. It takes about twice as long to do these maneuvers with a trailer. You will also need much more space for turning, since the trailer will not follow directly in the path of the car.

Backing is the most difficult maneuver that you will perform with a trailer. If you must back up, move slowly. Turning the steering wheel to the right causes the trailer to go left. Turning left makes it go right. Turn the steering wheel in the desired direction and then straighten it. Continue to turn the wheel and straighten it as the trailer responds. Do not turn the steering wheel too far and do not hold the steering wheel in a turn position too long. These actions will cause the trailer and car to *jackknife*. (A jackknife occurs when a car and its trailer turn suddenly to form the shape of an "L.")

If you must back up, you will usually find it easier if the trailer turns toward the left side of your car where you can see it. It will also help to have another person guide you. Practice is essential, particularly in developing the skill needed to park.

When you are driving a trailer on the highway, check traffic carefully. Signal every move early. Allow a much greater gap before merging into traffic, passing, or stopping.

If you are going to use the trailer on a trip, make sure that you check state laws on trailer operation in the states that you are going to drive through. For instance, in many states, a separate braking system is required for trailers that weigh over 1000 pounds when loaded. A breakaway switch to activate the trailer brake in the event of a failure may also be required. Also, when you travel, stop often to check to see that the load and the hitch are secure.

TO CONSIDER

1. Describe three users of the highway system that are not on foot or riding in cars or trucks.

2. Explain why the number of bicycle accidents has increased dramatically in the last few years.

3. Name three roadway conditions that are not hazardous to motor vehicle operators but create extreme hazards for bicyclists. How can a driver compensate for these hazards?

4. What do mopeds and bicycles have in common? How are they different?

5. Describe the special problems that moped operators have while riding in traffic.

6. Why are snowmobiles often difficult to see?

7. How would you adjust your driving in order to handle a recreational vehicle properly?

8. Why should drivers allow extra time and space to adjust to any maneuver a snowmobile may make?

9. How does visibility in a recreational vehicle compare with visibility in a car?

10. Describe the correct way to distribute the load on a trailer.

PROJECTS

1. Survey your area for safeguards that help drivers and other highway users safely share the roadways with bicyclists and moped drivers. Are school-crossing guards or safety patrols on duty at the right places and the right times? Are bicycle paths well marked and well maintained? Are there unnecessary hazards, such as unprotected sewer grates? Discuss with your class how the safeguards could be improved.

2. Ask a local police officer or traffic official these questions: Are laws relating to bicyclists and mopeds consistent throughout the state? If they exist, are these laws well enforced? Are the laws adequate? What do you think?

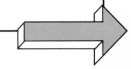

CROSSING

CAUTION

CHAPTER

21

YIELD

PEDESTRIANS AND ANIMALS

Vehicles are not the only hazard on the highway. Pedestrians and animals often cross a driver's path. More than 9000 pedestrians are killed and 100,000 injured each year in the United States.

Almost 85 percent of the pedestrians who get hurt are injured in urban areas. But accidents involving pedestrians in rural areas are often worse than those in cities. This is because vehicles travel faster in rural areas. The chance of a death in an urban pedestrian accident is 1 in 16. The chance in a rural area is about 1 in 7. Still, 67 percent of the total number of pedestrians killed are pedestrians in urban areas.

Children often run into the street and play behind parked cars without thinking of the dangers involved. Drive slowly and cautiously in areas where children play. Expect the unexpected.

Drivers should be extremely careful in areas where children are riding bicycles. A child having fun riding a bike may forget the hazards of motor vehicle traffic.

WHO IS INVOLVED?

Pedestrians between the ages of 5 and 6 and between the ages of 64 and 68 have more accidents than those in any other age groups. Boys have far more accidents than girls do. Among adults, about 25 percent of the pedestrians killed have been drinking alcoholic beverages.

WHERE MOST PEDESTRIAN ACCIDENTS OCCUR

People who live in the suburbs are not as aware of traffic hazards as people who live in cities. Since intersections are far apart and traffic is usually lighter, people often cross the street at places other than intersections. Other persons may step into the street while mowing their lawns or sweeping sidewalks. Parked cars and shrubbery limit both the driver's and the pedestrian's visibility. These factors, plus the behavior of young pedestrians, increase the chances of an accident.

Meter readers, postal employees, and people delivering packages have also been known to step into the path of moving vehicles. These people are usually thinking about their jobs, not about traffic.

Before you back into or out of a driveway, search for children. They may be hidden behind cars or shrubbery. Always check behind your car.

GROUND SEARCH

You have been taught to search at least 12 seconds ahead of your car. When you drive in residential areas, you must do a special type of scanning. It is called a *ground search*.

Parked vehicles or shrubbery may hide children or pets from view. Look for movement under and around these obstructions. Look from one side of the road to the other. Look for shadows that may tell you a person or an animal is near the street. Any movement should warn you that there may soon be a conflict.

BEHAVIOR OF YOUNGSTERS

Since young children are small, it is hard to see them. They are also apt to dart into the street. In residential areas, keep your speed low and your car as far from the curb or parked cars as is safe. That way, you will be better able to see children before they move into the street.

Young children often do not act the way we expect. Even when they are near heavy traffic, they may run or play games or push each other. When they are playing, children often forget about traffic and run into the street. Parked cars limit the escape routes for both driver and child.

Their height keeps children from seeing over the trunks or hoods of parked cars. Small shrubs block their vision. Therefore, every driver must look for danger signals. The main one is children playing near the street or road. Be careful, also, if you see a ball bouncing into the street or notice a pet or any wheeled toy. Check for a single child who may run across the street to join a group of children. Be alert near construction sites and playgrounds. Children are likely to be there. Look for them also at bus stops, in school zones, and where you see crossing guards or school patrols.

LACK OF SIDEWALKS

If there are no sidewalks, people are likely to walk in the street, and children tend to use the street as a playground. Children also like to ride bicycles, tricycles, wagons, or skateboards down steep, sloping driveways. Take great care when you drive past such driveways.

ACCIDENTS IN BUSINESS DISTRICTS

Most pedestrian accidents in business districts involve adults in intersections. Usually, the driver is looking at other vehicles or at traffic signals and does not see the pedestrian until the accident happens.

To make things worse, many pedestrians cannot judge the speed of traffic and the time needed to cross a street. They may run into the street or start across just as a traffic light changes. Braking takes time, and heavy traffic does not let the driver swerve far enough to avoid pedestrians.

Drivers can increase the number of hazards to pedestrians in business districts.

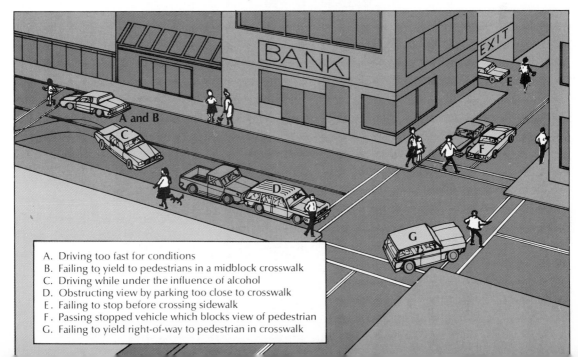

A. Driving too fast for conditions
B. Failing to yield to pedestrians in a midblock crosswalk
C. Driving while under the influence of alcohol
D. Obstructing view by parking too close to crosswalk
E. Failing to stop before crossing sidewalk
F. Passing stopped vehicle which blocks view of pedestrian
G. Failing to yield right-of-way to pedestrian in crosswalk

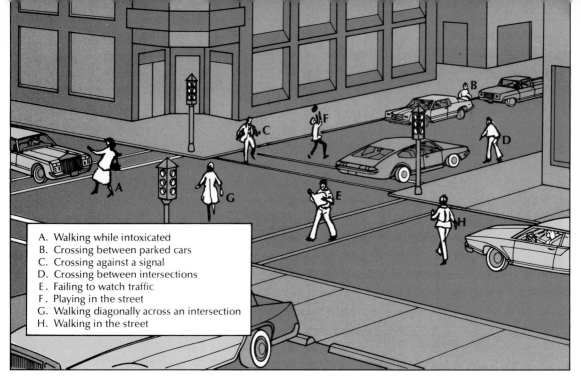

A. Walking while intoxicated
B. Crossing between parked cars
C. Crossing against a signal
D. Crossing between intersections
E. Failing to watch traffic
F. Playing in the street
G. Walking diagonally across an intersection
H. Walking in the street

Pedestrians can, by their own actions, endanger themselves.

Most pedestrians struck at intersections are hit just as they step into the street. The vehicle is in the lane closest to the sidewalk. Usually, the car is driving straight through the intersection.

Pedestrians, like drivers, must learn to judge the gaps in traffic. The typical young adult can cross a two-lane street in a residential area in 4 to 6 seconds. A child needs 7 or more seconds. An old person may need from 7 to 10 seconds to cross the same street. As a driver, you should estimate how much time pedestrians will need to cross the street. Then you should adjust your speed to avoid hitting them.

THE ELDERLY

Elderly people generally take longer than young people to cross a street. Sometimes, they fail to check traffic. They can also make errors in time-space judgment. In some cases, they need more time to cross than the "Walk" signal gives them. With this in mind, you should be careful as you come to a red light that is turning to green.

Slow-moving pedestrians can be a serious problem on wide streets. Vehicles stopped in other lanes may block your view. A pedestrian may suddenly step from behind a vehicle into your path. If you are not ready for this, you will have no place to go and no time to stop.

Blind people usually walk with a seeing-eye dog or carry a white cane. Give special consideration to blind pedestrians.

BLIND PEDESTRIANS

Blind people often carry a white cane or have a seeing-eye dog to lead them. Most of them have learned to cope quite well with traffic. A driver must always yield the right-of-way to a blind person.

STROLLERS AND CARRIAGES

A person who is pushing a stroller or a baby carriage may have trouble getting down off the curb. Once in a while, a carriage goes out of control. It may even roll into the path of traffic. If you are not moving too fast and can see danger as it approaches, you may have the time and space to avoid it.

If you are not sure that a pedestrian sees you, slow down and move as far away as traffic allows. You may also tap the horn lightly. However, do not blast the horn. A blast of the horn may scare someone and cause her or him to do the wrong thing.

SMALL ANIMALS

Pets often dart into the street or road. In trying not to hit the animal, a driver may swerve and strike a fixed object or another vehicle. A driver may also stop quickly and be struck from the rear. However, good visual search habits help to prevent accidents caused by animals. Use the same ground-search pattern that you use when you suspect that small children may be near.

235

Slow down when you see signs that warn of animals crossing. Do not blow your horn. Loud noises can frighten animals into a movement that could cause a collision.

LARGE ANIMALS

If you see signs that say "Cattle Crossing" or "Open Range," look for farm animals on or near the road. Be cautious. A collision with a large animal can be very serious, even if you are not moving fast. Slow down as soon as animals come into view. It is hard to predict what they will do. Be prepared to stop and to give them as much space as you can. Move over and pass the animals at a low rate of speed.

WILD ANIMALS

You have probably seen small birds or animals hit and killed by cars. Many deer and other large animals are killed by cars as well. A collision with such an animal can result in great damage to a car. It can cause injury or death to a driver or a passenger.

In some places, such as mountains, plains, and forests, wild animals are a major problem. They are not seen on the highway often. When an animal does come out, drivers panic. Also, many animals come out at twilight or after dark. With little light to see by, drivers may not notice an animal until it moves into the path of the car.

There are very few steps you can take to avoid these accidents. All you can do is to slow your speed when you drive in places where you know deer or other wild animals may cross the road. You can also look for movement or the reflection of light off the eyes of animals when it is dark.

TO CONSIDER

1. Describe two types of highway users who are on foot.

2. Why do rural pedestrian accidents result in fatalities more often than urban pedestrian accidents?

3. Define the term *ground search*. How is a ground search different from an ordinary visual search? When is a ground search most important?

4. List some reasons why young children are most often involved in pedestrian accidents.

5. How would you adjust your driving pattern to allow for the manner in which children behave?

6. Why is it dangerous to drive through an intersection without pausing first, even when the traffic light is green and the crossing traffic is stopped?

7. Why are the elderly often involved in pedestrian accidents? What can drivers do to lower the rate of pedestrian accidents involving the elderly?

8. What are some of the hazards pets create for drivers? If you were driving and saw a dog running near the roadway, what else would you look for? If a dog started to run in front of you, what would you do?

9. Discuss the bumper-sticker slogan "I brake for animals."

PROJECTS

1. Ask your local police department to supply information about pedestrian accidents in your area. Are there any streets or intersections that have especially high numbers of such accidents? What age groups are most often involved? How often is alcohol a factor? Are weather conditions and time of day important? Report your findings to your class.

2. Observe pedestrian and driver behavior at an intersection near your home. How many pedestrians check traffic in all directions before crossing? How many drivers adjust their speed and position in response to possible pedestrian hazards? Report your findings to your class.

CONTROLLING FAILURES IN VEHICLE SYSTEMS

UNIT

Unit IX is about maneuvers that should be used to avoid collisions. The unit also discusses how to control skids and vehicle breakdowns.

Chapter 22, "Evasive Actions," describes
• how to maneuver your car laterally to avoid a collision.
• how to return to the road from a shoulder (off-road recovery).
• when to accelerate to avoid a collision.
• how to brake to avoid an accident.

Chapter 23, "Skid Control," tells you
• what to do to avoid skids.
• how to recover from braking skids, power skids, cornering skids, and blow-out skids.

Chapter 24, "Vehicle Failure," discusses
• brake failure.
• steering failure.
• engine failure.
• hood fly-up.
• fire.
• flat tire.
• dead battery.
• wet engine.
• overheated engine.
• headlight failure.

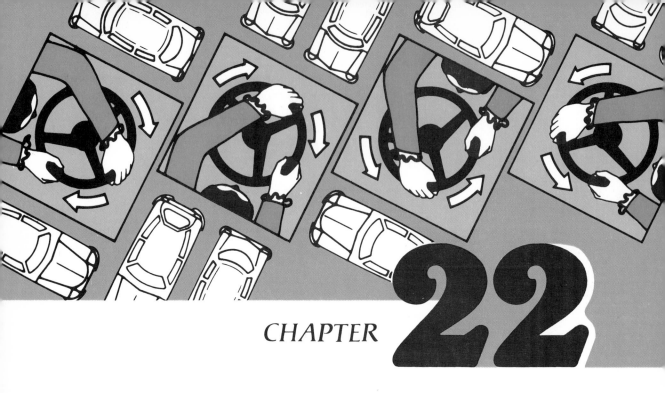

CHAPTER 22

EVASIVE ACTION

To avoid a collision, you may have to make an *evasive action* (a quick change in speed or direction). Evasive actions include quickly moving laterally (to the left or right), accelerating, and braking.

LATERAL EVASIVE

You make a *lateral evasive maneuver* when you turn the steering wheel hard and swerve sharply to avoid a collision. This is easiest to do if

1. the driver's seat is properly adjusted.
2. your hands are at the 9- and 3-o'clock positions on the steering wheel.
3. safety belts are fastened and properly adjusted.

Remember, it takes about 4 seconds to stop when you are driving at highway speed. To avoid crashing into an object less than 2 seconds from you, you have to (1) turn the steering wheel rapidly left or right as much as 160 to 180 degrees, (2) immediately turn the steering wheel 320 to 360 degrees back in the opposite direction, and then (3) turn the steering wheel left or right to bring the vehicle back to a path parallel to the original path of travel.

You must complete a lateral evasive maneuver quickly. If you do not, you may be on a collision course with an object off the road. You will not have time to look for an escape route after an emergency develops. Therefore, while you are driving, you should always scan the road and off-road areas ahead to find possible escape routes. For example, suppose you are driving at 90 km/h (55 mph) on a two-way road. As you reach the top of a hill, you see a car with a flat tire stopped in your lane about 3 seconds ahead. It is too late to brake to a stop. You must make a lateral evasive maneuver. Which way do you go? Are there vehicles following or coming toward you? Are there any off-road obstacles? How far are they from the road? What would happen if you crashed into these obstacles? What is the condition of the surface of the off-road areas?

To make a quick evasive movement to the right, you should steer right, then left, and then right again to recover a straight path. Your hands should start at the 9-and-3 position. Your head restraint and safety belt should be properly adjusted.

To get back onto the roadway when your right wheels are on the shoulder, do the following. (1) Steer to the right until your right wheels are ⅓ to ½ meter (1 to 2 feet) from the roadway. Straighten your wheels.

(2) Choose a spot where the shoulder and the road are level. Check traffic and signal a left turn.

Obviously, you cannot answer all these questions in the time you have. But you can make some fast decisions. If you have gathered information in advance, you will be able to assume certain things. For instance, you can assume that the shoulder on both sides of the hill will be more or less the same. You can assume that you could use controlled braking and steer off to the right in an emergency.

It will be harder to make a decision if the escape routes both to the left and the right are blocked. For example, suppose the right shoulder is lined with shrubs and there is oncoming traffic in the left lane. In such a situation, you should choose the route that holds the *least danger*. A move toward the oncoming traffic may result in a head-on

(3) Turn the steering wheel quickly to the left about a quarter of the way. As the right front wheel touches the edge of the roadway, steer back to the right to straighten your car in the right lane.

When your wheels are straight, steer straight ahead. *Note:* This recovery is the same if you are forced to leave the roadway completely, so that all four wheels are on the shoulder.

collision. Even if you make it to the left shoulder, an oncoming driver may panic and steer off the road or into your car. Your evasive move should, therefore, be to the right, even though the shrubs may hide some object.

OFF-ROAD RECOVERY

At times, you may have to steer part or all the way off the road to avoid a hazard. *Off-road recovery* (returning to the road from a shoulder), however, can be a dangerous maneuver.

SHOULDER HAZARDS

Steering may become hard if there is a difference in the level of the roadway and that of the road shoulder. If there is a difference, the front left tire of the car may drag against the edge of the road. This makes it difficult for the driver to control the direction in which he or she wants the car to go. Steering may be even more difficult if the shoulder area is not solid or smooth. Soft or loose sand, mud, and grass reduce traction, which is needed to control the car. If the shoulder area and the roadway have different types of surfaces, traction will suddenly change. The result may be loss of control.

Sometimes, drivers try to ease back on the road without slowing or properly positioning their cars. These drivers may not notice if the road surface is higher than the shoulder. The road surface is sometimes as much as 8 centimeters (several inches) higher. In trying to come back on the road, the left front tire may drag against the edge of the road, making control difficult. Or, the inside sidewall of the right front off-road tire may get caught on the edge of the pavement. This stretches the tire out of shape. The bottom of that front tire continues to point straight ahead, while the wheel points toward the road. Finally, the caught tire snaps up onto the roadway. If the steering angle is great enough, the vehicle will shoot across the road.

CONTROLLING OFF-ROAD RECOVERY

The best way to return to the road from a low shoulder is to

1. hold the steering wheel firmly, hands at the 9- and 3-o'clock positions.
2. check for traffic ahead and behind.
3. reduce your speed to about 30 to 40 km/h (20 to 25 mph) by letting up on the gas pedal and braking gently.
4. steer to the right until your right wheels are ⅓ to ½ meter (1 to 2 feet) from the pavement; straighten your wheels.
5. choose a spot where the shoulder and the road are level.
6. check traffic again and signal a left turn.
7. steer quickly to the left by making a quarter turn of the steering wheel. As the *right* front wheel touches the edge of the pavement, steer back 160 degrees to 180 degrees to the right. This steering reversal prevents your car from entering the oncoming lane. Straighten your wheels and move ahead.

EMERGENCY OFF-ROAD RECOVERY

If you have driven onto the right shoulder to avoid a collision, you may find yourself headed toward some other object. A bridge abutment, a large tree, or a pedestrian may force you to return to the road immediately. You will not have time for a routine off-road recovery. However, if you have both hands firmly on the steering wheel, you should still be able to control your car and recover.

Move your car far enough off the road so that the right front and right rear wheels are off the road and free of the pavement edge. Then do the following:

1. Take your foot off the accelerator and brake pedal. Quickly turn the steering wheel to the left 120 to 130 degrees.
2. As the *right* front wheel strikes the edge of the road, steer smoothly and quickly back to the right about 240 to 260 degrees. Immediately steer straight ahead.

In either a controlled or an emergency off-road recovery, you must remember to do three things: (1) steer smoothly and quickly back onto the road, (2) *countersteer* (turn the steering wheel in the direction you intend to travel) to control your lane position, and (3) brake gently if at all. The quickness and smoothness of steering must be precise to keep your car within a single lane. Quick, sharp steering back onto the road allows the leading edge of the front tire to climb up onto the edge of the pavement. Thus, the tire keeps its shape and maintains contact with the pavement.

ACCELERATION EVASIVE

The accelerator is the control device most often overlooked in an emergency. There are times, though, when speeding up may be your only means of escaping danger. These situations most often occur at intersections and in merging traffic. For example, you may be in an intersection when a car comes at you rapidly from one side. Braking will leave you directly in the car's path. A lateral maneuver will take too much time or be impossible because there are objects on both sides of you. If the road ahead is clear, a quick increase in speed may bring you to safety.

The car in the far left lane is quickly passing a possible collision. This is called an acceleration evasive maneuver.

BRAKING EVASIVE

In some emergency situations, a lateral evasive or acceleration evasive maneuver may not be possible. There may be no place to steer to. At speeds under 30 km/h (20 mph), it takes less time and distance to stop than to steer to another lane.

If you evaluate situations accurately and brake in time, you should be able to bring your car to a quick stop without losing control of steering. Press the brake pedal hard enough to stop fast without making the wheels *lock* (stop turning). Slamming on the brakes and locking the wheels may increase stopping distance, will cause a complete loss of steering control, and may result in a skid. The best ways to control braking are to use a steady, moderate pressure or to use quick, firm jabs on the brake pedal. (Each quick jab may lock the wheels for an instant, but not long enough to make you lose control.) Under stress, you may overbrake and lock the wheels. If you do, release the brake immediately and brake again, using a bit less pressure.

TO CONSIDER

1. Name three *evasive* actions. Give an example of each.

2. How will proper seat adjustment help you, the driver, in an emergency situation?

3. Describe the correct way to make a lateral evasive maneuver.

4. Why is it important to evaluate off-road conditions even when there are no immediate hazards?

5. Why are soft shoulders a serious hazard?

6. If your two right tires go off the road and onto the shoulder, what steps do you take to get your car safely back onto the road? What problems should you watch for?

7. What three steps will make it easier to perform an evasive maneuver?

8. In what situations can speeding up be a useful means of escaping danger? Give examples.

9. Why is it important *not* to lock the wheels when braking? What should you do if you overbrake and lock the wheels?

10. What is the best way to control braking in an emergency?

PROJECTS

1. Watch several drivers—including friends and members of your family—as they prepare to drive. How many of them make predriving checks and adjustments that will help them deal with emergency situations? Report your findings to your class.

2. Check the shoulders and off-road areas of three sections of local highway. Are the shoulders and other areas well designed and maintained? What hazards do they present to drivers? How could they be improved?

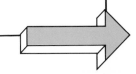

CHAPTER **23**

SKID CONTROL

SKID CONTROL

Skidding is loss of control over the direction in which your car is moving because of reduced traction. You can go into a skid any time there is not enough traction to start, stop, or change the car's position.

Among the most common causes of skidding are (1) changing speed or direction too quickly, (2) changing speed or position when traction is poor. If a skid does occur, you are not helpless. If you stay calm, you will be able to use the time and space available to regain control of the car. What you do will depend on what type of skid has occurred—braking, power, cornering, or blowout skid—and whether your car has front-wheel or rear-wheel drive. You must try to keep the car from swerving out of the lane or spinning around and facing in the wrong direction.

248

RESPONDING TO A SKID—REAR-WHEEL-DRIVE VEHICLE

If your rear-wheel-drive car begins to skid, do not step on the brakes. The rear wheels might lock before the front wheels, due to bad brake adjustment. Braking would cause the rear wheels to lose whatever traction might be available. Such a rear-wheel skid could cause the car to spin around completely.

When your car begins to skid in traffic, keep your foot off the brake and the gas. Steer in the direction in which the rear wheels are skidding. If the rear end skids out to the right, turn the steering wheel to the right. As soon as the skid begins to change direction, change the direction in which you are steering.

You should start the countersteering as soon as you start to skid. The longer you wait, the more the car will slide out of your intended path. Be careful not to *overcorrect* (oversteer). This could result in a *counterskid*—either a *fishtail* (a skidding back and forth of the rear wheels) or a *spinout* (a breaking of the traction of the rear wheels that will send the car spinning around). To avoid overcorrecting, you must

A. In a braking skid, release the brakes as soon as you begin to skid.

B. In a cornering skid, ease up on the accelerator. Steer in the direction in which the rear of your car is going.

Do not brake

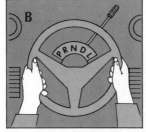

Grip the steering wheel

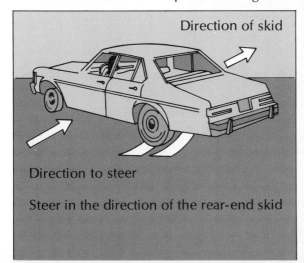

Direction of skid

Direction to steer

Steer in the direction of the rear-end skid

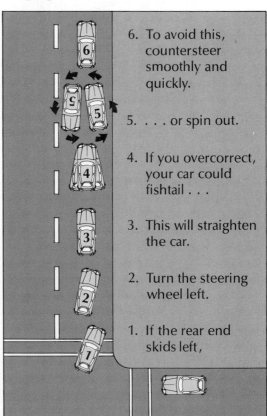

6. To avoid this, countersteer smoothly and quickly.

5. . . . or spin out.

4. If you overcorrect, your car could fishtail . . .

3. This will straighten the car.

2. Turn the steering wheel left.

1. If the rear end skids left,

countersteer smoothly and quickly. Each time the car changes direction, you must turn the wheel in the direction in which the car is skidding. Countersteering should be continuous until you are out of the skid and you have fully regained control of the car.

RESPONDING TO A SKID—FRONT-WHEEL-DRIVE VEHICLE

If your front-wheel-drive car begins to skid, step lightly on the gas pedal. If you take your foot off the gas suddenly, the front wheels will slow down and the skid will turn into a spinout. To get your car back under control, accelerate lightly, turning into the skid. If the road is too narrow to let you accelerate to get out of the skid, shift to *neutral* and continue to steer. But use care. You may have to take your eyes off the road. If the car has an automatic transmission, you may shift to reverse by mistake.

BRAKING SKID

A *braking skid* occurs when the brakes are applied so hard that one or more wheels lock. (If a car's brakes are properly adjusted, all the wheels will lock at the same time.) If one or more wheels lock, you will lose control of the steering. Your car may go into a braking skid if you stop suddenly. This skid can also occur if you brake too hard on a wet road or on a road covered with sand, gravel, wet leaves, ice, or snow.

When all four wheels or only the front wheels lock, a car will skid straight ahead. It will keep going straight unless something (such as a slope in the road) changes its direction. If only the rear wheels lock, the loss of traction makes the rear wheels slide sideways. The car could go into a 180-degree spin so that you end up skidding backward.

When only the rear wheels lock in a braking skid, these wheels slide sideways. The car can then spin around so that it faces the opposite way. Take your foot off the brake. When the wheels start turning, you will be able to control the steering wheel.

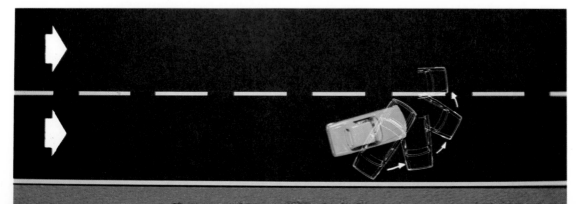

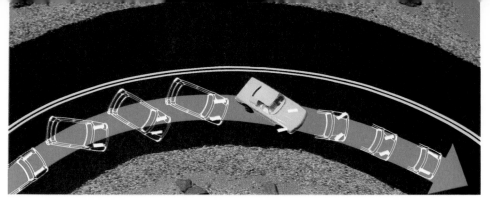

A cornering skid can also occur on a highway curve.

RESPONDING TO A BRAKING SKID

To get out of a braking skid, take your foot off the brake pedal. When the wheels start to turn and traction is regained, steering control will return. If you have to use the brakes again, use less pressure. This way, the wheels will continue to turn, and the car will slow down.

POWER SKIDS

A *power skid* occurs when you suddenly press on the gas pedal too hard. A power skid is much like a braking skid. If power is sent to the drive wheels in the rear too quickly, the sudden acceleration may cause the rear wheels to lose traction. The back end can then skid to the side. In a bad skid, the car may spin out. If the drive wheels are in the front, the car will plow straight ahead. Power skids occur most often when a driver accelerates quickly on a slippery surface. But they can happen even on a dry surface when there is a sudden, hard acceleration.

RESPONDING TO A POWER SKID

To correct a power skid, ease up on the gas until the wheels stop spinning. Make steering corrections as necessary. You may have to countersteer if the car starts to spin around.

CORNERING SKID

A loss of steering control in a turn is a *cornering skid*. A cornering skid can occur at any speed. If traction is reduced by poor tires or a slippery road surface, you may go into a cornering skid even at low speeds. If you try to turn a corner very fast, the car will be likely to skid. In a cornering skid, your car keeps going straight ahead no matter which way you turn the wheel.

Type	Reason	Conditions	What Can Happen	What to Do
Braking skid	The brakes are applied so hard that one or more wheels lock.	a sudden stop a wet, slippery, or uneven road	Steering control is lost. If the front wheels lock, the car skids straight ahead. If only the rear wheels lock, they slide sideways. The car might spin around.	Take your foot off the brake pedal. Steer. When the wheels start turning again and moving forward, steering control will return.
Power skid	The gas pedal is pressed suddenly, too hard.	a sudden, hard acceleration a slippery road surface	A car with front-wheel drive plows straight ahead. In a car with rear-wheel drive, the back end can skid to the side. The car might spin around.	Ease up on the gas pedal until the wheels stop spinning. Steer to straighten the car. Countersteer if the car starts to spin.
Cornering skid	The rear tires lose traction in a turn.	a turn made too fast poor tires or a slippery road surface	Steering control is lost. The rear wheels skid away from the turn. The car keeps going straight ahead.	In a rear-wheel drive car, take your foot all the way off the gas pedal. In a front-wheel drive car, ease up on the gas but don't take your foot off. Steer in the direction in which the rear wheels are skidding.
Blowout skid	A tire suddenly loses air pressure.	a punctured, worn, or overinflated tire an overloaded vehicle	There is a strong pull toward the side on which a front tire has blown out. A rear-tire blowout might cause a pull toward the blowout, side-to-side swaying, or fishtailing.	Do not brake. Make firm, steady steering corrections. Do not change speed suddenly. Slow down gradually and drive off the road.

RESPONDING TO A CORNERING SKID

To correct a cornering skid, ease up on the gas pedal. In a front-wheel-drive vehicle, however, do not take your foot all the way off the gas pedal. You must keep some power flowing to the drive wheels. In a rear-wheel-drive vehicle, take your foot all the way off the gas pedal.

BLOWOUT SKID

Whenever a tire suddenly loses air pressure, a car can go into a skid. Even if no skid occurs, there will usually be a sharp change in the way a vehicle steers. If a front tire blows out, there will be a strong pull toward the side on which the tire has blown. If a rear tire blows, the car will sway from side to side, fishtail, or pull toward the side of the blowout. Any blowout can cause a major skid or spinout.

If a tire blows out, do not slam on the brakes. Keep a firm grip on the steering wheel. Slow down, gradually. Put on your emergency flashers, signal, and steer off the road.

RESPONDING TO A BLOWOUT

If a tire blows, do not step on the brake pedal. Steer the car out of a blowout skid. Correct any change in direction caused by the blowout and avoid abrupt changes in speed. As soon as you get control of the steering, gradually reduce your speed and drive off the road. Just after a blowout, steering may be difficult; so you must keep a firm, steady grip on the steering wheel.

SKID PREVENTION AND RECOVERY

There are several things to keep in mind to help you to prevent a skid and to recover from any skid that does occur:

1. Watch out for conditions that cause skids. If you are prepared for a skid, you will be less likely to panic.
2. The sooner you respond to a skid, the easier it will be to correct the skid.
3. Do not speed up or brake suddenly. Skids are made worse by abrupt changes in speed.
4. Keep a firm grip on the steering wheel. This reduces the chance of a further loss of control.
5. Make steering corrections quickly and firmly. Do not steer so abruptly that you cause a skid in the opposite direction.

TO CONSIDER

1. Define the four types of skids and explain what causes each.

2. List the steps you would take to respond to each type of skid.

3. How is responding to a skid in a front-wheel-drive car different from responding in a rear-wheel-drive car?

4. Why is a car harder to control when a tire blows out?

5. If your car's front left tire blows out, which way will your car pull? How should you respond?

6. What are the most common causes of skidding? If your car begins to skid, what must you try to do? List five steps you can take to prevent skids and to recover from them if they do happen.

7. What can cause a *counterskid?* How can you avoid it?

8. What can happen in a front-wheel drive vehicle if you suddenly take your foot off the gas just after the vehicle starts to skid?

9. Why should you use care when shifting to *neutral* during a skid?

10. What is the difference between a braking skid in which all four wheels lock and a braking skid in which only the rear wheels lock?

11. In what ways is a *power skid* like a braking skid? How will a power skid affect front-wheel-drive vehicles? How will it affect rear-wheel-drive vehicles?

PROJECTS

Ask four experienced drivers how they would respond to skids. How many of them know how to steer out of a skid? What do they say about braking during a skid? How would you rate these drivers' ability to handle skids properly? Explain your ratings.

flat tire

VEHICLE FAILURE

No matter how well you maintain your car, it may break down suddenly. If your car is moving when a breakdown occurs, you must control the vehicle's speed and direction and drive out of the stream of traffic. Once you are safely off the road, you can deal with the breakdown with less risk of an accident.

BRAKE FAILURE

All new cars are equipped with a *dual-service brake system*. This means that there are separate systems for the front and rear wheels. Therefore, total failure seldom occurs. If it does occur, though, there are several things that you should do:

1. Pump the brake pedal rapidly. This action may build up some pressure in the brake-fluid lines and may, thereby, provide some braking force.

If the brakes in your car fail, follow the steps below. Do not put steady pressure on the parking brake.

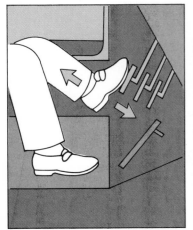

Pump the brakes.

Shift to low.

Pump the parking brake.

2. While holding open the release button or handle, release and pump the parking brake. Remember, the parking brake works only on the rear wheels. If you apply it suddenly, the rear wheels might lock and cause a spinout.

3. Shift to a lower gear. Slowing the engine and power train will provide a "drag" force. This will slow the car.

If none of these actions slows your car and gradually brings it to a stop, sound your horn to warn other highway users. Then do one or more of the following things to try to avoid serious danger:

1. Steer to the side of the street and try to rub the tires against a curb to slow the car.

2. Search for an open area, such as a field, a yard, or a parking lot. Drive into it, put the car into *neutral*, and coast around until the car slows to a stop.

3. Look for an uphill road that will slow you down and take you away from other highway users.

4. As a last resort, turn the ignition off and shift to low (*1* or *L*). This may damage your transmission, but it could help stop your car and avoid a collision.

5. If you cannot avoid a collision, try to make the move with the least serious consequences. Try to steer into large bushes or small objects. Steer to the side of the road to try to slow the car

by rubbing it against fences, guard rails, roadside embankments, or even parked cars. Any of these collisions is better than a head-on collision or a collision with a pedestrian or a large fixed object.

6. When your speed is reduced to about 15 km/h (10 mph), turn off the engine.

STEERING FAILURE

Total steering failure is rare. What does happen often is partial steering failure caused by a stalled engine in a car equipped with power steering. When the engine stalls, the power steering unit stops working. This makes steering hard. A broken drive belt, a faulty power steering system, or a defective hydraulic pump also make steering difficult. If any of these parts fail, the power steering stops working and the driver must work hard to turn the steering wheel. But steering control is not lost. If a power steering failure occurs, keep steering. Get your car safely off the road and brake to a stop.

An upper or lower control arm or balljoint breakdown is a more serious problem. This will make one front wheel collapse. If this happens, keep steering and take your foot off the brake pedal. Even

If your car breaks down, call a garage. A mechanic will come in a tow truck to haul your car to the garage. Before your car is towed, shift the car to neutral gear. Be sure to turn off the ignition and release the parking brake.

slight brake pressure can cause the car to pull sharply to one side. If you are traveling at highway speed, take the same steps you would take in case of brake failure. Shift to a lower gear and use the parking brake. (Remember that the parking brake release must be held open so that you do not keep the wheels in a locked position.)

ENGINE FAILURE

Engine failure is the most common vehicle failure. Many things can cause it, including a broken timing gear, a problem in the fuel system, lack of gas, electrical system failure, or a cold engine that stalls. As soon as you find that the engine is failing, try to steer off the road. If the engine stops completely before you can leave the road, try to coast to a safe area. Shift to *neutral;* the car will coast farther than it will in *drive.* You can also try to restart the engine in *neutral.* If the problem is a minor one, such as a stuck choke, shifting to *neutral* may work.

Remember, power steering and power brakes do not work the same when the engine is off, so it may be harder to steer or brake. With extra effort, though, you can still control the car.

If your engine stops running while you are driving, shift to neutral and turn on your warning flashers. Try to coast to a safe place.

If the gas pedal of your car sticks and the road ahead is clear, slide the toe of your foot under the pedal. Then lift the pedal with your foot.

STICKING ACCELERATOR PEDAL

Accelerator pedals sometimes stick. The cause may be a sticking linkage or a broken engine mount. When the accelerator sticks, leave the car in *drive* and turn the ignition off, thus shutting off the engine. Remember, if you have power steering, it will be harder to steer. You leave the car in gear so that you do not accidentally turn the key so far that you lock the steering column and lose steering. If you have power brakes, do not pump them. Without the engine to operate the power brake unit, pumping the brakes will quickly exhaust the system. Instead, apply steady, moderate pressure, signal a turn, and steer off the road. If you are slowing too quickly and you want to coast farther, shift to *neutral.* Only if you have a clear road ahead should you attempt to release the accelerator pedal. To do so, slip the toe of your shoe under it and pull up. Never try to release the accelerator by bending over and using your hands. You cannot control your car or see where you are going in that position.

HOOD FLY-UP

You must have a clear view to drive safely. Therefore, a hood that flies up is a great danger. Your best defense against hood fly-up is to prevent it. Before you drive, check the hood. Make sure it is fastened. After you or anyone else checks the engine, make sure the hood is locked. You can also check the hood as you drive. If the hood and fenders do not line up properly or if the hood seems to vibrate, it may not be fastened. Stop to check it.

If the hood does fly up, try to see through the side window. You may also be able to lean forward to see through the space between the dashboard and the hood. If you have no other choice, brake to a stop in your lane. You may be struck from the rear. However, if the driver behind you has a clear view, there should be time and space to avoid a rear-end collision.

If your hood flies up, put on your hazard lights. Slow down. Try to look through the space under the hood. Check your mirrors. Signal and pull off the road.

FIRE

Cars seldom catch on fire, even after a crash. If yours does, though, or if you see or smell smoke, pull off the road and stop immediately. As quickly as you can, turn off the engine and get all passengers out of and away from the car. If the fire is small and only in the passenger section, you can try to put it out with a fire extinguisher (a 1-pound dry-chemical extinguisher should be carried in the glove compartment or trunk).

If you do not have a fire extinguisher, use water, sand, dirt, or snow. If you cannot put the fire out quickly, get away from the vehicle before the fire spreads. It may cause an explosion.

FLAT TIRE

There may come a time when you walk out to your car and find that you have a flat tire. There are many causes of flats. Sometimes, the air leaks slowly from the tire while you are driving. When this happens, you may notice a gradual change in the way your car steers. As in a blowout, the car begins to pull toward one side if the soft tire is in the front. If a rear tire is leaking air, the car may start to fishtail. In either case, maintain steering control, signal, pull well off the road, and stop. As soon as you stop, set up flares or warning triangles 30 and 60 meters (100 and 200 feet) behind your car to alert other drivers.

A flat tire must be changed as soon as possible. If you are not careful, this can be dangerous. To be safe, take the following steps:

1. Make sure the car is parked on a level surface.
2. With the engine off, set the parking brake and place the selector lever in *park*. (In a manual-transmission car, put the gearshift lever in *reverse*.)
3. Get all the passengers out of the car.
4. Use a rock or a piece of wood 10 cm by 20 cm by 5 cm thick (4 inches by 8 inches by 2 inches thick) to block the wheel diagonally across from the tire that is flat.

All automobile manufacturers provide a list of steps to follow for changing a tire. The list can usually be found in the owner's manual or in the trunk. Here are the steps on most lists:

1. Remove the jack, jack handle, lug wrench (sometimes it is part of the jack handle), wheel block, base board, and spare tire from the trunk or storage area. Place the spare on the ground near the flat tire.
2. Remove the wheel cover from the wheel with the flat tire. Loosen the lug nuts that hold the wheel, but do not take them all the way off.
3. Following the instructions in your owner's manual, place the jack in the proper position on a solid base (the road shoulder, if

Changing a tire can be hazardous if you are not cautious. For the correct way to change a tire, read the steps outlined in the text.

flat, or a base board 15 cm by 30 cm by 2.5 cm thick (6 inches by 12 inches by 1 inch thick). Jack the car up until the flat tire clears the ground.

4. Check to make sure the wheel block is in place. Do not get under the car or so near it that you would be injured if the jack failed or if the car fell off the jack.

5. Take the lug nuts and place them in the wheel cover so they will not get lost.

6. Pull off the wheel.

7. Put on the wheel with the spare tire and replace the lug nuts.

8. Tighten the lug nuts, first by hand and then with the lug wrench.

9. Jack the car down to the ground and remove the jack. Make the lug nuts as tight as you can with the wrench. Replace the wheel cover.

10. Place the flat tire, jack, jack handle, lug wrench, wheel block, and base board back in the trunk or storage area.

After you change the tire, have the flat repaired or replaced right away. This way, you will always have a spare tire when you need one.

DEAD BATTERY

If you turn the ignition switch to start and nothing happens, the battery is probably dead. You can usually still start the car by attaching your battery to the battery of another vehicle. This is called *jump starting*. Jump starting is fairly easy to do if you have jumper cables. Follow these steps:

1. Place the vehicles so that the jumper cables will reach from the good battery of one car to the dead battery of the other.
2. Turn off the ignition and electrical equipment in both vehicles.
3. Shift both vehicles to *park* (*neutral* in a manual-transmission vehicle) and set the parking brakes.
4. Make sure both batteries are of the same voltage. Remove the cell caps and check the fluid level in both batteries. (If the fluid is frozen, do not try to jump-start the battery. It may explode.) Cover both batteries with a heavy cloth to protect against splashing of boiling battery fluid.
5. Attach one end of a jumper cable to the positive (P or +) post of the good battery. Attach the other end of the same cable to the positive post of the dead battery.

Old batteries will not always charge when a car has been standing for a long time. Learn the proper method for jump-starting your car.

6. Attach one end of the other jumper cable to the negative (N or −) post of the good battery. Attach the other end of the same cable to the engine block or frame of the car that has the dead battery. (This connection should be as far away from the battery as possible to protect against splashing in the event of an explosion.)
7. Start the engine that has the good battery. Hold down the accelerator pedal so that the engine runs at a high idle.
8. Start the engine of the car with the dead battery.
9. Take off the jumper cables, one at a time, in the reverse order from which you attached them—negative connections first.

WET ENGINE

When you drive through water, even at a slow speed, the water may splash the engine and make it stall. There are two reasons why a wet engine stalls:

1. Water may short out the electrical system.
2. Water may be drawn into the engine combustion chamber through the air cleaner and carburetor.

If your car stalls while or after going through water, steer to the side of the road. When you are off the road, turn off the ignition. Then raise the hood and check for water around the spark plugs. If the plugs are wet, dry the porcelain part of the plug with a cloth (be careful if the engine is hot). If the car still does not start, wait until the engine dries. If it is not raining, leave the hood up. The air can speed the drying.

OVERHEATED ENGINE

Engine overheating can be caused by driving in slow-moving traffic during hot weather; climbing up long, steep grades; a loose or broken fan belt; a broken water pump; not enough coolant in the cooling system; a stuck or broken thermostat; or a clogged radiator.

The most common problem is not having enough antifreeze or coolant in the radiator. In the winter, lack of antifreeze can lead to ice buildup in the radiator. This blocks the flow of water and causes the engine to overheat. In the summer, lack of coolant prevents proper

If your car overheats, pull off the road and turn the engine off. Let the engine cool. Then remove the radiator cap with a cloth or towel. Stand away from the radiator when you remove the cap.

heat transfer. Heat builds up in the engine, the fluid in the radiator starts to boil, and steam starts to come out of the front of the car.

If the needle of the temperature gauge is going toward *hot* or if the temperature warning light starts to flash, signal and pull off the road. Wait until the engine has fully cooled off before you open your radiator to check the fluid level in it. (If you remove the radiator cap, even when the radiator is operating at normal temperatures, the pressure inside the system could cause the fluid to boil over and scald you.)

While you wait for the engine to cool, see if you can spot any problems. Check for a broken hose or a loose hose connection that may need to be tightened. See if the fan belt is broken. After the engine has cooled, slowly unscrew the radiator cap and remove it. (Protect yourself by covering the cap with a cloth.) If the fluid in the radiator is low, add coolant or water. Cold water, however, could damage an overheated engine. To prevent damage, start the engine and let it run at idle speed as you add the water or coolant. (If it is winter or if you are using an air conditioner, you must add antifreeze to the water.) After you have filled the radiator to normal level, screw the cap on it tightly. Check the engine gauge to see that the engine stays cool. For most problems other than loss of antifreeze or coolant, you will probably have to call for emergency road service.

If you are caught in a traffic jam and your engine begins to heat up, shift to neutral. Race the engine by pressing on the accelerator. This will increase the flow of coolant around the engine and reduce overheating.

HEADLIGHT FAILURE

Both headlights rarely fail at the same time. But if one headlight goes out, you may not notice it until the second light fails, too. Headlight failure may have several causes. The most frequent ones are a blown fuse or a burned-out headlamp. No matter what the cause, you must bring the vehicle to a stop, off the road, as quickly and smoothly as possible. To do this, press the dimmer switch as you reduce speed. Headlamps seldom burn out on both high and low beams at the same time. If pressing the dimmer switch gives no light, turn on the turn indicators or the emergency four-way flashers. These can provide enough light to help you get off the road.

If you have no lights at all, look for the center- and side-lane markers on the pavement. They usually are bright white and provide some visibility. If other cars are coming toward or following you, their lights also will help you. When you bring your car to a stop well off the road, set up flares or reflective triangles to let other drivers know you are there.

Vehicle breakdowns range from minor inconveniences to serious hazards. Proper vehicle maintenance can help you avoid most breakdowns. Understanding what is involved will help you respond should a breakdown occur.

TO CONSIDER

1. Name four types of vehicle failure. Explain ways to avoid each type.

2. If your car is moving when a breakdown occurs, what is the first thing you must do?

3. If your brakes fail, what steps should you take, using your vehicle controls? If you cannot slow and stop your car using the controls, what actions should you take?

4. List three causes of engine failure. What steps should you take if your engine stops while you are moving in traffic?

5. If your car has power brakes and power steering, what will happen if the engine stalls? What should you do?

6. What should you do if your accelerator pedal gets stuck while you are driving in traffic?

7. What is the best way to change a flat tire? What precautions should you take when changing the tire?

8. Describe the correct way to jump-start a car that has a dead battery.

9. What should you do: (a) if your vehicle catches fire? (b) if your vehicle stalls while or after going through water?

10. List six causes of an overheated engine. What steps should you take if your car's temperature warning light starts to flash?

PROJECTS

Check a friend's or a family member's car. Is it equipped with a good spare tire, jacking equipment, jumper cables, flares or warning triangles, a flashlight, and a fire extinguisher? If any of these items are missing, ask the car owner why. Does the owner think they are unnecessary?

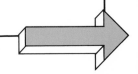

PERFORMING WELL AT THE WHEEL

10 UNIT

Unit X describes physical and emotional factors that can affect your ability to drive safely. Some of these factors may be temporary; others may be permanent. This unit tells you how to cope with both.

Chapter 25, "Drugs and Alcohol," discusses:
- how you can avoid the dangers of mixing drugs with driving.
- the effects of certain drugs.
- the effects of alcoholic beverages.
- some choices for drinkers who also drive.

Chapter 26, "Physical and Mental Impairments," discusses:
- how you can handle the effects of fatigue, emotions, and temporary illness.
- how you can make adjustments for vision, hearing, and physical handicaps.

DRUGS AND ALCOHOL

Some drugs impair a person's ability to drive. As a result, drug use is the cause of many accidents. Studies show that about 10 percent of the drivers involved in accidents had drugs other than alcohol in their bodies at the time of the accident.

DRUG USE AND ABUSE

Drug use means the taking of any drug, in any amount, under any condition—legally or illegally. Drivers who use drugs can be dangerous to themselves and to others. So keep these precautions about drugs in mind:

- *Avoid excessive drug use.* Do not take drugs when you do not have a medical reason to do so.
- *Avoid illegal drugs.* If possible, avoid any drugs that affect the skills critical for safe driving.
- *Read the label.* If you are taking an over-the-counter (or nonprescription) medicine, read the label carefully before you use it.
- *Ask your doctor.* Ask your doctor if the prescribed drug will affect your driving.
- *Avoid taking other people's drugs.* Drugs are prescribed for certain conditions. If they are not prescribed for you, do not take them.
- *Be cautious.* When a new ''superdrug'' is advertised, be especially critical. When using drugs, consider the risk and the effect of the drug. Avoid taking drugs that interfere with what you have to do. Remember that besides their intended purpose, drugs may have side effects. Drugs can also have different effects on different people. They can also have different effects on the same person at different times.

Do not take drugs when you have to drive. Legal as well as illegal drugs can greatly affect a person's ability to drive well.

PRESCRIPTION DRUGS

By law, prescription drugs can be prescribed only by a doctor or dentist. They can be bought only from a pharmacy. Directions for their use are usually printed on the label that the pharmacist puts on the container in which they are purchased. These directions must be followed exactly. If not, the drugs may not do what they are intended to do. In addition, they may cause dangerous side effects. Some drugs may affect your ability to stay alert. After you take them, you may fail to recognize and react to dangerous driving situations.

NONPRESCRIPTION DRUGS

Nonprescription drugs, or over-the-counter drugs, include lozenges, capsules, tablets, and syrups. By law, these drugs must provide "adequate directions for use." Before taking any nonprescription drug, read the label carefully. Check to see if driving after taking the drug is discouraged.

ILLEGAL DRUGS

Illegal drugs, or street drugs, are illegally sold without identification or prescription. One obvious danger in buying street drugs is not knowing their content. Even when the pushers know the content of a drug, they cannot be trusted to report it correctly or honestly. People have also purchased nondrug substances, thinking they were buying drugs. With street drugs, buyers also run the risk of having one drug substituted for another without their knowing it.

EFFECTS OF DRUGS

Drugs produce both wanted and unwanted effects. Unwanted effects are also known as *side effects*. Most drugs act by speeding up or slowing down the central nervous system. *Stimulants* speed it up. *Depressants* slow it down. *Hallucinogens* affect the way the drug user sees things. Some hallucinogens also have effects like stimulants or depressants. Stimulants and depressants can also affect the user the way hallucinogens do.

Many motor vehicle accidents are the result of a person's driving while under the influence of drugs. A driver's ability to react and to make decisions quickly can be affected by the use of drugs.

Let's take a look at some drugs and their effects.

Amphetamines speed up the central nervous system. When tired, some people use amphetamines to "keep going." A person taking amphetamines may feel more alert and self-confident. When the effect wears off, the user may be very tired and depressed.

Barbiturates have an effect that is similar to alcohol. They slow down the central nervous system. Some people use barbiturates to calm nervousness. When the effects of the drug wear off, depression often follows. If combined with alcohol, barbiturates can cause depression.

Tranquilizers, also called "downers," are depressants. They also slow down the central nervous system. They are used by people with nervous and emotional problems. Tranquilizers cause drowsiness, especially at first. People who use tranquilizers often combine them with alcohol. This combination of depressants and alcohol can stop the heart, reduce blood pressure, and stop the supply of oxygen to the brain.

Marijuana is a mild hallucinogen. Its effects vary widely. It can act as a stimulant or a depressant, depending on the user's mood and experience with the drug. The strength of marijuana also makes a difference. A small amount of strong marijuana may have a deep effect. Often, the use of marijuana results in drowsiness. People who use marijuana report problems in judging time and space. While under the effect of marijuana, people also tend to concentrate on one thing at a time, ignoring everything else around them.

Among young people, alcohol and marijuana are the most widely used drugs. Because marijuana causes a loss in driver skill, it can be a major threat to highway safety. Marijuana affects mood, vision, reaction time, and the ability to judge time. The drug has the greatest effect on new users.

MISUSE OF ALCOHOL

About one-half of all drivers admit to drinking and then driving at least once in a while. Some of them do not know the dangers involved. Others enjoy drinking and then find that they have to go someplace else by car. Some simply do not care. Others reduce the risk by not driving until they have sobered up.

SERIOUSNESS OF THE PROBLEM

If you drink an alcoholic beverage and then drive, you risk having an accident. Here are some figures:
- Alcohol is a factor in about one-half of all highway deaths. About 400 people a week die in alcohol-related crashes.
- About half of those killed in alcohol-related crashes are not the people who were drinking.
- Alcohol-related crashes account for about 60 percent of the young people (16 to 24 years old) killed on the highways. Some 40,000 young people who survive end up disfigured.

The percentages of alcohol in beer, wine, and hard liquor are not the same. However, the amount of alcohol in an average serving of each is about the same.

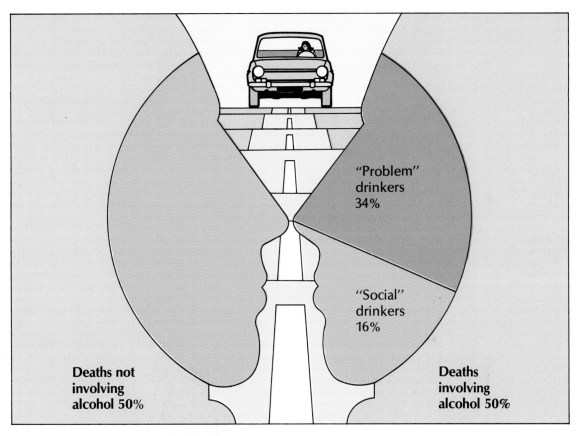

Alcohol is a factor in about half of all traffic deaths.

The more alcohol you drink before driving, the greater the chances of your having an accident. The increased accident risk begins even before you feel drunk. The following are the odds that an average driver who drinks alcoholic beverages 1 hour before driving will have an accident:

- 1 to 2 drinks—chances of an accident are slightly greater than if no alcohol were drunk.
- 3 to 4 drinks—chances of an accident double.
- 5 to 6 drinks—chances of an accident are 6 times greater.
- 7 to 8 drinks—chances of an accident are 25 times greater.

WHY ALCOHOL AFFECTS DRIVING

Alcohol is a clear, odorless, depressant drug. It impairs the brain and nervous system and prevents them from functioning properly.

The effects of alcohol begin with the first drink. In 1 hour's time, a standard serving of beer, wine, or liquor has the following effect on a person who weighs about 150 pounds:

- After one drink, inhibitions are lessened. The drinkers become less critical of themselves and others. Judgment begins to be affected. (BAC [blood-alcohol concentration]: 0.01 to 0.02 percent.)
- After two drinks, reaction time slows. Drinkers are even less critical of themselves and others. They appear relaxed and friendly. (BAC: 0.03 to 0.04 percent.)
- After three drinks, judgment is not sound. Drinkers do not think clearly. Their reasoning is less reliable. They say and do things that are rude and unreasonable. (BAC: 0.05 to 0.06 percent.)
- After four drinks, hearing, speech, vision, and balance are impaired. (BAC: 0.08 to 0.09 percent.)
- After five drinks, body parts do not seem to work together. Performing any task using hands and feet—even walking—is difficult. (BAC: 0.10 to 0.11 percent.)
- When average people drink twelve drinks each, their BAC reaches about 0.30 percent. At this level, they fall into a deep sleep or a coma. If and when the BAC reaches 0.50 percent, they will be in a deep coma and near death.

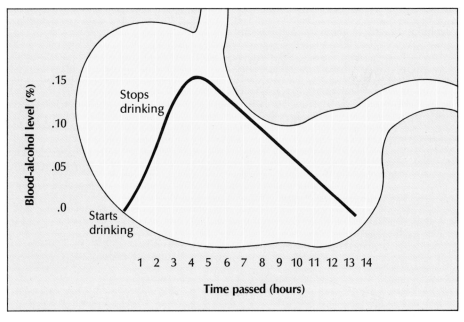

Alcohol enters the stomach and is absorbed into the bloodstream. Note that the level of alcohol in the bloodstream increases even after a person stops drinking.

HOW TO CONTROL THE EFFECTS OF ALCOHOL ON A GROUP

Drinking alcoholic beverages can be dangerous if it is not done with care. Mixing drinking with driving is *always* dangerous, no matter how much care is taken. There is only one sure way to control alcohol rather than letting it control you or your friends: Don't drink.

RESPONSIBILITY TO OTHERS

Everyone is responsible for keeping a drinker from driving. However, the person who is providing alcoholic beverages has the greatest responsibility. The one who gives a party, for example, knows who drinks, who drives, and who is most likely to combine the two.

KNOW THE SIGNS

Remember, judgment is one of the first things affected by alcohol. This includes the ability to judge the effect the alcohol is having. People who have had too much to drink generally do not recognize it. If they do, they may not admit it. So it is important for you to recognize these signs of too much drinking.
- Loud talking, slurred speech
- Dropping things, spilling drinks
- Walking unsteadily, using hands for support
- Perspiring, turning pale or red in the face

Any unusual behavior is also a possible sign. For example, a normally loud person may become quiet.

DECIDE IN ADVANCE

If you care about your friends and are concerned about road safety, you must decide in advance to prevent your friends from drinking too much. You must also be willing to prevent further drinking by those friends who have already drunk too much.

In making these decisions, it may help to realize that people who drink too much rarely remember what took place. Those who remember are likely to thank you for sparing them a hangover. They should also appreciate your caring about their safety.

GET HELP

If you host a party, try to get a few friends to help control the drinking. Arrange for these friends to (1) keep other people from drinking too much; (2) help cut off the supply of drinks to people who have had too much; (3) help if someone tries to continue drinking; (4) take charge of serving drinks to control the supply.

CONTROL THE SUPPLY

Do not have a lot of alcohol around. Putting the supply out all at once encourages people to drink. It also makes it hard to tell how much has been drunk. So set out a limited amount of alcohol. Do not serve a drink to someone who is already holding one. This only urges the person to drink more rapidly. It is also a mistake to pass the bottle. Passing the bottle around encourages people to drink too much. In order to get "their share," they often feel they must take some more each time the bottle is offered to them.

DO SOMETHING ELSE

Get your friends involved in activities other than drinking. Dancing, and games (except drinking games) that require people to set their drinks down, are good choices. Remember, a person who is holding a drink is likely to sip it.

HOW TO CONTROL YOUR OWN DRINKING

If you make the decision to drink, find your drinking limit and stay within it.

SET A LIMIT IN ADVANCE

Under the effects of alcohol, you cannot tell when you have had enough. Therefore, you need to set a limit in advance. Your body can get rid of about three-fourths of a standard drink in 1 hour. If your limit is 2 drinks in 2 hours, do not drink a third. If you do, you had better wait another hour before you drive.

Try to stay below your limit. It is harder to stop drinking if you become impaired. At that point, your control and your ability to make decisions are reduced.

Amount of beverage	Concentration of alcohol in bloodstream	Typical effects		Time required for all alcohol to leave body
1 highball (1½ oz. whisky) 1 cocktail (1½ oz. whisky) 3½ oz. fortified wine 5½ oz. ordinary wine 2 bottles (24 oz.) beer	0.03%	Slight changes in feeling		2 hours
2 highballs 2 cocktails 7 oz. fortified wine 11 oz. ordinary wine 4 bottles beer	0.06%	Feeling of warmth, mental relaxation, slight decrease of fine skills, less concern with minor irritations and restraints.	Increasing effects with variation among individuals and in the same individual at different times	4 hours
3 highballs 3 cocktails 10½ oz. fortified wine 16½ oz. (1 pt.) ordinary wine 6 bottles beer	0.09%	Buoyancy, exaggerated emotion and behavior, talkative, noisy, or morose.		6 hours
4 highballs 4 cocktails 14 oz. ordinary wine 22 oz. ordinary wine 8 bottles (3 qts.) beer	0.12%	Impairment of fine coordination, clumsiness, slight to moderate unsteadiness in standing or walking.		8 hours
5 highballs 5 cocktails 17½ oz. fortified wine 27½ oz. ordinary wine ½ pt. whisky	0.15%	Intoxication—unmistakable abnormality of bodily functions and mental faculties.		10 hours or more

STICK TO YOUR LIMIT

Do not drink more just because you do not feel the effects of the first few drinks. The BAC builds up in your body for a while even after you stop drinking. When you begin to feel the effects of alcohol, it may already be too late.

USE TIME

Give your body time to get rid of the alcohol. Follow these two simple guidelines: (1) Allow 1 hour for each alcoholic drink to leave your body, and (2) drink no more than one alcoholic beverage per hour.

KNOW YOUR CONDITION

Take yourself into account. Limit your drinking of alcoholic beverages in terms of your emotions, the situation, and your physical health.

ALTERNATIVES TO DRINKING AND DRIVING

PUT TIME BETWEEN DRINKING AND DRIVING

If you drink and have to drive, allow time for your BAC to decrease. Wait until you are no longer under the influence of alcohol.

DRINK AT HOME

The best way to avoid driving home drunk is not to leave home in the first place.

FORM A CARPOOL

If you are going to a party, get a group to drive there together. Arrange for one person not to drink and to drive the others home. If the one who was supposed to stay sober gets drunk, but another member of the group manages to stay sober, be sure your sober friend drives.

INVITE NONDRINKERS

Do not exclude your friends because they do not drink. They can drive the drinkers home.

Never allow a friend who has been drinking to drive. Call a taxi or help the person to the back seat.

Never allow a person who has drunk too much to drive home. Have that person stay overnight. An overnight stay allows the alcohol to get out of the system.

PLAN OVERNIGHT STAYS

If you are going to drink at someone's home, ask if you can stay overnight. Then there will be no need to drive.

CALL A FRIEND

If you drink too much, call a friend on the telephone and ask for help. Your friend may be willing to come over and give you a ride or drive your car.

HITCH A RIDE

If you find you have had too much to drink, park your car and leave it. Ride with a sober friend. You can pick up your car later.

STAY PUT

Stay where you are until you sober up. It may be only a few hours.

CALL HOME

Call home and tell your parents or another relative that you will be late. If necessary, ask one of them to pick you up. It may be hard to admit to them that you have had too much to drink, but it is better than driving in that condition.

TO CONSIDER

1. What are some precautions that you should remember concerning drugs and driving?

2. What can you do to cut down on your use of drugs?

3. Name four drugs and explain their effects on the behavior of drivers.

4. Why is drinking and driving a serious problem? Give examples to support your reasons.

5. Is alcohol a drug? How does it affect the human body?

6. Discuss how alcohol affects your decision-making abilities.

7. What are some of the things you can do to control the drinking at a party?

PROJECTS

1. Ask several experienced drivers what drugs besides alcohol they take before or while they are driving. Report your findings to your class.

2. Invite a local police officer and a traffic official to talk to your class about drinking and driving. Ask them what problems they face in trying to enforce laws relating to drinking and driving.

3. Ask your local pharmacist what precautions about driving he or she recommends to customers who purchase prescription drugs. Does the pharmacist feel that most customers follow the recommendations?

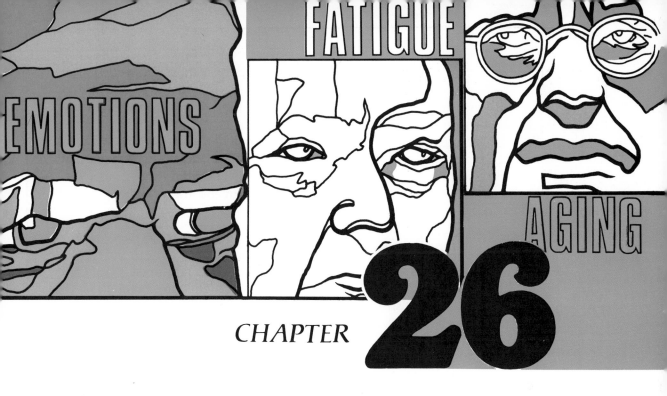

PHYSICAL AND MENTAL IMPAIRMENTS

Drugs and alcohol are not the only things that can impair your mental or physical abilities. Fatigue, emotional stress, and a variety of physical problems can, too. When they affect you, you must decide if you are fit to drive. If you must drive, is there any way to make up for the disability?

FATIGUE

Fatigue is a temporary condition that affects everyone. Fatigue impairs vision and the other senses. It weakens your judgment and ability to make decisions. If you are tired, you may ignore or fail to recognize emergency situations. You may also misjudge speed and distance and take unusual chances. Many tired drivers become irritable and overreact to minor irritations.

Fatigue can be caused by many things: a hard day at work, a day at the beach, emotional stress, or boredom. Other causes are the glare of the sun, illness, overeating, drinking alcoholic beverages, an overheated room or car, and nonstop driving over long distances.

WHAT CAN BE DONE ABOUT FATIGUE?

There is only one way to overcome fatigue. You must sleep. But there are a few things you can do to delay fatigue and maintain alertness, especially on long trips:
- Be well rested when starting the trip.
- Let plenty of fresh air circulate in the car.
- Wear good-quality sunglasses in bright sunlight.
- Avoid heavy foods and alcoholic beverages before you start and when you stop to eat.
- Stop periodically for rest and light exercise.

On long trips, 10-minute stops every 2 hours, plus regular stops to get fuel and food and to go to the restroom, can do a great deal to prevent fatigue and enable you to continue driving.

There is no fixed rule about how far you should drive. Just do not overexert yourself. When you have driven a reasonable distance, stop driving for the day. It is usually not a good idea to sleep in a car at the

On long trips, stop every 2 to 3 hours to rest. If you begin to yawn, or when you begin to rely on the radio, singing, or conversation to remain alert, do not continue driving.

Do not drive when you are very tired. Public rest areas are provided for drivers to take short naps and to walk around before continuing a trip.

side of the road. If possible, find a hotel, a motel, or a campground. If you must stop along the roadway to rest, follow these practices:
- Make sure you are as far off the highway as possible.
- Try to find a lighted area.
- Give yourself a little outside air, but keep the window closed enough to prevent entry from outside.
- Lock all the doors.
- Have parking lights on but all other electrical equipment off.
- Before beginning to drive again, get out of the car and make sure you are *completely awake*.

EMOTIONS

Strong emotions, such as fear and anger, can affect the way we grasp and use information. Therefore, emotions can and do affect the way we drive.

HOW DO STRONG EMOTIONS COME ABOUT?

Strong emotions are responses to the things that happen to us. Quite often, one emotion leads to another. For example, you are driving on a freeway when another motorist cuts in front of you. Your first response is fear. This quickly changes to anger, and you honk your horn.

Emotions such as fear, anger, and depression can affect your ability to think, reason, and make judgments. Delay or stop driving when you are emotionally upset.

Any number of situations may leave a person too upset to drive safely. Here are examples: (1) You have an argument, jump into the car, and drive off. (2) You are excited about a closely played ball game. As you drive home, the events of the game race through your mind. (3) A driver goes through a red light or cuts in front of you. You get furiously angry. (4) You become impatient and frustrated while following a slow-moving car along a winding roadway. As the minutes tick by, you grow more and more eager to move out and pass.

GUIDES FOR CONTROLLING EMOTIONS

The following guidelines can help you keep strong emotions from interfering with your driving:

1. *Identify situations that can lead to upsets.* People often become emotional when they are faced with threatening situations.
2. *Plan your trip to allow enough time.* Many common traffic situations become frustrating when you are late. Avoid this by planning a trip well.
3. *Expect other drivers to make mistakes and have upsets.* All drivers make mistakes. Some persons may not have the skill or knowledge that they should have. But remember that the mistakes others make may be ones you have also made. If you have not already made them, you may make them in the future.
4. *Direct your emotions to the driving errors of persons rather than to the persons themselves.*
5. *Remember that your goals may conflict with the goals of others.* Other drivers do not have anything against you. They are only trying to meet their goals.
6. *Delay driving when upset.* Most emotional upsets are temporary. It is best, therefore, to wait until the emotion subsides.
7. *Stop driving if you become upset.* When you are upset, find a place to stop. Take a short walk around the car. This would be a good time to stop for gasoline or refreshments.
8. *Do not drive if you are depressed.* Some emotional upsets, such as grief and anxiety, may last for several days. A person in such a depressed state should not drive.

TEMPORARY ILLNESSES

The temporary illness of a usually healthy driver can be a serious safety problem. A driver with a temporary impairment often is not able to cope as well as someone with a permanent disability. For example, a person with one eye may drive more safely than a hay fever victim whose eyes are filled with tears.

Everyone suffers minor illnesses from time to time—headache, toothache, cold, upset stomach. Many of these temporary illnesses can reduce your vision; make you dizzy, drowsy, or nauseated; or cause you pain. They can also affect your timing and coordination. Any of these conditions make driving difficult and dangerous.

The medications you take for an illness can sometimes cause more problems than the illness itself when you try to drive. Read the labels on medicines carefully to find out if you can drive when you use them. When in doubt, ask a doctor or a pharmacist.

When you are sick, but not sick enough to be in bed, find out what effect the sickness will have on your driving. Then, if you can, take steps to minimize the effect. Finally, decide whether you should delay driving until you feel better. Your doctor can help you with these matters.

In small amounts, carbon monoxide can cause headache, dizziness, nausea, and loss of muscle control. In large amounts, it can cause death. When you drive, always leave the air vents or a window open to let in fresh air.

CARBON MONOXIDE POISONING

Carbon monoxide gas is a by-product of burning gasoline. It is colorless, odorless, tasteless, and poisonous. If a car's exhaust system does not work right, carbon monoxide may be drawn into the passenger compartment. Keep fresh air circulating in your car by adjusting the air vents or opening a window. This will reduce the effects of carbon monoxide.

AGING

Our ability to see and react is reduced as we grow older. Many of these changes are due to hardening of the arteries. This process can affect the entire body, including the heart, brain, nervous system, eyes, and ears. The changes occur gradually. In early stages, their effect is minor. But they can cause a person to become an unsafe driver.

The effects of aging vary from one person to another. Therefore, there is no specific age when a person should stop driving.

VISION AND HEARING

Good driving decisions are based on accurate information. You use your eyes to gather most of the information you need to drive safely. Therefore, if your vision is impaired, your ability to make decisions is also impaired.

Good hearing is also important for safe driving. However, people with hearing impairments can usually drive well. They make up for their poor hearing by using their eyes more effectively.

VISUAL ACUITY

Visual acuity is the ability to see clearly. Impaired visual acuity is the most common visual problem. If your visual acuity is not good, you may have difficulty identifying signs, signals, and roadway markings. You may also fail to notice objects that can influence your selection of a path of travel.

Most states require drivers to wear glasses when their visual acuity falls below a certain level. Some people's visual acuity, even when wearing glasses, cannot be made better than 6/22 (20/70). That means that they can accurately identify letters or objects 0.93 centimeter (3/8 inch) high at a distance of 6 meters (20 feet), when they should be able to identify them at 22 meters (70 feet). Some states grant these people restricted licenses. They are allowed to drive only under certain conditions, such as during the day.

If you need glasses, wear them. They will help you to gather the information you need to make sensible driving decisions.

50	**L D A T**	15.24
40	**T A L O E**	12.19
30	**A L D O T F**	9.14
20	**F L O T D E X C**	6.10
15	**F X V T D E A L**	4.75

FIELD OF VISION

The area to the left and to the right that you can see without turning your head is called your *field of vision*. It is important to have a broad field of vision when you drive. There is always a chance that objects may come at you from both sides. The sooner you see these objects, the easier it will be to avoid them.

Most people are able to see or detect motion at right angles to either side of them. This means that they have a field of vision of almost 180 degrees. Some people, however, have a very narrow field of vision. This is called *tunnel vision*.

A field of vision that is less than 140 degrees is considered an impairment.

Drivers whose field of vision is restricted can usually compensate for this handicap by glancing to the sides frequently and by using their side-view mirrors more than other drivers. However, this solution reduces the amount of attention the driver can give to the path ahead.

COLOR VISION

Color attracts attention. You can use your sense of color to organize your search of the traffic environment. For example, the color red from a traffic signal, a stop sign, or the brake lights of the car ahead should immediately tell you that you have to stop. Yellow indicates a warning sign. Blue or brown signs indicate no danger. They tell drivers about recreation areas and services available.

Color blindness should *not* seriously impair a person's ability to drive. For example, on nearly all traffic signals, red is at the top and green is at the bottom. A color-blind person can tell the meaning of traffic lights by their location and of warning signs by their shapes.

DISTANCE JUDGMENT AND DEPTH PERCEPTION

To drive safely, you need to be able to judge depth and the distance between objects. If you have difficulty judging depth or distance, you may not be able to control space in traffic. Distance judgments are more difficult to make when you are moving than when you are standing still. An accurate judgment of distance requires that both your eyes work together. Therefore, distance judgments are also more difficult if one eye is impaired. By practicing, though, it is possible to improve depth perception. To do this, you must learn to compare the sizes and shapes of objects at different angles and distances.

NIGHT VISION

Humans cannot see as well in the dark as they can in light. However, the ability to see in reduced light varies from person to person. Just because you can see well in the daytime does not mean that you will be able to see well at night. At night, you have to depend on the artificial lighting of street lamps and headlights to see the road. Artificial light is not as effective as daylight. Although artificial light helps you to see at night, its glare presents a problem for some drivers. The most frequent cause of glare is the headlights of oncoming vehicles. This glare can temporarily blind you. Avoid looking directly at the headlights of oncoming cars. Look at the right edge of the road ahead until an approaching car passes you. Even with this precaution, glare may affect your vision. Most people can adjust to glare and recover from it within a few seconds. If you find night driving difficult because of glare, have your eyes tested. It may be wise for you to avoid night driving whenever possible.

HEARING

It is hard to identify the direction or source of sound while driving a car. This is particularly true in the city. However, sound can give you information about other vehicles and about the condition of your own car. It can also alert you to hazards, such as trains, trucks, motorcycles, and emergency vehicles that are using sirens. You may hear these vehicles before you can see them.

PHYSICAL HANDICAPS

Most states issue a restricted driver's license to people with physical disabilities. This license permits them to operate only vehicles that have been equipped with special controls. With such vehicles, people who do not have the use of one or more limbs can still become skillful, safe drivers. A driver's license is very important for such people. It opens up job opportunities and provides them with the mobility that they otherwise would not have.

Restricted driver's licenses permit people with physical disabilities to operate vehicles equipped with special controls.

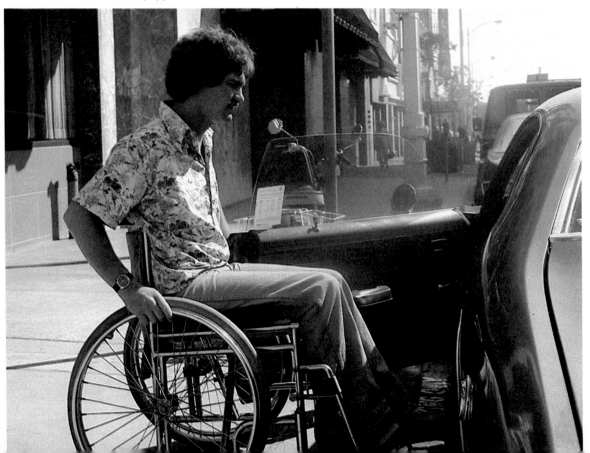

TO CONSIDER

1. List some causes of fatigue for drivers of motor vehicles. What can a driver do about fatigue?

2. How can drivers control their emotions? Give three examples.

3. Explain how illnesses can create special hazards for drivers.

4. Should people older than a certain age be allowed to drive? Why or why not?

5. Are good hearing and good vision of equal importance to safe driving? Explain your answer.

6. How do automobile manufacturers assist drivers who have physical handicaps?

7. If you must stop along the roadway to rest, what practices should you follow?

8. What causes carbon monoxide to be drawn into the passenger compartment of a car? What steps can you take to lessen the risk of carbon monoxide poisoning?

9. Define the term "visual acuity." What problems could you have if your visual acuity were poor?

10. What is the purpose of granting a restricted driver's license to people whose vision is not as good as it should be?

11. What clues to danger do we normally receive through hearing? Which of those clues would we also be able to see, as soon as we heard them?

PROJECTS

Investigate your state's rules about driver impairments. How often are drivers examined for impairments? Report to your class. Do you and your class think these examinations are adequate? Are the examinations given often enough?

LEARNING ABOUT MOTORCYCLES

Unit XI will help you become familiar with those aspects of motorcycling that are important for safe driving.

CHAPTER 27, "General Information about Motorcycles," tells you
- how to choose a motorcycle.
- why noise level should be kept down.
- why you should be insured.
- how to protect yourself on a motorcycle.
- what you should know about the motorcycle controls.
- how to conduct a premount inspection.
- how to start a motorcycle.
- how to drive a motorcycle.

CHAPTER 28, "Riding a Motorcycle in Traffic," discusses
- how to drive safely in traffic.
- how to carry a passenger safely.
- how to handle problems created by wind and fatigue.

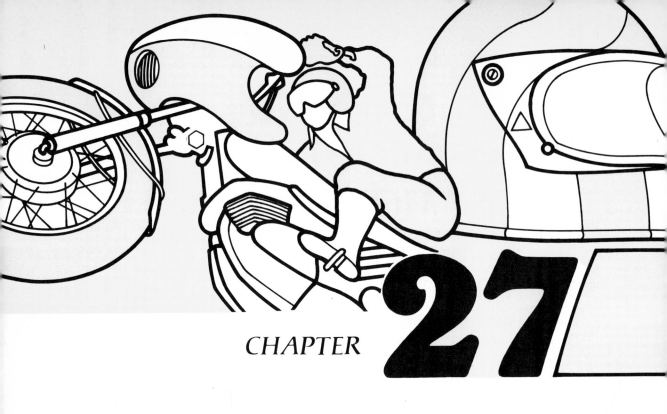

CHAPTER **27**

GENERAL INFORMATION ABOUT MOTORCYCLES

The number of motorcycles in use in the United States grew from 1.3 million in 1967 to over 5 million in 1976. This was due partly to their low price and low operating cost. But it was also because a motorcycle, or "bike," can be fun to drive. However, it can be very dangerous if it is not driven properly.

SELECTING A MOTORCYCLE

Think about the kind of driving you expect to do before you buy a motorcycle. Do you want one that handles best on pavement or on off-road trails? For local use, a motorcycle with a 100- to 200-cubic-centimeter engine will generally have enough power. If you plan to travel widely, a 350- to 500-cubic-centimeter engine will be better. If you plan to buy a used motorcycle, shop carefully; have the motorcycle inspected by a good mechanic. Avoid bikes with equipment that may make them hard to ride or to handle.

Shop carefully if you plan to buy a motorcycle. Inspect it thoroughly for safety features.

NOISE

Motorcyclists need the good will of motorists. Do not offend motorists by making unnecessary noise. Do not use modified exhaust systems that increase noise levels or drive in low gear at high engine speeds in residential areas.

INSURANCE

Motorcycle coverage and rates vary. Shop for the best buy. Make sure your insurance covers passenger injury as well as property damage. Since motorcycle accidents often result in injuries, buy coverage for medical payments if you can.

EXPOSURE AND THE MOTORCYCLIST

Motorcycle riders have very little protection against bad weather or injuries caused by falls or collisions. They are also exposed to greater physical demands than a person driving a car. Motorcyclists are pushed constantly by wind and air resistance. They are exposed to engine vibration and engine noise. These things tire the rider after a short time. Alcohol and drugs are especially dangerous to a motorcyclist. Even a slight lapse of attention may result in loss of control.

VISIBILITY

Motorcycles are smaller than most other vehicles; so they are often not seen by other drivers. Some drivers may not even think to look for a motorcycle in their blind spot. Because of their size, motorcycles do not fill a traffic lane; therefore, drivers of cars often crowd motorcycles. Many drivers do not realize that a bike needs at least as much room as a car to maneuver.

PROTECTIVE DEVICES

Motorcycle riders are not protected by a steel passenger compartment, as in a car. In an accident, their primary protection is proper clothing. So it is important for the cyclist to choose clothing that provides good protection.

HELMETS

Head injuries are the major cause of deaths among motorcyclists. Without a doubt, a helmet is the most important piece of equipment a motorcyclist can wear. Buy a helmet that meets or exceeds U.S. Department of Transportation safety standards. Select a bright-colored one so that you can be seen more easily. The helmet should fit comfortably. It should be strapped on securely so that it will not come off if you fall. (Avoid helmets with snap fasteners.) It should also cover your ears to cut out much of the road noise that causes fatigue.

EYE PROTECTION

Proper eye protection, such as goggles or a face shield, makes it easier for the motorcyclist to see in glare, dust, or wind. It also protects the eyes from bugs, grit, and other objects. The goggles or shield should be free from scratches and made of material that will not shatter in a crash. A face shield should provide clear vision to either side. It should be fastened securely to the helmet so that it cannot be blown off. For bright daylight use, gray- or amber-tinted lenses help to reduce eye fatigue. But do not use tinted lenses at night. If you wear prescription eyeglasses, make sure they are shatter-resistant.

This motorcyclist is properly dressed for riding a motorcycle. He is wearing heavy-duty pants, a heavy jacket, helmet, goggles, leather gloves, and leather boots.

JACKETS AND PANTS

All parts of your body should be protected by a tough covering. The best protection for your skin is leather clothing. If you do not want to buy leather clothing, then wear a heavy cotton twill, such as denim.

Wear light colors. They are easier to see than dark colors. If you have a dark leather jacket, wear a reflective vest over it. A jacket should fit snugly enough so that it will not catch the wind and cause problems with balance. But there should be room to put on bulky underclothing in cold weather. A jacket should not ride up, exposing the small of your back. Sleeves should be long enough to cover your wrists. Pants should fit snugly but should not cut into you as you sit on the motorcycle. The cuffs should stay down at your ankles.

GLOVES

You usually put out your hands to cushion a fall. In a motorcycle fall, your hands can be badly injured if they are not well protected by gloves. For riding in cold weather, long gloves are best. They prevent the wind from blowing up your sleeves. For warm weather, use wrist-length driving gloves.

BOOTS

Always wear boots to protect your feet and lower legs from scrapes and burns. Motorcycle boots should have nonskid soles and heels, steel toes, and heel guards. The tops of the boots should be at least 8 centimeters (3 inches) above your ankles to shield you from contact with the exhaust pipes or engine. Anything less than a high-cut, solid leather boot could result in serious foot and ankle injuries.

RAINSUIT

You should not ride a motorcycle in the rain or during bad weather. But if you must ride under such conditions, a rainsuit specially designed for motorcyclists will help protect you against the weather. It should fit properly at the neck, wrists, and ankles. It should be large enough to wear over your regular motorcycle outfit.

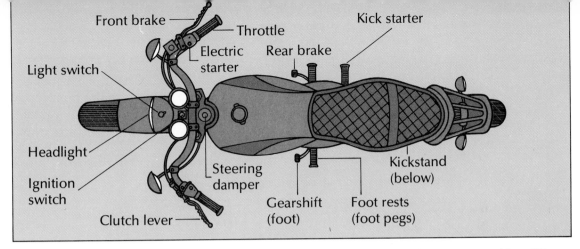

Front brake — Throttle   Kick starter
Light switch   Electric   Rear brake
starter
Headlight
Ignition   Steering   Kickstand
switch   damper   (below)
Clutch lever   Gearshift   Foot rests
(foot)   (foot pegs)

A motorcycle has many of the same controls as a car, but they are operated in a different way.

CONTROLS

To operate a motorcycle, you must be seated comfortably in the saddle. If the seat is adjusted properly, you will be able to use the controls without straining or throwing the motorcycle off-balance.

All the controls are not the same on all motorcycles. Before you use an unfamiliar motorcycle, first learn where all the controls are and how they are operated.

BRAKES

The front and rear brakes should be used together. The lever for the front brakes is on the right handlebar. The front brake provides most of

The rear brake is operated with a pedal on the right side. The front brake is operated with a lever on the right handlebar. The rear brake should always be applied lightly just before the front brake.

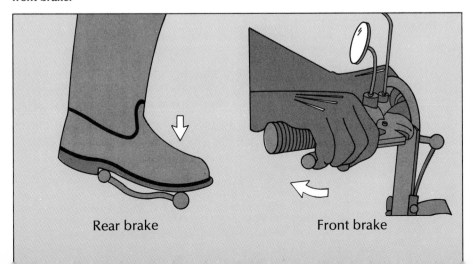

Rear brake   Front brake

the braking power (about three-quarters of the braking effort). Therefore, it should be squeezed gradually. If the brake handle is squeezed hard and quickly, the brakes may lock. This could cause the motorcycle to go into a skid, especially on wet pavement. The rear brake pedal, which is on the right side of the cycle, is operated by pressing down with the right foot.

The throttle is operated with a hand grip on the handlebar.

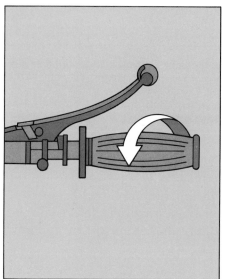 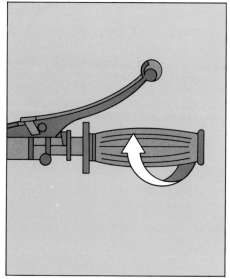

To increase engine speed   To decrease engine speed

THROTTLE

The *throttle* (accelerator) is controlled with a twist grip at the end of the right handlebar. Twisting the grip toward you increases engine speed. Twisting the grip away from you slows down the engine.

CLUTCH LEVER

Most motorcycles have a manual clutch, operated by a lever near the end of the left handlebar. Closing your hand (pulling the lever toward you) disengages the clutch. This allows you to change gears. Opening your hand gradually to release the lever engages the clutch again. Motorcycles equipped with an automatic transmission do not need a clutch.

302

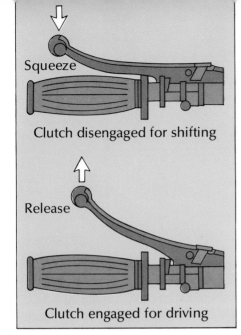

Squeeze

Clutch disengaged for shifting

Release

Clutch engaged for driving

The clutch lever

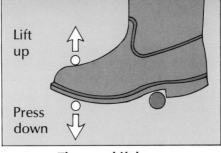

Lift
up

Press
down

The gearshift lever

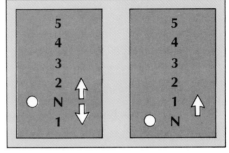

Common gear patterns

The clutch is operated with a lever on the left handlebar. The gearshift lever is usually a pedal on the left side of the motorcycle.

GEARSHIFT LEVER

The *gearshift lever* on a motorcycle is foot-operated. The lever is located directly ahead of the left footrest. Generally, there are four or five gears, plus a *neutral* position. There is no *reverse*. Your owner's manual will explain the gear-shift pattern for your motorcycle.

IGNITION SWITCH

Motorcycles have a key-operated ignition switch below the fuel tank or near the middle of the handlebars. The standard positions are *off* and *on*. There are many motorcycles that have *light* and *park* positions, too. Both the *on* and *light* positions turn on the ignition and start the engine. (On some motorcycles, both headlights and taillights are on when the switch is in *on* and the engine has started.) When the switch is in the *park* position, only the taillight is on. You can remove your key when you are in *park* or *off*.

ENGINE CUTOFF SWITCH

The *engine cutoff switch*, also called the *kill switch*, is on the right handlebar. In an emergency, you can stop the engine with this switch.

For example, if the throttle sticks, you can stop the engine without taking your hand from the handlebar. If you use this switch to shut off the engine once you have stopped, turn off the ignition also.

LIGHT SWITCH

Most motorcycles have a light switch that is not part of the ignition switch. It may be located on either handlebar.

DIMMER SWITCH

The *dimmer switch* may be part of the light-switch control. It sets the beam of the headlight to either *high* or *low*. It is located on the left handlebar.

HORN BUTTON

This button is found on the left handlebar.

TURN-SIGNAL SWITCH

This directional switch is located on the left handlebar. When you push the switch to *L*, the left front and left rear signal lights flash on and off. When you push the switch to *R*, the right signal lights flash on and off. On most motorcycles, turn signals do not go off by themselves after the driver has made a turn. They must be switched off.

STARTER

Most motorcycles have either an electric starter or a kick starter. Some have both. The *electric-starter* button is usually on the right handlebar. You push in this button to start the engine after you have turned the ignition switch to *on*. The gear-shift lever must be in *neutral*. The *kick starter*, located behind the right foot peg, has the same function as the electric starter. Usually, it must be flipped out before it can be kicked to start the engine.

CHOKE

The *choke lever* controls the air-fuel mixture that goes to the engine. It can be found on either side of the engine or on one of the handlebars.

To start a cold engine you must

1. turn the choke lever to *on.*
2. start the engine.
3. turn the lever to *off* when the engine is warm; otherwise, the engine will stall.

FUEL-SUPPLY VALVE

The *fuel-supply valve,* or *fuel cock,* controls the fuel flow from the fuel tank to the engine. Located below the fuel tank, it has three positions: *on, off,* and *reserve.* The *reserve* position releases fuel from the reserve tank and lets it flow into the main fuel tank when that tank is dry.

INSTRUMENT CLUSTER

At the center of the handlebars are the speedometer, odometer, high-beam indicator light, *neutral* indicator light, and turn-signal indicator light. Some motorcycles also have a *tachometer* (which shows engine revolutions per minute) and a *tripometer* (which shows kilometers or miles ridden).

STEERING DAMPER

Some motorcycles are fitted with a *steering damper.* The damper reduces the tendency of the front wheel to kick or wobble. Screwing down (tightening) the damper makes the front wheel more stable at high speeds. Loosening the damper makes the front wheel more maneuverable in city traffic.

PREMOUNT INSPECTION

The motorcycle should be checked each time you plan to ride it. The inspection of a motorcycle is more detailed than the predriving inspection of a car. A faulty motorcycle can endanger your life. Therefore, defects must be found and repaired.

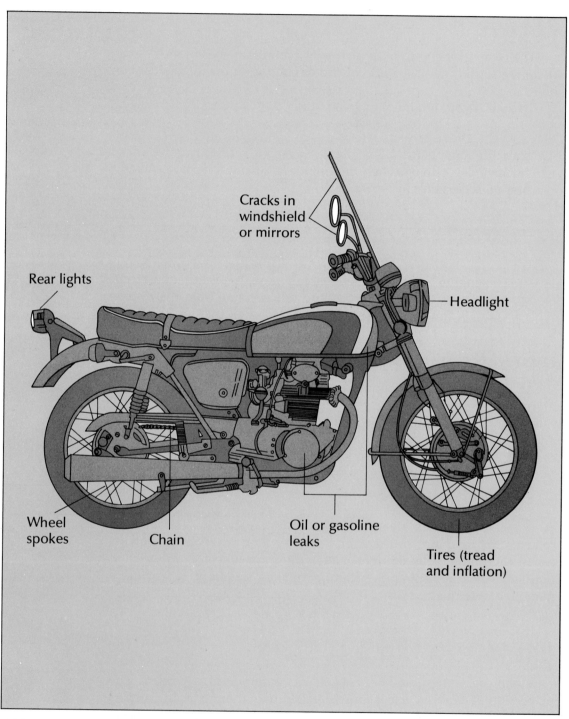

Make a premount inspection of all these items each time you prepare to drive.

TIRES AND WHEELS

Check the tires to be sure they are inflated to the right pressure. Look for wear and cuts in the tire sidewalls and tread. Remove any small objects stuck in the tread. The front tire usually wears more quickly on the sides of the tread than the rear tire does. The rear tire wears more quickly in the center. A front tire that has a thin side tread will have less traction on turns. A rear tire that has a thin center tread may skid while turning or when braking hard. Check the wheel rims for dents and make sure that all the spokes are tight.

CONTROL CABLES

Check all control cables, especially the clutch and the brake cables. Look for signs of wear, loose connections, and broken cables. Lubricate the cables at regular intervals. Replace worn cables.

BRAKES

Check the front hand-brake lever and its mounting bracket for cracks and loose screws. If the front brake is a hydraulic-disc brake, check the fluid-reservoir level. Check the rear brake by stepping down on the brake pedal. The pedal should feel solid and move down only a short distance.

GASOLINE AND OIL LEAKS

Gas or oil leaks can be very dangerous. At highway speeds, leaking gasoline or oil may be blown onto the rear tire, reducing traction. Check the engine and transmission oil levels and make sure all seals are tight. A lack of oil in the engine could cause it to *seize* (suddenly stop moving). This could lock your rear wheel and make you lose control. Check to see that you have enough gasoline. Running out of gas can be dangerous if it happens in a place where you cannot get off the road quickly.

CHAINS

Check the drive chain to see if it is adjusted properly. A chain that is too tight wears rapidly. A chain that is loose can jam around a *sprocket* (a toothlike gear on the edge of a wheel that holds the chain). This would cause the rear wheel to lock. Also, the chain should be lubricated   to prevent unnecessary wear.

ELECTRICAL ACCESSORIES

Make sure all four turn signals flash when they are turned on and are bright enough to be seen. Make sure that both the high and low beams of the headlight are working. Try each of the brake controls to be sure that each one flashes the brake light. Check the horn.

WINDSHIELD

If the motorcycle has a windshield, check it for cracks. Under strong wind pressure, a small crack can result in a completely shattered windshield. Also, spots and cracks in the rider's path of vision make it difficult to see the road.

MIRRORS

Clean and adjust both mirrors before you start. Never steer with one hand while you try to adjust the mirror with the other. Adjust each mirror to let you see about half the width of the lane behind you and part of the lane next to you.

HANDLING A MOTORCYCLE

A motorcycle handles very differently from a car. For instance, a motorcycle is far more affected by weather and road conditions. Like a bicycle, a motorcycle is not very stable. It can easily be *spilled* (tipped over). A pothole in the road that would not be a serious problem for a car might put a motorcycle out of control. Bumps or dips in the road, lane markings, grease, oil, and loose material on the road can affect a motorcycle's traction. Strong, gusting winds reduce stability. This can be a very serious problem at high speeds.

PREPARING TO GET UNDERWAY

After you have completed the premount checks, follow these steps to get ready to drive the motorcycle:

STARTING THE ENGINE

1. Open the fuel cock.
2. Straddle the motorcycle and balance it.
3. Pull in on the front brake lever to keep the bike from moving.
4. Set the choke if the engine is cold; turn on the ignition.
5. Check to make sure the transmission is in *neutral*.
6. Open the throttle by turning the throttle grip slightly toward you.
7. Pull in the clutch lever.
8. Press the ignition button or kick down on the kick-starter lever. (Use the ball of your right foot and kick all the way down to avoid injury in case it kicks back.)
9. If the engine is cold, allow it to run at idle speed for a moment. Gradually, turn the choke off until the engine begins to run evenly.

PUTTING THE MOTORCYCLE IN MOTION

Getting a motorcycle moving is similar to making a lateral maneuver with a car.

Follow these steps to start the motorcycle. If the engine is cold, give it time to warm up.

1. Open fuel cock.

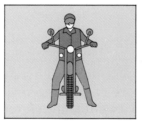
2. Straddle the motorcycle.

3. Apply rear brake.

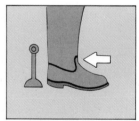
4. Release kick-stand.

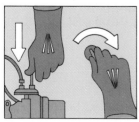
5. Set the choke or prime with kick starter and turn on ignition.

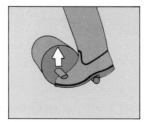
6. Shift to neutral.

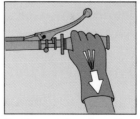
7. Open the throttle slightly.

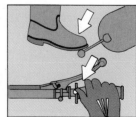
8. Start the engine with the electric starter or kick starter.

1. Signal your move into traffic.
2. Pull in the clutch lever and shift into first gear.
3. Place your left foot on the ground and your right foot lightly on the rear brake pedal. Doing this prevents the motorcycle from moving.
4. Check the mirrors. They should be adjusted to give as wide a view as possible of traffic to the rear. Look over your shoulder to make sure there is a clear path of travel.
5. Increase the throttle slightly and gradually engage the clutch lever.
6. Place both feet on the footrests as soon as possible.
7. Shift upward through the gears without gunning the engine.

GEAR SELECTION

The different gears allow you to keep the engine speed at the most efficient level. First gear is used for moving the motorcycle from a stopped position. It can also be used when driving in slow-moving traffic or when climbing very steep hills. As your speed increases, higher gears should be used. The highest, or top, gear is used for *cruising* (maintaining steady, constant speed while driving long distances). To gain more pulling power on steep upgrades, you sometimes have to *downshift* (change to a lower gear). You may also have to downshift when you reduce speed or prepare to stop.

SHIFTING UP

To shift up through the gears, use the following procedures:

1. Pull in the clutch lever with your left hand and turn the throttle away from you to reduce engine speed slightly.
2. Shift to the desired gear with your left foot.
3. Gradually release the clutch lever and twist the throttle toward you with your right hand.

As you increase your speed, repeat these steps until you are in the proper gear.

DOWNSHIFTING

This is almost the same as shifting up through gears. However, as you pull in the clutch, twist the throttle away from you to reduce engine speed. At the same time, move the gear selector to the next lower gear.

STEERING AND MOTORCYCLE STABILITY

On a motorcycle, steering and stability are related. A motorcycle is balanced so that it steers in the direction in which it is leaning. Heavy or poorly distributed loads make a motorcycle less stable, especially if the load is improperly tied down.

CORNERING

Before driving through a curve or around a corner, (1) estimate its sharpness, (2) check the available visual lead, and (3) judge whether the road surface is banked, crowned, rutted, or slippery. This will help you choose the best speed. You may have to downshift. If you have to brake, do so before you enter the curve. Use gentle acceleration as you go around. This will keep the motorcycle more stable.

Apply your brakes as you approach a curve, not while you are in it. Then, as you leave the curve, accelerate.

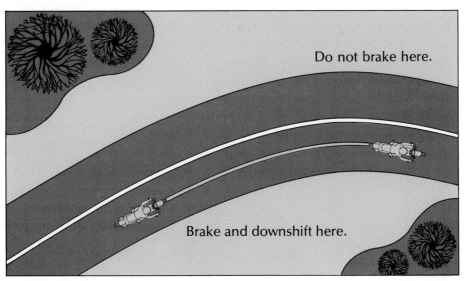

USING THE BRAKES

Apply the front and rear brakes together. Increase the pressure on the brakes gradually to avoid losing traction. The front brake has greater stopping force than the rear brake because the weight of both the driver and the motorcycle is thrown forward when the brakes are applied. This weight transfer presses the front tire more firmly on the road surface and produces more traction. If you use the rear brake only, you lose most of your braking power. The rear wheel can also slide more readily than the front wheel. It is a good idea for new motorcyclists to spend time practicing braking in a large, clear area.

ADJUSTING BRAKING TO THE ROAD SURFACE

It is very important to learn to adjust your braking to the road-surface conditions. Scan the road ahead. Avoid braking where the surface looks slippery. If you have to slow down quickly on a slippery surface, pump the brakes.

PARKING AND SECURING THE MOTORCYCLE

A motorcycle must be parked in a legal parking space. Parking at a right angle between two closely spaced cars is illegal. It can also result in damage to the motorcycle if one of the cars is maneuvered out of the space. When parking a motorcycle, leave it in a well-lit area. A case-hardened, heavy link chain with a strong lock is a good investment. Use a chain that is long enough to anchor the frame of the motorcycle to a solid object, such as a lamp post or a street sign. Alarm systems are also useful for discouraging thieves.

When you park, always secure your motorcycle. Use a heavy chain, or similar material, and a strong lock.

TO CONSIDER

1. What are some things you should consider before purchasing a motorcycle?

2. Why is it important to include coverage for medical payments in your motorcycle insurance policy?

3. Describe proper motorcycling clothing. Why are certain types of clothing better than others?

4. Explain how the controls of a motorcycle are different from the controls of a car.

5. List and explain the main controls of the motorcycle.

6. What should be checked in the premount inspection?

7. Describe the steps you should follow to start a motorcycle, to shift up and down, to corner, and to brake to a stop.

8. What steps should be taken to secure a parked motorcycle?

9. What special visual problems do motorcyclists have? Do motorcyclists have any visual advantages?

PROJECTS

1. Watch the behavior of motorcycle drivers in traffic. How many drivers have very noisy vehicles? How many take unnecessary risks? In general, are motorcycle drivers better or worse than automobile drivers? Tell your class what you find.

2. Report on the regulations for owning and operating motorcycles in your state. How do these regulations differ from those relating to automobile ownership and licensing?

3. Interview a motorcycle dealer. Ask for suggestions on protecting your motorcycle against theft.

CHAPTER

28

RIDING A MOTORCYCLE IN TRAFFIC

To drive safely, motorcyclists must use defensive driving tactics. They should have a good visual lead and scan the road ahead.

SEARCHING THE ROAD

A well-developed visual search is essential for avoiding accidents. Motorcyclists sit higher than car drivers. Therefore, they enjoy a better field of vision. Furthermore, they do not have blind spots.

BLOCKS TO GATHERING INFORMATION

Motorcyclists do have some problems, though. For example, rear vision is poor if the rear-view mirrors vibrate too much or if the mirrors are not adjusted properly. Tinted visors or goggles reduce vision in poor light. Goggles with thick frames reduce side vision. (You must wear goggles, however, to keep your eyes from watering or from being struck by flying objects.)

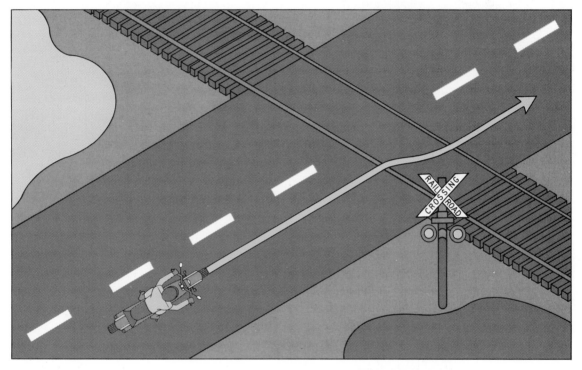

Drive across railroad tracks at as close to a right angle as you can. This will prevent the rear wheel from spinning or the front wheel from getting caught between the tracks.

SCANNING THE ROAD SURFACE

Never assume that the road ahead is clear of hazards. Scan the road for oil, gravel, holes, sewer drains, bumps, railroad tracks, and so on. Sewer drains can be especially hazardous. The front tire of the motorcycle may wedge into the grating. If you must ride over a bump, reduce speed and stand up on the footrests. This will keep you from bouncing off the motorcycle. Cross railroad tracks as nearly as possible at a right angle to the tracks. This prevents the rear wheel from spinning or the front wheel from getting caught.

315

Groups of motorcyclists should drive offset, not side by side. By riding offset, they can swerve safely, if necessary.

OBJECTS IN THE ROADWAY

Motorcyclists have a special reason for keeping a good following distance. An object that falls from another vehicle may force you to take evasive action. For instance, you may suddenly see a muffler lying on the road. The only way to avoid it may be a quick lateral maneuver. If you turn quickly, however, you risk being hit by other vehicles. To reduce this risk, try to squeeze by the object without leaving your lane. To do this, you must move quickly. If you must leave your lane, check first for other vehicles coming up alongside. Only under the most extreme conditions should you change lanes without checking.

If you cannot safely swerve or stop to avoid striking an object in the road, keep your cycle up straight and go over the obstacle in a straight line. If you are forced to drive over a sharp object, get off the road as soon as possible and check your tires.

As you drive, scan the road ahead. The following hazards often can be found on the road: water, oil, mud, ice, wet leaves, and other slippery substances. These can cause a sudden loss of traction. Shaded portions of the road can be especially slippery when the leaves fall during wet or freezing weather. Under such conditions, any changes in speed or direction should be made as gradually as possible. Avoid driving in the center of a traffic lane. Oil and water that leak from cars collect here. This problem is especially bad at intersections. Painted lane markings can also become slick, especially when wet.

RESPONDING TO ANIMALS

Animals, particularly dogs, can be dangerous to motorcyclists. Try to anticipate their movements. If you can, accelerate away from them. *Do not swerve to miss an animal.* Animals will often dodge out of the way if the driver keeps going straight. If the animal does not dodge, you are more likely to keep control if you strike the animal while you are in an upright position.

SEEING AND BEING SEEN

After automobile-motorcycle collisions, most car drivers claim that they did not see the motorcyclist. To increase your chances of being seen by other drivers, drive with your headlight on. Also wear a bright-colored helmet and reflective clothing.

POSITIONING TO BE SEEN

Ride in the path of the left wheel of the vehicle ahead. This will let the driver ahead see you in the rear-view mirror. You will also be more visible at intersections, and you will avoid the slippery center part of the lane.

Anticipate times when other drivers' vision will be limited. This is especially true at intersections.

Do not get in other drivers' blind spots.

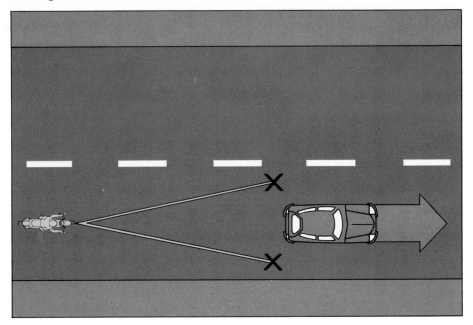

POSITIONING TO SEE

Stay well behind any vehicle you are following. This lets you see past the vehicle ahead and helps you anticipate when you may have to stop. If you are forced to ride on the right side of the outside lane, you should

1. scan for parked cars about to pull out.
2. check for car passengers about to open doors.
3. watch for pedestrians (particularly children).
4. look for vehicles that may turn left in front of you.
5. watch for vehicles approaching from the right side or backing out of driveways.

SPECIAL TRAFFIC CONDITIONS

When a large vehicle, like a trailer truck, comes toward you from the opposite direction, move to the right side of your lane. Doing this will cut down the effect of wind drafts and turbulence.

Driving in the space between lanes of cars is illegal and very dangerous. Drivers do not expect you to be there. The small gap between lanes can close suddenly. When you drive with other motorcyclists, do not drive side by side. Instead, drive *offset* (one behind the other on

Driving between lanes of cars is illegal and very dangerous. A car may swerve suddenly and cut you off.

opposite sides of the lane). This ensures that both drivers will have room to swerve, if necessary.

CHECKING INTERSECTIONS

Approach intersections, pedestrian crossings, and traffic signals cautiously and at a reduced speed. Double-check side streets, oncoming traffic, and sidewalks. If a traffic light changes to green as you come to it, scan for drivers hurrying through. Scan twice at any intersection; you may have missed something the first time.

TURNS

Signal and move into the proper position well before you turn. Downshift as you approach the turn. Then give your full attention to the road and traffic ahead.

If you are being passed, stay to the left of your lane. If you move to the right, the passing driver may not see you.

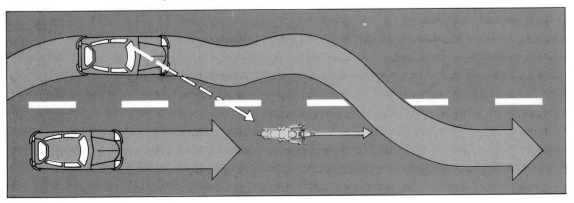

If you are alongside another motorcyclist and you want to pass a vehicle ahead, do it one at a time.

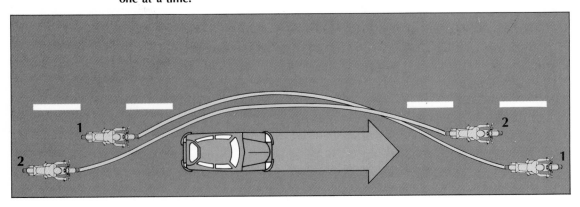

CHANGING LANES AND PASSING

Do not pass on the right of cars on single-lane roads except in an emergency. Before passing, signal to alert other drivers. (Sound your horn in the daytime. Flash your lights at night.) If you and a friend are on separate motorcycles, each of you should pass other vehicles one at a time. When you are being passed, stay on the left side of your lane. You will be more visible.

BEING TAILGATED

If someone is tailgating you, accelerate slightly. However, do not do so if you have to reduce the space between you and the car ahead. If accelerating does not work, signal and pull off the road. Avoid high-speed roads if you cannot maintain traffic speeds. (This problem is most likely to arise on upgrades.)

STALLING IN TRAFFIC

If your engine stalls when you are moving, check traffic to the rear, signal, and steer off the road. If traffic is crowded and you cannot move off the road, warn traffic to the rear. You can do this by waving your arm and flashing your brake light. Shift to *neutral* so that you can get off and push the cycle off the road.

HAZARDOUS CONDITIONS

A motorcyclist is at the mercy of the weather. Extreme cold can numb your arms, legs, and face, even if you are properly dressed. It will impair your ability to use hand and foot controls. Rain makes you less able to maneuver safely and more likely to skid. Poor weather conditions also make you less visible.

RAIN

Rain makes road surfaces slick. When it rains, slow down and scan for obstacles, such as potholes, that may be hidden by puddles. Make steering, braking, and acceleration movements gradually. Try to avoid driving through puddles; they could make your motorcycle hydroplane. Do not depend on the ability of other vehicles to stop. To stay dry and maintain your vision, wear proper rain gear and a face shield or goggles. Coat the inside of your face shield with an antifog solution to keep it clear. A windshield is especially helpful in rain and in cold weather. This piece of optional equipment is highly recommended.

SNOW AND ICE

If the roads are covered with snow or ice, do not drive. Blowing snow, near-zero traction, controls that ice up, gloves that freeze to the grips, iced boot soles, and foot pegs spattered with slush impair your ability to control a motorcycle.

NIGHT DRIVING

Being seen is one of the motorcyclist's major safety problems. Night riding reduces your visibility even further. On weekends, your problems will be increased by drunk drivers. To compensate, wear reflective clothing. Make sure that all lights and signals are clean and working. Be extra alert for the errors of other drivers. Reduce your speed so that you have enough time to scan the road for hazards.

SKIDS

Skids can be caused by slippery road surfaces and by braking too hard. Motorcycle skids are also caused by accelerating too quickly and by cornering improperly.

BRAKING SKID

If the brakes are applied too hard, one or both wheels may lock. To correct a braking skid, ease off the brakes until the wheels roll again. On a slippery surface, pumping the brakes will help you to stop without locking the wheels.

ACCELERATION SKID

Too much acceleration will make the back wheel spin. This may cause the back of the motorcycle to slide to the side. Ease off the throttle immediately.

CORNERING SKID

Cornering skids are the most difficult to correct. They can be caused by driving around a curve too fast. They can also be caused by braking too hard while leaning over or swerving to avoid a collision.

If the rear wheel begins to skid, steer in the opposite direction.

Both driver and passenger should know how a motorcycle operates. They should be properly dressed and should hold onto the proper grips. Are these riders properly dressed?

THE EXPERIENCED DRIVER

Before carrying a passenger, do a lot of solo driving under various traffic conditions. With a passenger aboard, your acceleration and handling will be impaired. So drive more slowly. Also, carry out all maneuvers gradually and smoothly.

AN INFORMED PASSENGER

If your passenger has never been on a motorcycle before, explain what a passenger must do while being ridden. The passenger should (1) be dressed the same as the driver, (2) sit still, (3) not distract the driver, (4) keep both feet on the passenger foot pegs and grip the passenger hand holds, (5) lean with the driver when making turns, and (6) lean in the same direction as the driver, and lean as far as the driver.

This motorcyclist's bike is well packed. An overloaded motorcycle could cause your motorcycle to become unstable when cornering.

HOW TO PACK THE MOTORCYCLE

Any load should be evenly distributed and placed as low and as far forward as possible. If you have a rear-mount luggage rack, do not overload it. Mount anything you carry securely with heavy-duty, adjustable stretch cord. Consider buying saddlebags or a tank-mounted bag.

TOOLS OR SPARE PARTS

Because motorcycles often need repairs, you should always carry replacement parts. Include pregapped spark plugs, a set of points, headlight bulbs, and other bulbs. Fuses, replacement cables, a variety of nuts and bolts, a spare chain, and a master chain link are other parts which you should always have on hand. To make needed repairs, you should have electrical tape, a chain breaker, a tire patch kit, and a tire pressure gauge. Also have tools needed for changing oil, tools for setting the ignition, and an assortment of screwdrivers, pliers, and open-ended wrenches. A first-aid kit is also essential.

TO CONSIDER

1. Why is it so important for a motorcyclist to be seen by car drivers in traffic? What can a motorcyclist do to become more visible?

2. Describe some roadway conditions that are more important for a motorcyclist to be aware of than a car driver. Explain your answer.

3. Explain what motorcyclists can do about riding in poor weather conditions.

4. How can you control a motorcycle that begins to skid?

5. Why is it better to have packs mounted up front rather than at the rear?

6. Explain why motorcyclists often suffer from fatigue. What can a motorcyclist do to reduce the likelihood of fatigue?

7. How should a motorcyclist's visual search differ from a car driver's visual search?

8. What steps should you take if you are forced to ride on the right side of the outside lane?

9. What problems can be created by riding in the space between lanes of cars?

10. Describe the steps you should take when being tailgated.

11. What can a passenger do to help the motorcycle operator drive safely?

PROJECTS

1. Observe and report on motorcycling practices in your area. How many motorcyclists are properly dressed? How many adjust their speed and position for safe driving? How many have their headlights on in the daytime? Do other highway users seem to cooperate with the motorcyclists?

2. Talk to a local police officer about motorcycle use in your area. What does the officer think are the major causes of accidents involving motorcycles? What suggestions does the officer give to remedy the situation?

Glossary

accelerate To gain speed. To go from a slower rate of motion to a steadily increasing one.

accelerator The gas pedal. This pedal is used to control the amount of fuel fed into the engine cylinders. It controls speed.

accessory (acc.) The position of the ignition switch that permits turning on electrical equipment (radio and air conditioner, for example) without starting the engine.

administrative law A law regulating driver licensing, vehicle registration, financial responsibility of drivers and vehicle owners, or minimum equipment and care standards for vehicles.

airbag A safety bag that becomes filled with air automatically upon impact in a collision by means of an electric signal. The inflated bag is a cushion that keeps occupants of the car from striking the interior parts of the automobile.

alternate path of travel An emergency route to be taken if the intended (immediate) path of a vehicle is suddenly blocked. This escape route should be 4 seconds ahead at any given time.

alternating current Electric current whose direction of flow is reversed at regular intervals.

alternator A device that is driven by the engine and that produces electric current.

alternator gauge or **light** An ammeter.

ammeter An instrument that tells whether the car battery is being charged or discharged, by means of a gauge or a light.

angle parking Parking so that cars are arranged side by side, at an angle with a curb or other boundary.

antifreeze A chemical preparation used in a motor vehicle's cooling system to reduce the possibility that the coolant will freeze.

automatic transmission A system in which gears are changed automatically by means of a selector lever set by the driver.

axle The shaft upon which the wheels revolve.

banked Sloping up toward the outside. A well-designed road is banked at curves or turns.

battery A group of electric cells connected as a unit to furnish current by means of chemical reaction. After the cells have been discharged, they can be charged again (recharged). This is done by passing current through the cells in a direction which is the reverse of the flow of current in the discharging process.

blind spot An area outside a vehicle that is not visible to the driver, even in the mirrors.

blind turn A turn along which the driver's vision is blocked. Only the section of the road immediately ahead is in sight.

blood-alcohol concentration (BAC) The amount of alcohol found in the blood. (Usually a BAC report is made on a driver charged with drunken driving.)

blowout The sudden bursting of a tire, resulting in loss of air.

blowout skid A skidding movement caused by a blowout and resulting in a pull toward the side, swaying, or fishtailing.

bottleneck **1** A narrow or blocked section of a road that slows traffic. **2** A slowdown in an otherwise clear section of roadway caused by the breakdown or slowing of a vehicle.

brake lights Part of the taillight assembly. They light up when the brakes are applied.

braking skid A skidding movement caused when the brakes are applied so hard that one or more wheels lock.

breathalyser A device for testing blood-alcohol concentration (BAC). It examines the breath of a person charged with drunken driving.

camper A vehicle that also serves as a dwelling place, usually on long trips or vacation.

carburetor The part of an engine that combines fuel with air so the mixture will burn properly.

catalytic converter A device that reduces the harmful gases carried off by the exhaust system.

charge To pass or receive electrical energy into something, such as an automobile battery, where the energy is stored for later use.

chassis The steel frame that holds together a vehicle's major operating parts. They include the engine, transmissions, brakes, wheels, etc.

choke A valve that controls the engine's fuel and air mixture. To choke an engine is to reduce the amount of air so that the engine will start and warm up easily.

citation A ticket or summons to appear in court to answer a charge of breaking a law.

closing movement A movement by another vehicle or other highway user that may lead it into a driver's path and cause a collision.

clutch A pedal or lever that controls the coupling and uncoupling of two sections of a rotating shaft. One section is connected to the engine, the other to the drive shaft. The clutch connects and disconnects the source of power and the drive wheels.

compact A rather small automobile. A size between an intermediate car and a subcompact.

controlled slipping A method of returning the steering wheel to a straight position after making a turn. The steering wheel is permitted to slip back through the driver's hands until the car is pointed in the desired direction.

coolant A liquid added to a motor vehicle's radiator to reduce heat.

cornering ability The ability of a vehicle to be steered through a turn without going out of control.

cornering skid A skidding movement on a turn, caused by turning too fast, poor tires, or a slippery road surface.

countersteer To turn the steering wheel in the direction you intend to travel.

crankshaft The shaft that is turned as the pistons move up and down in the cylinders of the engine.

crosswalk A pathway marked off for use by pedestrians when they cross a street.

crowned Higher in the center than at the edges. A road that is crowned at curves is good for right turns but dangerous for left turns.

cruise, or **speed, control** A system by which speed is maintained automatically by setting a control button, rather than manually by keeping the foot on the accelerator. The speed stays the same until the control is released.

dead end A street having one end closed off instead of connecting two streets.

decelerate To slow down.

deductible policy An insurance policy providing that the driver pay a given amount of the damage (the first $100, for example) and the insurance company the rest.

defog To remove fog from (windshield and windows).

defroster A heating unit that clears moisture from the inside of the front and rear windows and ice from the outside surfaces.

differential An arrangement of gears that connects two shafts and permits them to rotate at different speeds. It is used on the drive axle to allow the drive wheels to turn at different speeds when going around a corner or curve.

directional control The ability of a motor vehicle to hold to a straight line.

directional, or **turn, signal** A signal that tells other drivers that a motor vehicle plans to turn or move to the right or left. The signal may be given by blinking a light on the right or left side on the front and rear of the vehicle. Or it may be a hand signal given by putting the left arm out the window.

discharge To give up an electric charge that has been stored within something, such as a battery.

distributor The engine switch that sends electric current to each spark plug in proper order and at the proper time.

downshift To shift down to a lower gear.

drive The basic gear used for forward movement. This is the gear used for most driving in a car equipped with an automatic transmission.

drive shaft A rotating shaft that sends mechanical power to the place in a vehicle where the power is being demanded.

drive train The engine, transmission, and clutch.

drive wheels The wheels to which power is sent by the engine to pull the vehicle.

driving while impaired Driving while under the influence of alcohol or drugs. This is usually a law violation by a driver showing only a limited amount of alcohol in the body, and therefore less serious than the charge of **driving while intoxicated (DWI).**

dual-service brake system An arrangement of separate braking systems for front and rear wheels.

electric starter A button on a motorcycle handlebar that is pressed to start the engine after the ignition switch is on.

emergency brake The parking brake.

emergency vehicle A police vehicle, fire engine, ambulance, or the like.

emission-control device A device that prevents or controls pollution by regulating exhaust gases.

escape route A path or route that permits a driver to stay out of a collision. This route is made available by identifying an alternate path of travel to steer to in case of an emergency.

evasive action A quick change in speed or direction to avoid a collision.

exhaust system The parts of a motor vehicle that, working together, get rid of waste gases and vapors from the engine and reduce the noise of the explosions within the engine cylinders.

expressway A divided highway with limited access that has more than one lane running in each direction. It is designed for high-speed travel.

fifth (gear) In vehicles with a five-speed transmission, the gear that produces the highest speed.

first (gear) Low gear.

fishtail A side-to-side skidding movement of the rear end of a vehicle while moving forward.

fixed, or **absolute, speed limit** A speed limit that may not be exceeded for any reason. In some localities, there are also limits on the lowest allowable speed.

flexible, or **prima facie, speed limit** A limit that varies according to existing driving conditions. The set (posted) limit is for ideal road conditions, but a lower top speed may be required if conditions are less favorable.

following distance The time-space gap between vehicles traveling in the same lane in traffic.

four-speed transmission A manual transmission with four forward gears and a reverse gear.

fourth (gear) In vehicles with a four- or five-speed transmission, the gear that produces the next higher speed after third.

friction Resistance between tires and the road surface, caused when they rub against each other to create a force to check a vehicle's movement.

friction point While the clutch pedal is being released, the point at which the clutch and other power-train parts begin to come together.

fuel cock A valve on a motorcycle that controls the flow of fuel from fuel tank to engine.

fuel gauge An indicator that shows the amount of gasoline in the fuel tank.

fuel-supply valve A fuel cock.

gas pedal The accelerator.

gear A wheel with teeth that interlocks (meshes) with another toothed part and, in so doing, transmits motion or changes speed or direction. The choice of gears determines a car's direction (forward or reverse), power, and speed.

gear-selector lever The selector lever.

gearshift An assembly of parts that permits changing from one gear to another by engaging and disengaging the transmission gears.

gearshift lever A lever with which a driver changes gears (shifting). It is also called a **stick-shift lever.**

generator A machine that is driven by the engine and that converts mechanical energy into electrical energy.

ground search A low-level search by a driver for objects in or near the vehicle's path that may be hidden by shrubs or parked cars. The search can be accomplished by road scanning.

guard rail A steel or concrete fence designed to keep a vehicle from going off the road.

hand brake The parking brake.

hand-over-hand steering A method of steering on turns that ensures the greatest control of the steering wheel through use of separate movements of both hands. For example, in making a right turn, the left hand begins the turn of the steering wheel. Then the right hand is reached across to the left position and supplies the remaining force needed to make the wheels move in the desired direction.

hazard flasher A warning flasher.

headlight A light that is mounted on the front of a motor vehicle. It provides illumination of the road ahead at night or during heavy rain or fog.

head restraint A fixed or adjustable safety device designed to prevent injury to the head and neck in the event of a sudden stop or rear-end collision.

high (gear) The gear, or gear setting, that permits the greatest output of speed for a given engine.

high-beam Bright: said about headlights.

highway A main public roadway, especially one that runs between cities. It includes roads, streets, bridges, and tunnels.

hydraulic brakes Brakes that work on the principle that fluid cannot be compressed. The fluid in the master brake cylinder is pushed, under pressure, through brake-fluid lines. The resistance to this forcing activates brake cylinders in each wheel.

hydroplane To ride on top of a film of water instead of with tires maintaining firm contact with the road.

idle To run at a slow speed with little or no pressure on the accelerator: said about an engine. Generally, the transmission is in neutral gear.

ignition A system, controlled by a switch, which provides the spark that causes the fuel and air mixture in the engine to burn.

ignition interlock A system that automatically keeps a car's engine from starting when certain safety conditions are not met, as when safety belts are not properly buckled.

immediate path of travel The route to the point where a driver hopes to be, in normal traffic, 4 seconds from a given time.

impact-resistant Especially made to absorb the force resulting from striking an object: said about a bumper.

implied consent law A law that requires a driver charged with being under the influence of alcohol to consent to take a chemical test that measures the amount of alcohol in the blood.

inertia The tendency of a car in motion to resist any change in direction.

internal-combustion engine The kind of engine (used in automobiles) in which a fuel mixture is burned within the engine. The energy that produces the car's motion comes from burning within the engine cylinders, not from burning outside, as in a steam engine.

intersection A place where two or more streets cross.

interstate Involving, or connecting, two or more states.

jackknife To form the shape of a letter L—a 90-degree angle (the action of a vehicle and its trailer in making a turn improperly).

jump starting Starting a car by attaching its battery (which is dead) to the charged battery of another vehicle by means of cables.

kickstarter A motorcycle starter switch, on the right foot peg, that is operated by kicking downward to start the engine.

kill switch A switch on the right handlebar that can be used in an emergency to turn off the engine on a motorcycle; also called **cutoff switch.**

labor To run or to cause (an engine) to run with great difficulty because of improper engine adjustment or gear selection.

lap belt See **safety belt.**

lateral On, toward, or from the side or sides. Sideways or sidewise.

liable Responsible according to law.

lock The position of the ignition switch by which the steering wheel, ignition switch, and automatic transmission are locked.

low (gear) The gear, or gear position (first), that permits the smallest output speed (actual speed of a vehicle) for a given engine speed. It provides the greatest pulling power of the forward gears.

low-beam Of low-degree brightness: said about headlights.

lubricating system A system that reduces heat by coating the engine parts with oil.

magneto A small machine (generator) that produces alternating current used in the ignition system of some internal-combustion engines.

manual Operated by hand.

moped A bicycle that runs on power from a small engine.

muffler An attachment that reduces engine noise caused by the explosion of the air and fuel mixture.

multiple-lane highway A highway having more than one lane running in each direction.

network A group of connecting roads that bring points along them into contact.

neutral The position in which the car gears are not engaged, and no power can be transmitted.

odometer A gauge that shows the total distance that a car has been driven.

offset A road position of motorcyclists driving together. One cycle is behind and to the right or left of the cycle ahead in the same lane.

oil-pressure gauge A gauge that shows the pressure at which oil is being pumped to the engine's moving parts.

optional equipment One or more extra features that a car buyer is not required to take.

overinflated Having too much air pressure.

oversteering Too much movement of the front of a car to the inside of a turn.

parallel parking Parking so that a given car is in line with a group of cars arranged one behind the other, parallel to and close to a road edge.

park The reading on the selector quadrant which shows that the transmission is locked.

parking brake The brake, separate from the hydraulic brakes, that holds the rear wheels. It is used to keep a parked car from moving.

passive safety belt (passive restraint belt) A shoulder strap that connects from the center of the seat to the car door. It is used with a regular lap belt.

pedestrian A person traveling on foot rather than in an automobile or on a motorcycle, bicycle, or other vehicle.

perpendicular parking Parking so that a car forms a 90-degree angle with a curb or boundary.

piston A steel cylinder that is enclosed in a cylinder within the engine. As the piston moves up, it compresses a fuel and air mixture. The piston is forced down by the explosion of this mixture. This up-and-down movement turns the crankshaft.

play The amount of free movement in a lever, foot pedal, or steering wheel that is possible without affecting the device being controlled.

points The electrical contacts in the distributor of a car engine which make and break the connection, permitting a flow of current.

positive crankcase ventilation (PVC) system A system that recycles gases in the crankcase so that they can be burned again in the cylinders.

power-assisted brakes (power brakes) Brakes that make it easier to slow or stop by increasing the pressure beyond that exerted by the foot.

power skid A skidding movement caused when the gas pedal is pressed suddenly, too hard.

power steering A system of steering in which the front wheels are turned by a force supplied by an extra (auxiliary) source of power, together with the regular force provided by the driver.

race To run at high speed: said about an engine.

radiator A cooling device in a car which, by a fan, air-cools liquid pumped from the engine.

regulatory sign A roadway sign that indicates certain legal controls over a driver's actions.

restraint Any device, such as a safety belt, that checks the movement of a car occupant at the time of a sudden stop or a collision.

reverse The gear used for backward movement.

revoke To take away (a driver's license, for example) permanently.

right-of-way The right of a vehicle or pedestrian to go first, before other traffic moves, when there is a conflict. It is granted by law or custom.

rotary motion Rotating movement.

safety belt A restraining belt attached to the floor of a vehicle, designed to protect the driver and riders in the event of a collision. **Lap belts** are fastened across the hips; **shoulder belts,** across the shoulder and chest. **Lap-and-shoulder belts** combine the two kinds of protection.

scan To move the eyes over a wide area (of a road), rather than to look at one fixed point.

seat belt A safety belt.

second (gear) The gear that permits a vehicle to run at the next-to-lowest speed: 25 to 40 km/h (15 to 25 mph).

selector lever A device that permits the driver to choose the desired gear.

selector quadrant An indicator that shows which gear a car is in.

shift To change (gears) by means of a mechanism.

shock absorbers Devices that act as cushions for a car's frame against the impact of bumps in the road. They also control bouncing.

shoulder The off-road area running along the edge on either side of a road.

shoulder belt See **safety belt.**

side-marker lights Lights that mark the sides of a car. They are operated by turning on the headlight switch.

sideswipe To strike (another vehicle) along the side while passing or trying to pass it.

simulator A model of the interior of an automobile, used in training beginning drivers.

snowmobile A motor-driven vehicle for travel on snow or ice.

space margin The amount of space around a vehicle, separating it from possible sources of danger in traffic. Also called **space cushion.**

spark plug A device in a cylinder head of an engine that ignites the mixture of fuel and air by means of an electric spark.

speedometer A gauge that shows how fast a vehicle is moving, in kilometers or miles per hour.

spinout A spinning movement by a car, resulting from lack of traction of the rear wheels.

standard equipment Those parts of an automobile that the owner must take, and pay for, when buying a car.

start The position to which the ignition switch is turned in getting the engine to begin running.

starter An electric motor that starts the engine.

steering-column lock The locked condition of the steering wheel when the ignition switch is in the *lock* position.

steering damper A motorcycle device that controls the front wheel. Tightening this device makes the wheel less likely to kick or wobble at high speeds. Loosening it makes the wheel easier to manage in city traffic.

stick shift A hand-operated gear shift. It is also called a **manual shift.**

stop sign An 8-sided sign, with white letters on red. It means: "Come to a full stop and do not move until it is safe to do so."

subcompact A small automobile.

sun visor A shield fastened above the windshield that can be adjusted to protect the driver and front-seat riders from sun glare.

suspend To take away (a driver's license) for a time.

suspension The assembly of springs, shock absorbers, and related parts that insulate (protect) the chassis of a vehicle against road shocks coming through the wheels.

tailgate To drive behind another vehicle too closely to permit stopping or swerving quickly.

tail pipe The part of the exhaust system that carries exhaust gases out from under a vehicle.

temperature gauge A gauge, or sometimes a warning light, that shows whether the engine is running at a proper temperature.

third (gear) **1** The gear that produces the next higher speed after second. It is used for speeds above 40 km/h (25 mph), usually up to 50 or 60 km/h (30 or 40 mph) in vehicles with a four- or five-speed transmission. **2** In vehicles with a three-speed transmission, high gear.

three-point turn A turnabout beginning from a stop at the far right of a street. The turn is made by (1) a left turn into the opposite lane of traffic, (2) a brief stop while in a position across that lane, (3) movement in reverse gear, followed by (4) another brief stop, and (5) a second left turn, which completes the change of direction.

three-speed transmission A manual transmission with three forward gears and a reverse gear.

throttle The accelerator of a motorcycle, controlled with a twist grip at the end of the right handlebar.

time-and-space gap The distance separating a vehicle from the vehicle directly ahead of or behind it. The gap is measured in time and space necessary to stop or swerve safely in emergencies.

tow To pull along, as a trailer.

tracking Keeping a vehicle steadily and smoothly on a desired course by making the necessary steering corrections.

traction **1** The pulling power of a vehicle. The vehicle's ability to move over a surface, under its own power, in a controlled way. **2** The friction (between tires and road surface) that keeps wheels from slipping or skidding.

transmission The gears and related parts by means of which power is carried from the engine to a driving axle.

tread The outer surface of a tire, with its pattern of grooves and ridges.

turnabout A turning maneuver in which a driver moves a vehicle so that it faces in the opposite (reverse) direction.

turn signal A directional signal.

two-point turn A turnabout carried out by first backing into a driveway or alley. It can also be made by heading into an alley or driveway and then backing into the desired street and stopping in the through-traffic lane.

underinflated Having too little air pressure: said about tires.

understeering Failure of the front of a car to respond satisfactorily to a turn of the steering wheel.

universal joints Joints that connect the drive shaft to the transmission and differential and allow the drive shaft to move up and down or sideways.

U-turn A turnabout carried out by a full, U-shaped, left turn. The turn is made starting from the far right of a road and ending with the car in the opposite far right lane, headed in the other direction.

V-8 engine An eight-cylinder engine. There are four cylinders on each side of a V-8 engine.

vehicle A machine with wheels or runners for carrying people or goods.

violation A breaking of a law.

visibility **1** The distance and area a driver can see. **2** The ability of a vehicle or pedestrian to be seen.

visual acuity Sharpness of eyesight.

visual lead time The distance ahead to which a driver should be scanning and which the vehicle will reach in a given time. The minimum visual lead time is 12 seconds, or one block ahead, in city traffic. At higher speeds or on an expressway, the visual lead time may be 20 to 30 seconds.

warning flasher A signaling device, worked by a switch, that makes all four turn-signal lights (at the front and rear of the car) flash at the same time. It is used to warn other drivers that a vehicle on or off the road ahead has stopped or is moving very slowly.

water jacket The passageway that surrounds an engine cylinder, through which coolant flows to cool the engine.

weaving lane A lane of traffic near the entrance or exit of an expressway, made up of cars preparing either to enter (speeding up) or exit (slowing down).

whiplash An injury to the neck resulting from a sudden jerking of the head, backward or forward, at the time of a collision or an abrupt stop of a car.

yield sign A red and white triangular sign that tells a driver to be ready to give the right-of-way to another highway user. It means: "Be prepared to stop or slow down."

Index

Photo Credits

2 3 4 5 6 7 8 9 10 DODO 88 87 86 85 84 83 82 81 80

Antoniette
Loves
Rich

2/01/90